An Adventure in Two-Party Politics

Holm Bursum III, the Young Republicans, and the Revitalization of the GOP in New Mexico in the 1960s

An Adventure in Two-Party Politics

Holm Bursum III, the Young Republicans, and the Revitalization of the GOP in New Mexico in the 1960s

JUDITH L. MESSAL

© 2022 by Judith L. Messal
All Rights Reserved
No part of this book may be reproduced in any form or by any electronic or mechanical means including information storage and retrieval systems without permission in writing from the publisher, except by a reviewer who may quote brief passages in a review.

Sunstone books may be purchased for educational, business, or sales promotional use. For information please write: Special Markets Department, Sunstone Press, P.O. Box 2321, Santa Fe, New Mexico 87504-2321.
Printed on acid-free paper
∞
eBook 978-1-61139-671-3

Library of Congress Cataloging-in-Publication Data

Names: Messal, Judith L., 1947- author.
Title: An adventure in two-party politics : Holm O. Bursum III, the Young Republicans, and the revitalization of the GOP in New Mexico in the 1960's / by Judith L. Messal.
Description: Santa Fe, New Mexico : Sunstone Press, 2020. | Includes bibliographical references and index. | Summary: "The story of New Mexico Young Republicans, under the leadership of Holm O. Bursum III, who helped restore a two-party system in New Mexico in the 1960's"-- Provided by publisher.
Identifiers: LCCN 2019049355 | ISBN 9781632932464 (paperback)
Subjects: LCSH: Bursum, Holm O., III, 1934-2018. | New Mexico Young Republican Association--History. | Politicians--New Mexico--Biography. | New Mexico--Politics and government--1951-
Classification: LCC F801.4.B87 M47 2020 | DDC 978.9/053--dc23

LC record available at https://lccn.loc.gov/2019049355

WWW.SUNSTONEPRESS.COM
SUNSTONE PRESS / POST OFFICE BOX 2321 / SANTA FE, NM 87504-2321 /USA
(505) 988-4418

Dedication

In memory of Anita Dickenson Menger, who, in 1960, gave her eighth-grade social studies students an intriguing assignment. They were to visit the political party headquarters of their choice and select candidates to study, bringing their platforms back to class to present and defend. Mrs. Menger expected her students to handle all aspects of the assignment with the utmost decorum. Thus, a group of thirteen-year-olds in Alamogordo, New Mexico learned that they were trustworthy enough to go out into the real world of electoral politics and meet adults engaged in a democratic process. They learned that, in political discussions with one another, all sides should be heard with respect. I was fortunate to be one of her students, and I am thankful.

Contents

Foreword ‡ 8
Preface ‡ 10
Acknowledgments ‡ 12
1. A Young Challenge to One-Party Politics ‡ 14
2. The First Bursums in a New and Ancient Land ‡ 19
3. Democratic Dominance: One-Party Rule in the 1930s and 1940s ‡ 47
4. Republican Persistence: Cracks in the One-Party System ‡ 56
5. Holm O. Bursum III: Growing Up in the GOP ‡ 69
6. 1959–1960: Early Young Republican Revitalization Photographs ‡ 78
7. 1961: Young Republican Leaders in the State and Nation ‡ 94
8. 1962: Local Organizing and Midterm Surprises ‡ 113
9. 1963: Tensions, Toil, and Tragedy ‡ 128
10. 1964: Traces of Progress in a Profound Defeat ‡ 146
11. 1965: Transitions at Home and a Peace Mission Abroad ‡ 162
12. 1966–1968: A Party Set to Celebrate ‡ 176
13. And Then: Seven Young Republicans in Middle Age and Beyond ‡ 186
Notes ‡ 206
Epilogue ‡ 235
Bibliography ‡ 236
Index ‡ 244

Foreword

The well-being of the Republican Party has been important to me all my life. I grew up during a time when New Mexico was under one-party rule by Democrats. I was raised in an active Republican family. My grandfather was a sheriff, the Republican Party chairman for New Mexico Territory, the mayor of Socorro, and a United States senator. My father was a successful mayor of Socorro for twenty-two years and was a Republican Party state treasurer. He took part in all of Edwin L. Mechem's campaigns for governor. My mother also was a Republican and was active in women's organizations locally and statewide. She and First Lady Dorothy Mechem were very close friends and worked Republican politics throughout New Mexico. I had no choice about being a Republican and have enjoyed every minute of it.

When I became active in the 1960s, people were surprised that our Young Republican movement took off and exploded all over the state. I don't think they had any idea there was so much pent-up emotion in young people about corruption in state government. Many, from teenagers to thirty-year-olds, were frustrated with the party in power. One example of the corruption was that people who held government jobs with the Democrats in Santa Fe and statewide had to give a portion of their salaries to the party. Governor Ed Mechem put a stop to that practice and others like it. With Republican revitalization, New Mexicans finally had a choice!

When I was elected president of the Young Republican Association of New Mexico in 1961, Republicans had been sidelined for so long, but we had a very sincere governor in Ed Mechem. He agreed with the idea that the senior Republican Party needed new young blood and appreciated that we were willing and able to do the legwork for the senior party and that we were not trying to take over. The timing was good for us because Mechem had just been elected to his fourth term as governor. He was an outstanding public official and a good example for the younger generation. We wanted to help him build up the party and had no trepidations about what we were going to undertake. There was no mission impossible!

Many people gave their support to revitalizing the young wing of the Republican Party in New Mexico. First among them is Edwin L. Mechem. Many others also worked hard to help us succeed. They include John Mitchell, Bill Gardner, Fanny Bliss, Hoyt Pattison, Colin McMillan, Richard Cheney, Frances Lee, George McKim, Merle Tucker, Jack Ryan, Bob Botts, Jim Parker, LeRoy Hansen, Bob Davidson, Paul Robinson, Brad Zeikus, Chuck Monette, Charlotte Monette, Don Tripp, Rosie Tripp, Joe Skeen, Pete Domenici, Manuel Lujan, Edward Lujan, Earle Bursum, George Cowart, Jane Cowart, Tom Bolack, Rowena and Adolpho Baca, and Leo and Don Murphy. Our work brought results. We became and remain a two-party state. The Republican Party is still competitive in New Mexico! That fact is a source of great satisfaction to me.

To young people becoming politically active today, I offer my view that the two-party system is one of the greatest reasons for the success of the U.S. system of government. Not three parties or four; not one. Two parties. We must have responsibility. If we elect a Democrat as president or governor or as a member of Congress and he or she does not perform well, we can put a Republican in office or vice versa. With more than two parties, it is hard to pin down responsibility, and with only one in power, the problems are clear. New Mexico has learned from its past that it is important to keep our two-party system vital.

—Holm O. Bursum III
Socorro, New Mexico
September 7, 2018

Preface

This is a story of young New Mexicans in politics in the 1960s. In particular, it is a story about Holm O. Bursum III and his peers as they revitalized their state's Young Republican Association. My own young eyes were on the developments as they were unfolding then. I had become a political volunteer at thirteen, first reporting to party headquarters in my hometown on November 8, 1960. That morning before school, I sat down at a telephone bank and went to work to get out the vote in a presidential election. By 1964, I had joined my county's new Teen Age Republican Club. In the process, I met Governor Edwin L. Mechem and Holm Bursum III, who led the senior and young wings of New Mexico's Republican Party at the time.

Governor Mechem's and Mr. Bursum's benevolent outreach to new generations built the young wing. Under their guidance, we felt important politically even though some of us were not yet old enough to vote. We learned to do party work, but we also learned to cherish broader civic engagement. It was exhilarating for young people to be welcomed into the power and policy world of our elders and to glimpse the processes and institutions of a democratic republic.

Fifty years later, when I was researching the career of Edwin L. Mechem, Holm Bursum agreed to an interview. It was our first extended conversation, and he was great fun to talk to. He remembered virtually every player and event on the New Mexico political stage of the 1950s and '60s. As we delved into the era, I found Mr. Bursum's own story absorbing. His work as a political organizer serves almost as a handbook on how to enter civic life in one's young years. It demonstrates how to involve other young people in promoting healthy competition at the polls with ethical governance as a goal. He agreed that we could write up his story.

As we talked, I learned more than just the facts of political organizing. I learned that Holm Bursum's love of New Mexico—its people, land, and history—gave him a fine perspective. It kept his focus on the long-range well-being of the polity and made inclusiveness first nature to him. In the 1960s, men held most of the high posts in politics and government, but a young Holm Bursum sought guidance from both the women and men in the senior party. He served with women officers in the young wing. He wanted all their work noted. His state's cultures and languages were other elements he appreciated. When I admired his ability to speak Spanish, he indicated that for him, it was a way to extend courtesy and friendship to his fellows.

The backdrop of New Mexico history that Holm Bursum constructed during our conversations was captivating. I learned more about the past and present riches of his home county, Socorro. I also learned about the first Holm Bursum, the grandfather who inspired him. Both his forebears and Socorro's lands were so integral to his identity that they became part of his story as a young politico. A private man with a humble nature, he never placed himself front-and-center in his recounting. He credited others. He was one among many colleagues, and they too appear prominently in this telling of events.

Holm Bursum's other kinds of civic work came into the frame of his public life. His passions for improving the state's highways and preserving his community's history did not develop separately from his caring about New Mexico's electoral system and governance. The story that grew out of our visits is about a man whose values and actions were well integrated, who was characterized, as his associate Cindy Lam points out, by honesty, kindness, generosity, and a gift for listening. His firsthand knowledge of political history was a treasure. I am honored that he shared that knowledge with me, and I hope to pass some of it along to others.

Acknowledgments

Many people contributed to the story of Holm Bursum III and the Young Republicans (YRs). I am grateful to all and will mention a few. First is the Bursum family. Holm IV (Cuatro) Bursum, Elizabeth Spencer, Julia Bursum, and Michael Bursum generously provided photographs, documents, and insights. Cindy Lam wrote eloquently about the Mr. Bursum she knew in a professional setting. Several of his colleagues from the 1960s YR days granted me interviews. Some were in person. It was a great pleasure to visit with the former minority leader of the New Mexico House of Representatives, Hoyt Pattison, and his wife, Joy Pattison. We met on their lush green farm in eastern New Mexico on a summer day and shared a beautiful lunch at their dining room table. On a sunny winter afternoon at an outdoor venue in Silver City in 2019, I enjoyed coffee and conversation with Ron Hamm. He had written a Bursum family biography and shared his archival material generously.

From afar, I got to know Leonard J. Nadasdy of Minnesota, who in the early 1960s chaired the Young Republican National Federation. In 2018, while contending with a terminal illness, he wrote extensively about the exciting young politics in his era. It was a great gift. Thank you to the Dona Ana County Historical Society for publishing my overlapping work on mid-century politics in *Southern New Mexico Historical Review*.

Thanks also to Rozanne Kalsbeek and Joe Alexander, who read drafts of this book and helped improve it. Many people offered encouragement. Terry Messal and Christina Miller are among them. As my younger sibling, Terry remembers being subjected to tedious sessions poring over my Nixon scrapbooks. When Christina was my little seven-year-old, she complained in her school journal that talk at the family dinner table was about nothing but politics. Despite the bombardments, both are good and fully engaged citizens today. Thanks to Paul Mapes and Cynthia Saylor Banerjee, my fellow Teen Age Republicans, who, in recent years, helped me explore the Mechem era. Thanks to Sharon Ellis, who always took an interest and reminded me that a manuscript under endless revision is not preferable to a finished one. Finally, I am very grateful to the people of Sunstone Press for their guidance and great patience.

Note: When I used interview and email information from Holm Bursum III and Len Nadasdy, I identified the sources but did not formally cite them. Regarding all the sources I used, I hope my interpretations are accurate and take full responsibility in cases where they are not.

1
A Young Challenge to One-Party Politics

A big part of my philosophy is a strong belief in the two-party system of the United States.

—Holm O. Bursum III, 2012[1]

It was a spring morning in Albuquerque in 1961, and the workers at the Alvarado Hotel were attending to the final details of what was to become a transforming political event. The Alvarado was a fitting site for notable New Mexico occasions. It was one of the grandest of the Fred Harvey Houses along the Atchison, Topeka, and Santa Fe Railway line. Built in 1902 in the California Mission Revival Style, its complex of buildings sprawled along Albuquerque's First Street, all pale stucco and red-tile roofs with long arcades, gables, towers, and lush gardens.[2]

One of the people making his way through the Alvarado's doors that morning in 1961 was a dark-haired young man of long stride and striking appearance. His name was Holm Olaf Bursum III, and he was there to address delegates to the Young Republican Association's state convention. It was going to be an auspicious event for him and them. Twenty-six years old and a candidate for association president, he was ready to launch a movement that would challenge New Mexico's political status quo and help restore its two-party system.

Political history had been made at the Alvarado for decades, some of it involving Bursum's family. On October 15, 1909, his grandfather, the first Holm O. Bursum, and other New Mexico territorial leaders gathered at the hotel to fete U.S. President William Howard Taft. That night's ceremonial dinner was the culminating event in a campaign to solidify the president's support for New Mexico statehood. Bursum, the head of the Territorial

Republican Central Committee, was among the evening's speakers. By that time, he had helped lead the statehood movement for half a decade, and, in 1909, success seemed near.

New Mexico, indeed, succeeded in joining the Union during President Taft's administration, and the first Holm O. Bursum was on hand at the White House in 1910 to witness the signing of the enabling legislation. When Bursum's grandson, Holm III, stepped into political leadership half a century later, the state faced a governance challenge. For much of the younger man's life, New Mexico had operated as virtually a one-party state under the Democrats. Politics in his grandfather's time had not been that exclusive. Holm Bursum III thought that Republicans could retrieve their place in a bipartisan government and that the party's young wing could help.

Young Republicans (YRs) had a long tradition in New Mexico, but by the late 1950s, they needed organizational renewal. Bursum presented his platform to the convention delegates on May 6, 1961, winning a unanimous election as their president. In that luxurious moment of political unity, he and his colleagues were about to demonstrate what a motivated group of young people could do to effect change.

The revitalization of the young wing of the Republican Party was going to help remake the electoral landscape and impact state governance. It would be a little like a lavish rainfall in the desert that brings long-dormant plants to life. The political scene had been dry ground for the Grand Old Party (GOP) since the 1930s. In three decades, only two Republicans had been elected to any of the state's nine executive-branch offices. Only one Republican was elected to New Mexico's congressional delegation, incumbent Senator Bronson Cutting, who died just months into his new term and was replaced by a Democrat. In the state legislature, the Republicans' minority status was extreme. In 1961, only seven Republicans served in the New Mexico House of Representatives, whereas the Democrats had fifty-nine members. In the Senate, four Republicans served alongside twenty-eight Democrats. The two-party system in New Mexico was not in good health, and young people were gathering in Albuquerque to remedy the situation.

As the state YR president, Holm Bursum wanted to build up the whole party by motivating young people to become politically active "twenty years before they otherwise might have gotten involved," he said. He mapped out a plan: get the state association in top condition, build an executive team, and move out into the counties to re-charter existing clubs and establish new ones. He could imagine a network of Young Republicans expanding throughout New Mexico, even into regions where the GOP had few footholds. Next, the young people in the network would get into their counties' party headquarters, on the telephones, and into the neighborhoods. They would do the senior party's legwork, assisting with the day-to-day tasks of building a voter base, fundraising, and campaigning. Recently, the party's two wings had fallen a bit out of step with each other, and Bursum wanted to bring them together. In his mind, a party in greater harmony could elect people to office, thus sharing again in New Mexico's governance.

Already one individual had opened a path to bipartisanship in state government in a spectacular way. His name was Edwin L. Mechem, and Holm Bursum III knew him as a lifelong family friend, one of his father's closest colleagues. In 1950, Ed Mechem, then a young attorney, had run as his party's gubernatorial candidate and was the first Republican elected to any state executive office in twenty-two years. Returned to the governorship three more times, he was a politician who appealed to voters in both parties and a public official who operated deftly in a bipartisan government. Although Mechem had not planned on a political career, the GOP enlisted him to run for statewide offices on every ticket from 1950 through 1964. Through the years, he mentored younger leaders, and among those he took under his wing was Holm O. Bursum III.

Bursum was a born organizer who wanted to learn from senior party women and men and channel their insights back to the young wing. In the Young Republican (YR) movement of the 1960s, he worked at all levels, from county and university clubs to the state association and the national federation. He met presidential candidates such as Richard Nixon and Barry Goldwater and worked with Young Republican National Federation officers like Leonard Nadasdy and Patricia Hutar.

The state Young Republican Association had a meager treasury during the organizing years, but Bursum worked around that. He recruited people to spend their evenings and weekends with him, traveling the long, mostly two-lane roads of New Mexico in their own cars, staying with friends and relatives when they could—all to help build a young adults' political organization. The clubs in the revitalized network worked hard, taking on the legwork to which Bursum had referred. They also sponsored Teen Age Republican clubs, and they studied the big issues of their day, getting their perspectives into the newspapers and policymakers' offices. In the years between elections, they engaged in bipartisan and nonpartisan good-government projects. It was political involvement with breadth and depth, and Holm Bursum III had the personality to make it both compelling and fun.

The collaboration that Bursum envisioned between the young and senior wings of the GOP worked. By the second half of the 1960s, the whole party was showing signs of sustainable growth. More of its candidates did well at the ballot box. Some of the new generations of elected officials in the 1960s and 1970s came directly out of the Young Republican movement. They included Hoyt Pattison, who became a legislative leader with a talent for building bipartisan coalitions. Another Young Republican, David F. Cargo, became governor and helped make structural changes that also revitalized the two-party system.

Through the reflections of Holm Bursum III and his colleagues, through newspaper archives and politicians' memoirs, we retrace the steps of a group of young organizers in the 1960s. First, however, we set the stage by looking at the early years of the twentieth century. The great political challenge of the time was New Mexico's admission to the Union. It had been a long time in coming. Since Bursum's grandparents were involved in the statehood movement's ultimate success, we open, in Chapter 2, with their story. In particular, we see how his grandfather worked for New Mexico's admission and helped write the state's constitution. We see both of his grandparents in public service. In Chapter 3, we check in on the political and governmental systems in New Mexico as they were operating in the 1930s into the 1950s. They were the years of Bursum's youth, the years when one party dominated to the near exclusion of the other. As in any one-party state, the methods of maintaining power at times were not commendable.

For Holm Bursum III and his colleagues to help restore a two-party system in the 1960s, their parents' generation had to have kept the GOP alive during the arid years, running candidates for office no matter how futile the races. In Chapter 4, on Republican persistence from the 1930s into the 1950s, we meet the father of Holm Bursum III and his father's friend Edwin L. Mechem. They were two of the young Republicans in their day who ran those seemingly futile races. They were among the first to find the hairline cracks in the one-party system, open them wider, and push their candidacies through to win public offices.

With the political stage thus set, we come to the second part of the story, the young Holm Bursum's introduction to politics and later his joyful and engaging party organizing. "We tried everything. We thought we could do anything. We didn't know any better," Holm Bursum III said with a smile in 2017 as he recalled his young years. In those times, the horizons seemed barrier-free, and aspirations were limitless. In a spirit of indomitability, the Young Republicans accomplished more than might have been expected during a time when the Democrats in New Mexico enjoyed more than a five-to-two voter registration advantage.³

2

The First Bursums in a New and Ancient Land

...[T]he Bursums of New Mexico, an impressive assemblage of hombres.
—Ron Hamm, Journalist, Educator, and Historian, 2012[4]

For Holm O. Bursum III, becoming a Republican leader in New Mexico at the age of twenty-six was not out of the ordinary. It was part of being a Bursum. A passion for politics and government service always had animated his family's life, making it impossible, he said, to pinpoint the time when he first became interested in political activity. He had a great love for his state, party, and community, and he grew up knowing that his family had helped build them all.

The family gave him mentors, Holm Bursum III said—his father, of course, and his father's friend Edwin L. Mechem—but no one gave him more inspiration for his political work than his grandfather. The first Holm Olaf Bursum was a towering family figure. The child of immigrants, he had settled as a young orphan in Socorro County in the nineteenth century. He grew up to be a leader in the Republican Party and a United States senator. Parts of his story appear in many New Mexico histories. More intensive documentation of his life also exists. The first Holm Bursum appears as the subject of a doctoral dissertation by Donald Moorman and a manuscript by Paul Harden. Martina Franklin's 1970s interview with Bursum's son provides more insights. Ron Hamm's biography, *The Bursums of New Mexico: Four Generations of Leadership and Service*, offers a fresh and comprehensive treatment of the triumphs and challenges of Bursum's life.

In gratitude to those who have given us histories of the Bursums, we review the first Holm's childhood and political organizing years. We look especially at the accounts of his work for New Mexico's statehood.

They are among the stories that inspired his grandson. In them, we meet Lulu Moore Bursum, the woman who shared her life with the first Holm Bursum and made her own mark in public service. We also meet William A. Keleher, a distinguished New Mexican whose links with the extended Bursum family give a special dimension to the narrative. The stories set the stage for Holm O. Bursum III, who, like his grandfather, took on political organizing at a young age.

The First Holm O. Bursum
Migrating from Iowa to New Mexico Territory

In 1881, a fourteen-year-old named Holm Olaf Bursum made his way out of Denver and traveled south along the Front Range of the Rocky Mountains into New Mexico Territory.[5] His destination was San Antonio, a small town south of Albuquerque along the Rio Grande. There his uncle Augustus Halvorson Hilton had a thriving business and a job for him. It had been a very long trek for the Bursum child and his family.

For Bursum's parents, the journey had begun in Norway, a country challenged by population growth and the agricultural failures that affected mid-nineteenth-century Europe. Frank O. and Maria Bursum left their Norwegian home and came to the United States after the Civil War, settling in Fort Dodge, Iowa. One of the newer states in the Union then, Iowa presented an enticing landscape of gentle wooded hills and grasslands. It was well-watered, its borders formed by the Mississippi River on the east and the Missouri on the west.

Around the time the Bursums settled there, the state was near the U.S. frontier. Far to the west, California, Oregon, and Nevada had been admitted to the Union. Nebraska soon would be, but between those states and Iowa lay a broad swath of territorial land. Throughout the region, land divisions were being established with Indigenous people, resulting for many in displacement and economic disruption. About twenty years before the Bursums arrived in Fort Dodge, the Meskwaki people of Iowa had been compelled to relocate to Kansas. According to a Meskwaki Nation history,[6] white settlers who witnessed the Native people's exodus described the great sorrow that it caused. The somber removal proceeded peacefully, but in 1849, something unusual happened, something sanctioned by the state a few years later. Members of the Meskwaki community began returning to Iowa. They arranged to purchase and hold title to part of their old lands. Some of their neighbors, specifically German, Swedish, Danish, and Norwegian immigrants, advocated that they stay. The state and private transactions set the Meskwaki community apart from most Indigenous nations, whose land was allotted by the federal government and held in trust.

At a time of such social flux, the Scandinavian and German immigrants' goodwill toward Indigenous people had made a valuable statement. In 1867, Holm Olaf Bursum was born into one of the Scandinavian communities where he absorbed some of what it meant to live in a new and diverse republic. By age ten, he would be headed to a distant land of even greater diversity. He would settle in a U.S. territory a thousand miles away, and there he would enter the history books. The reason for his journey was tragic and all too common in his era.

The Bursum family's life in Iowa quickly became difficult. The father, Frank Bursum, taught school and farmed, but he was ill, possibly with tuberculosis.[7] He died as a young man. Maria Bursum was left with two small children to support, Holm and Louise. Eventually, Maria remarried, and in 1877, she and her family left the mellow green hills of Iowa to join her brother Augustus Hilton in New Mexico Territory.[8] It was a long trek south and west across the Great Plains. Travelers on the route would have had that moment, that first faraway sighting of the Rockies, blue, snow-crested, and floating like a vision above the prairie. For Maria, the image must have been beautifully reminiscent of her native Norway. Her party turned south along the mountains, headed for New Mexico, but Maria would not go much farther. She died on the journey, probably of tuberculosis, and was buried in Colorado Springs.[9] Holm Bursum, not yet an adolescent, was on his own. He gave little Louise funds to travel on to New Mexico, and he stayed in Colorado to find a job.[10]

Bursum's youthful days of hardship and hard work became part of a nineteenth-century story of immigration and life on the frontiers of the United States. Many years later, when he had moved to Washington, DC to serve in the U.S. Senate, the International News Service reporter J. Bart Campbell wrote a description of his childhood:

> An orphaned boy of eleven years bent over a tub filled with bottles in a Denver drug store. There were holes in his shirt, patches in his worn knickerbockers. His shoes were the worse from wear. But he whistled cheerily as he washed bottles, his hands red from frequent

immersion in scalding water and yellow soap. He had a job. Although his parents were dead, he was sure of a bite to eat and a place, however hard, to rest his tired little body when night intervened between him and his toil.[11]

After three years of various kinds of work, the boy resumed his journey to New Mexico, finally arriving in San Antonio in Socorro County. There he took a job with Gus Hilton, his uncle, and helped mentor his young cousin, Conrad.

As part of the Hilton household, Bursum learned business practices, made connections, and resumed his studies. His circumstances had disrupted his formal education, but in San Antonio, he attended public school as it fit around his work schedule.[12] He also became fluent in Spanish, one of the languages of his new land. In his twenties, he started a freighting business and joined the Republican Party. In 1891, he saw his sister Louise married to George Wolfinger. Within the decade, the couple would move over a hundred miles away to the new railroad town of Alamogordo, where they would purchase a mercantile business.[13]

In 1894, Bursum, a Republican, was elected sheriff of Socorro County. Thus at twenty-seven, he began serving as the law enforcement officer of one of the largest jurisdictions in New Mexico Territory. The tall teenager had grown into "...a big, broad-shouldered, deep-chested powerfully-built man," Campbell wrote. His hands were "...large gnarled ones accustomed in youth to manual labor." His square jaw gave him the look of a "...born fighter. But withal he is good-natured—a hail fellow well met," Campbell concluded.[14]

Settling in the Ancient Land of Socorro

When Holm Bursum settled in Socorro County in the late nineteenth century, it was spectacular in many ways. One of New Mexico's nine original counties, it was vast. Over time it would lose territory to Lincoln, Sierra, Torrance, Catron, and Cibola counties, but in Holm Bursum's time, Socorro County stretched all the way to Arizona. It is a beautiful land near the point where the Colorado Plateau, Chihuahuan Desert, and High Plains grasslands converge. Rows of blue mountain ranges rise in the west, some peaking at almost 11,000 feet. Snow-topped in winter, shadowed in the summer by monsoon clouds, the ranges are habitats for mountain lions, bears, bighorn sheep, and elk. In the east, a greenbelt of farmland lies along the Rio Grande, and beyond that, ranchland stretches toward another row of mountains.

The Socorro region has attracted waves of humans for thousands of years, reflecting a part of the world's ongoing story of migration. To set the stage for Holm Bursum's arrival in the 1880s, we look briefly at the region's past. Over five hundred years ago, an Indigenous farming culture of Piro-and Tompiro-speaking people flourished along the middle Rio Grande in and near today's Socorro. They rose from a culture known today as Ancestral Puebloan. By the 1500s, the people in the mid-Rio Grande area numbered in the thousands, living in well-organized towns of stone or adobe and participating in a far-flung trade network.

Meanwhile, Athapascan groups, migrating from the subarctic north, were en route to Piro lands. By perhaps the thirteenth century, they had reached central North America.[15] Eventually, branches known as Apaches came into the mountains of central New Mexico. They operated hunting, gathering, and trading economies and, at times, raided Piro and other Pueblo towns. In a later century, Apache leaders in the area would include those whose names we remember today: Cochise, Mangas Coloradas, Victorio, Lozen, Nana, and Geronimo.

In the late sixteenth century, another group migrated into Piro lands, this one coming up from the south. The newcomers were European colonists, mostly Spanish in origin. They used an old Indigenous trade route, which they called the Camino Real. It brought them across the Rio Grande at El Paso and, several days later, right up to the Piro towns. By then travel-weary and low on food, the colonists approached a local leader named Letoc, Paul Harden tells us.[16] From Letoc and his town of Teipana, the colonists received sustenance and sound counsel on the journey ahead. Not long after Onate's visit, other Europeans settled among the Piro people to convert, farm, mine, marry, and govern. They made the neighboring town of Pilabo an administrative center for the area and renamed it Socorro for the humanitarian aid they had received nearby. Early in the seventeenth century, a Catholic church went up in the town, and new religious practices came into the Piro world.

For communities like the Piros, the sixteenth and seventeenth centuries brought extraordinary challenges. The arrival of migrating groups meant that the scarce resources of the region, including products of the Piros' own labor, had new claimants. The Europeans, in particular, changed life profoundly. The Piro and other Pueblo people soon found themselves subsumed into an empire that ruled them from the other side of the world.

As the seventeenth century wore on, another change materialized—a hard drought. Under environmental and social pressure, people reacted, and strong opposition to European colonization began to build in Pueblo communities north of Socorro. Resistance spread, and in 1680, the Pueblo Revolt erupted. Years in the planning and led by Po'pay of Ohkay Owingeh, the conflict unfolded over days and drove the Europeans back to El Paso. In Socorro, several families had blended, with both Piro and Spanish members. Some joined the retreat south.[17]

Just twelve years later, the Spanish Reconquest was launched from El Paso. Socorro was out of the mainstream of the revolt and the restoration of European power, but it felt the effects. The Spanish government, short on military resources, allowed no resettlement on the Rio Grande south of Belen for many years, Paul Harden writes.[18] The town entered a long quiet period. Eventually, the rules relaxed. In the early 1800s, the mission church of San Miguel went up on the base of Socorro's earlier church, and the community began to revive.

During the 1821-1822 transition from Spanish control, New Mexico became part of a newly-independent Mexico. The relationship held for a quarter of a century. Then another colossal change occurred. In 1846, the United States, in a war with Mexico, took Santa Fe and installed a military governor. Two years later, the U.S. annexed most of New Mexico through the Treaty of Guadalupe Hidalgo. From that point forward, people of many heritages began migrating to the new territory, and a number of them settled in Socorro, the town once called Pilabo. Holm Bursum, with his Nordic roots, was among them.

In the 1880s, when Holm Bursum first knew Socorro, it had taken on the sheen of wealth as U.S. mining companies extracted silver, gold, and copper from the nearby mountains. With its economy humming, the little city grew rapidly, competing for a while with Albuquerque to be the territory's urban center. Soon, Socorro could count an institution of higher education, several churches, and an opera house among its refinements. Its older features were part of the young man's daily landscape too: the seventeenth-century Catholic Church and the old Camino Real. Prizing all of Socorro, vintage and new, became a Bursum value.

"Socorro was a town to stir a man's blood as well as his imagination," wrote Bursum's cousin Conrad Hilton, who grew up nearby.[19] "Everybody who was anybody in New Mexico was in Socorro at one time or another," Bursum's grandson, Holm III, said of that era. The city drew both the illustrious and the infamous. Among the former were Judge Merritt Mechem, a future governor; Trinidad Romero, an ex-delegate to the U.S. Congress; Elfego Baca, the legendary sheriff, and the entrepreneurial Hiltons. Among the latter were outlaws like the High Five and Blackjack gangs.[20] Holm Bursum, political leader and law enforcement officer, knew them all.

Meeting Lulu May Moore

Bursum had done well. Coming to central New Mexico in his teens and becoming a businessman and an elected official in his twenties, the young man was ready for a new stage in his life. Romance caught up with him in a town called Shakespeare. As a sheriff traveling an expansive jurisdiction of deserts and mountains, he sometimes crossed into other counties on business. On one of those trips, he stopped in Shakespeare, his son said.[21]

Shakespeare, a silver-mining town in Hidalgo County, was on the Butterfield Stagecoach Line. It was not far from the newer railroad town of Lordsburg. Both were gateways to the Bootheel of New Mexico, a spectacular land of mountain ranges and valleys spilling down to the border with Mexico. In that remote spot, Holm Bursum met a young woman. It happened at a dance. The sheriff had prolonged his stay in Shakespeare into the evening and had gone to the dance. At one point, he took his turn at making music. As his son Holm, Jr. heard the story, Bursum, a good player, tucked a violin under his chin and "...spelled the fiddler" for a while.[22] At some point, the wife of a Lordsburg banker introduced him to Lulu May Moore. It was an encounter with a future.

Dark-haired, known as charming and beautiful, Lulu Moore was a decade younger than Bursum. She and her family had come from Arkansas around 1880 and settled in San Lorenzo in the pretty hill country of pinones and junipers along the Mimbres River. Lulu had attended a normal school, an educational advantage in a frontier society. Bursum courted the young woman, and in 1898, when he was thirty-one, they married. The new bride came to Socorro to share in her husband's life of ranching, politics, and elective office, and together they raised a family of three daughters and a son. In due time, Lulu Bursum would take on her own political organizing and public service work.

Organizing for Statehood, 1906–1911

Toward the end of the nineteenth century, Holm Bursum became a rancher. His work in the GOP also intensified. In territorial days, an elite group controlled the party, but "an emergent group of younger Republicans" challenged them, according to David L. Caffey.[23] The young leaders were known as the Colts, and Holm Bursum was among them. They allied themselves with the also-youthful Governor Miguel A. Otero II, Robert W. Larson noted.[24] Their allegiance put them in some tension with an older leader, attorney Thomas B. Catron. Catron, a Missourian, had an unusual profile. He had served as a Confederate Army officer and later joined the Republican Party. Once he settled in New Mexico, he helped establish a machine known as the Santa Fe Ring. More than a few times, he went up against Miguel Otero.

As Bursum navigated the factional seas of the GOP, he was building his resume. In 1899, Governor Otero appointed him superintendent of the territorial penitentiary in Santa Fe. There, the young ex-sheriff had reunions with some of the criminals he had pursued in Socorro County. Bursum, a young administrator at thirty-two, had humanitarian ideas and a belief in rehabilitation. His approach led a penal expert of the time to praise his work.[25] Under Bursum, the prisoners ate well and worked in good conditions on road building and brick making. Thus, they learned skills and earned money for the time of their release.

In 1904, at thirty-seven, Holm Bursum began to chair the New Mexico Territorial Republican Central Committee. Caffey evaluated Bursum's party work, drawing on the perspective of the young man's contemporary, attorney and historian Ralph Emerson Twitchell:

> Not until the new century did the [Republican] party find a leader with the vision, energy, and organizational skill to seize and exert persistent, controlling influence from the chair. When such a man came along, he was not a protégé of the old Ring, but the representative of a new generation of Republican leaders. Holm O. Bursum of Socorro was elected chairman in 1904 and served until 1911 … In Twitchell's view, the chairmanship was "a position which he filled with great credit, leading his party to victory in every campaign down to and including the election of delegates to the constitutional convention of 1910."[26]

Caffey's view that Bursum was not a product of the old Santa Fe Ring is significant. The Ring emerged in post-Civil War times as newcomers to New Mexico dove into land speculation. Sometimes unethically, they amassed fortunes and wielded political power.[27] One of their mightiest was Thomas B. Catron. Holm Bursum was not part of Catron's inner circle. He was Catron's junior by twenty-seven years and had different motivations. Nonetheless, David V. Holtby considers the younger man one of "the Generation of 1890," a Euro-American GOP leader who, like Catron, had established himself in the territory by the end of the nineteenth century.[28] Perhaps Bursum served as a bridge between the old guard and the new politicians of the early twentieth century. He helped refresh the party and shift the focus to its young wing.

Bursum led the GOP during an exciting, anticipatory time. After many attempts to join the Union, New Mexico finally seemed close. For the prior half-century, Washington power players had considered the territory too foreign. It was bilingual, they said, and it was Catholic. Other reasons emerged too, such as balancing power between slave and free states. The Civil War had resolved the power-balance problem but not the "foreign" one. Statehood might not have happened in 1912 without New Mexicans who could organize politically and negotiate diplomatically with the U.S. government. Bursum was one of the strategists and chief ambassadors of the cause. Consistently, he maintained that the territory's people were worthy of being part of the Union, and he judiciously used political pressure and rhetorical eloquence to make his point. In the process, he met presidents and helped design a government.

1906: Selling a Super State

In 1906, New Mexico decided to approach its long journey to statehood in a new way, partnering with Arizona Territory to enter the Union as one state. But there were a few hurdles to clear. The U.S. Congress passed a bill requiring the electorate in both territories to approve the single-state plan by a vote.[29] Getting those votes presented a challenge. Each territory had its sense of identity, based in part on different settlement patterns and distinctive constituencies. In Arizona, the Hispanic and American Indian presence was estimated to be five to twenty percent of the population.[30] By contrast, New Mexico's percentage was over half.

GOP chairman Holm Bursum, who initially had opposed jointure, became a great proponent. He knew others had their doubts, but he was undaunted. He was in an excellent position to win the territory's support for joint statehood—especially if he could maintain his political leadership. In 1906, he was elected to the first of his six terms as mayor of Socorro. He also was about to stand for reelection as chairman of the Territorial Republican Central Committee. Bursum was thirty-nine that year, his face still showing the smooth fullness of a young man, his hair thick and carefully groomed. He had reached that time of life when he had an ideal combination of experience, reputation, and energy to devote to his political activism. He was an influential and popular leader, one who found himself cheered in some circles at just the mention of his name.[31]

On September 29, 1906, the Republican Party met for a convention in the northern New Mexico town of Las Vegas. The meeting was one of harmony, reporters stated. Important matters were on the agenda: the election of the central committee chairman and the question about New Mexico's entering the Union with Arizona. Bursum and his allies brought the matter of joint statehood to the delegates in a resolution, and it was only that resolution which rippled the calm waters of the convention.[32]

Solomon Luna, chairman of the resolutions subcommittee, began his report. He was a notable man of New Mexico, well educated, affluent, and prominent. He had a fashionable look, his dark wavy hair cut short, oiled and parted in the middle, and his bounteous mustache setting off the handsome curve of his nose. He wore beautifully cut suits and starched white shirts. A rancher, banker, and local official, he lived with his family in Los Lunas. Their mansion, with its soaring white columns, still stands today and has been called by Richard Melzer the 'Downton Abbey' of Valencia County.[33] Luna's prominence extended to the political realm. He was a strong Republican who served as his party's national committeeman for years, and he was Holm Bursum's comrade. Addressing the convention, he thanked Bursum "...for his faithful work for the party.... We not only recognize in him an able, loyal and consistent republican [sic], but we regard him as a man possessing the confidence of the people for his candor, honor and integrity."[34] The convention roared in agreement with the commendation.

Then, Luna presented the resolution for joint statehood. A rollicking debate on the convention floor ensued. It was, as one press report said, "a three-corner fight,"[35] and it was going to be up to Bursum to manage the outcome. Some contended that New Mexico possessed all the attributes—population, geography, wealth, industry, and education—to enter the Union as a single state. The commanding Thomas B. Catron stood at this corner of the fight. He and his group pushed for a party plank that would repudiate jointure. Another faction argued that supporting or rejecting jointure was not the business of the party. In this group were the aristocratic Don Eugenio Romero and his big San Miguel County delegation. They urged that each New Mexican should vote at the ballot box according to his own thinking.

Holm Bursum spoke for the third group. First, he expressed regard for President Theodore Roosevelt, praising him for economic-growth sustaining policies, global leadership, and support for New Mexico statehood. Then, Bursum addressed the jointure issue. Like Catron and his group, he spoke of New Mexico's rich resources. He went on to cite the numbers of people migrating in, eager to settle, but unlike the Catron faction, Bursum thought statehood with Arizona was the best way forward. He himself was working for jointure, he said, "with the zeal of a recent convert."[36] His speech brought loud applause from much of the convention but, as a reporter noted, "coldest silence" from Romero and his San Miguel group.

As Bursum left the stage, a band played a bouncy dance tune, and the convention prepared for its next phase. Before the day was over, the delegates had reelected Bursum as chair of the central committee and passed the resolution for joint statehood with Arizona. Two days later, the *Albuquerque Citizen* editorialized about the young leader, noting that the ovation he received at the convention was one "...of which even President Roosevelt could have been proud."[37] As a public figure, Bursum had grown over the past several years. He had developed himself as a thinker; he was a good speaker, and he could organize—all attributes that could advance him to some sort of national position, the editorial concluded.

Bursum was in good standing with his party. Whatever his long-term political ambitions might have been at the time, his most immediate task was to promote New Mexico's statehood through jointure. To that end, he was in motion, going from Las Vegas in the northeast to Silver City in the southwest.[38] His willingness to get on the roads and rails of New Mexico to promote a cause created a family norm. Half a century into the future, his namesake, Holm III, would follow those same roads—sometimes even taking to the air—to organize for political purposes.

While the first Holm Bursum built support for jointure in New Mexico, the Arizona proponents formed their arguments.[39] They offered their electorate the vision of a spacious new state. The territories together would form the second-largest state in the U.S. and would have more power in Washington than they enjoyed at the time. At the time, each territory had one delegate in Congress with no vote. As a joint state, they would have two senators and at least two representatives, all of whom could vote. It was an attractive point, but it was not enough. Worries sprouted over cultural differences between the two territories.

Some Arizonans had trepidations about their neighbors, given that many New Mexicans were of a different European-American background than they were. In their view, not enough in New Mexico were fluent in English, and too many practiced Catholicism.[40] The dubious in Arizona argued that it was not wise to merge two such different populations. The pro-jointure Arizonans rebutted.[41] Was it good, reasonable, and just, they asked, to oppose joint statehood because of a bias against people who lacked fluency in English? Many immigrants who came to the West from around the world also were not fluent in the language, they pointed out. People of Mexican heritage at least were native-born and Americans, they said. As for New Mexico's Catholicism, the advocates appealed to people's respect for religious freedom and to an overall keen love of liberty that characterized the frontier.

On November 6, New Mexicans elected to enter the Union with Arizona, voting 26,195 to 14,735 for jointure.[42] Their neighbors did not reciprocate, and the effort failed. Bursum did something that he passed down to his grandson. He looked for the positive message in a vote he did not win. In 1906, the message was that, regardless of the outcome, organizing for jointure had given the statehood movement some traction. New Mexicans had supported the proposal by a substantial margin, and that reflected well on Bursum and his party.[43]

1908: Working a Convention

With joint statehood out of reach, New Mexicans regrouped. In 1908 three territorial leaders, Governor George Curry, Solomon Luna, and Holm O. Bursum, met at the White House with President Theodore Roosevelt.[44] Roosevelt had decided not to run for a third term and wanted to secure the New Mexicans' support for his preferred successor, Secretary of War William Howard Taft. Bursum was dismayed. He wanted another term for Roosevelt for the sake of New Mexico statehood and said so. He was more than slightly acquainted with the president. Roosevelt, passing through New Mexico by train, had "...stopped in Socorro once to say hello," Bursum's daughter, Ruth Harban, remembered.[45] Despite the urgings of many, the president did not change his mind about reelection; he would not run in 1908.

Bursum and his colleagues got on board for William Howard Taft at the Republican National Convention in Chicago in June 1908.[46] Bursum worked the convention floor to win the support of the District of Columbia and the territories of New Mexico, Arizona, Puerto Rico, Alaska, Hawaii, and the Philippines.[47]

He had another role, one that entailed deal-making with the party's leadership. It produced GOP support for the individual admissions of New Mexico and Arizona to the Union. Credit for the platform plank went to Bursum, but the endorsement did not happen without a trade, Robert Larson noted.[48] The Roosevelt administration wanted to appeal to labor voters in the coming election by having a strong anti-injunction plank. Some delegates opposed the provision, however, fearing it would cut into judicial power. Bursum went to work. A member of the powerful resolutions committee, he had leverage. The anti-injunction plank was modified, and with the help of Bursum's territorial voting bloc, it passed.[49]

1908 was not the last time a Bursum worked a national convention floor to build an alliance. The first Holm Bursum might have been interested to see his grandson act similarly in 1961 at a national Young Republican convention. From a small-population polity, the two men had the ability to build greater power through bloc voting.

1909: Hosting President Taft in New Mexico

Feting the President at the Alvarado

In the 1908 election, Theodore Roosevelt's wish materialized. William Howard Taft won the presidency, and in New Mexico, his supporters began tracking his work for statehood. In 1909, when the U.S. House of Representatives resisted bringing the territory into the Union, the new president did not move vigorously on the matter. The New Mexicans regrouped once more. They learned that President Taft, on a train tour through the West, planned to stop in Albuquerque on October 15. They would be ready. This time their appeal for statehood would be an elaborate and ceremonial one. The territorial leaders set to work on a program that would begin as Taft entered New Mexico from Arizona.

October is just the time to be in the Southwest. The skies turn a deep and cloudless blue, and the sun streams light at such an angle that the land appears unearthly. The heat of summer is retreating, and a touch of crispness might invade the day. It was a good season to host a president. As William Howard Taft traversed the high Colorado Plateau spanning upper Arizona and northwest New Mexico, he must have been struck by its red-rock beauty. It was morning when he and his entourage crossed the territorial border and stopped in Gallup. There, at the edge of the Navajo Reservation, New Mexico's political and business leaders had gathered to greet him. Among them was celebrated Navajo weaver Elle of Ganado, who presented one of her blankets to the president as a gift for First Lady Helen Taft.[50]

Traveling east along the rails, the retinue stopped at Laguna Pueblo, a Keresan-speaking community settled in 1699. Against the backdrop of mesa and mountain, Taft spoke, assuring the Laguna people and their Acoma neighbors that the U.S. government was committed to their welfare. He encouraged them in their artisanal and agricultural work and touted quality education for their children so that they could "grow up to be good men and women and good citizens of the United States."[51] The people responded to the friendly Taft with their own warmth, generously not reacting to the paternalistic notes in his well-intended message.

Then, after a day of spectacular scenery and heartwarming hospitality, the president and his party came into the Rio Grande Valley, its cottonwood bosque along the river beginning to turn a shimmering gold. Taft stepped off the train in Albuquerque to cheering crowds. William Keleher, a young reporter for the *Albuquerque Journal*, recalled the scene as the president addressed the public on the lawn of the Alvarado Hotel.

That evening the crowning affair of the visit took place, a great banquet. New Mexico's territorial leaders were going to stand before the president of the United States and make their best case for statehood. Holm Bursum was to be among the evening's speakers. The program "... had been prepared and rehearsed, carefully and religiously, for weeks in advance," Keleher said.[52] But, as the night progressed, the event almost imploded. Keleher continued:

The Alvarado Hotel..., the then pride of the Fred Harvey system, had made every preparation to extend unusual hospitality to President Taft. Blue point oysters were brought from the Atlantic seaboard and the finest food and drink had been procured for the banquet on the evening of October 15th. The west veranda of the hotel was enclosed to permit the placing of tables for sixty-five carefully chosen guests, selected from the most prominent men in New Mexico.... Speakers for the banquet had been selected with utmost care. H. O. Bursum of Socorro responded to the toast "Statehood."[53]

Bursum's speech, according to *The Santa Fe New Mexican*, was splendid. In part he said,

New Mexico has been a part of this union for more than sixty years, a result of conquest. At the time of its annexation, her people had been reared and educated under the flag of our sister republic yet within a short period of twelve years, she demonstrated a keen appreciation of American liberty: her ideals of a successful constitutional government [and] her fidelity and devotion to those principles....[54]

Bursum moved on to speak about New Mexicans' loyalty to the United States during wars. They had offered their lives to preserve the Union "...by furnishing more soldiers to the cause of the Civil War proportionate to population than any other state," he said. He also praised the actions of New Mexicans in the Spanish-American War of 1898. Despite their shared heritage with Spain, they had demonstrated their American patriotism, he pointed out, by "...sending four troops of the famous Rough Riders regiment commanded by that great American Theodore Roosevelt."[55]

Then, Bursum pointed out that "[t]he federal government has never expended a single dollar for educational purposes within our boundaries. No such liberal broad-minded policies as were instituted in the Philippines and Puerto Rico were ever here inaugurated...."[56] At that point, Bursum praised Taft, who had served as governor of the Philippines in 1901 and 1902.

He commended New Mexico families. They valued education, he assured Taft, and made every effort to find schooling for their children. Those who had the means sent their children on long, perilous journeys from New Mexico Territory to St. Louis to be educated, he said. He pressed his point with an example. One of the men dining with the president that very night represented precisely the background Bursum was describing: Solomon Luna of the illustrious family of Valencia County. Luna, whose family had been in New Mexico since the late 1600s,[57] was educated, accomplished, and affluent. He was "...fully equipped," Bursum stated, "in every respect for American citizenship."[58]

Democrat Owen N. Marron, Albuquerque's ex-mayor, followed Bursum on the agenda. Republican Thomas B. Catron, former delegate to Congress, came next. Like Bursum, they stayed on message. Then the evening changed dramatically as Albert Bacon Fall stepped into the spotlight to speak.[59] At first, no one suspected that disaster was lurking in the well-rehearsed and heretofore smoothly unfolding event.

Albert B. Fall's presence at the Alvarado that night was a story in itself. A Kentucky native, he was known for his thick, longish curls, black cowman's hat and formal dress, his ever-present cigar, and a decorative cane that reportedly could be weaponized on occasion.[60] Fall had started his career in New Mexico as a Democrat. However, anticipating statehood and wanting a seat in the U.S. Senate, he pondered his political affiliation. He realized that the Republican Party had the greater share of power in New Mexico in those days.[61] The territory's time as a U.S. possession had coincided with a long line of Republican presidents, and, given that the presidents appointed the top territorial leaders, the GOP had built a robust infrastructure in New Mexico. After considerable thought, Albert Bacon Fall changed parties.

On the night of October 15, 1909, with President Taft just feet away, Fall began his speech. Going off-script, he began to criticize the president and the national Republican Party for their tepid support of New Mexico statehood.[62] Like other New Mexicans, Fall was disappointed that Taft and Congress had not acted earlier that year to bring New Mexico into the Union. Furthermore, the president's speech in front of the Alvarado earlier that evening—one which counseled more patience on the part of New Mexicans—had greatly irritated Fall. The territory had been patient long enough. As he continued to reprimand their distinguished guest, the leaders in the room grew alarmed. "Aghast," "crestfallen," and "embarrassed" are among the terms Keleher used to describe their reactions as Fall spoke.[63]

Taft had given his address earlier in the day, but when Fall concluded, the president felt moved to speak again. He "...was on his feet," Keleher said, "plainly agitated ...." He defended his position on New Mexico, ending with a witty assurance that he would stick with the statehood cause despite Fall's words.[64] Fall drew widespread criticism for his lack of "western hospitality" and for behaving without courtesy to "a great man," Keleher noted.[65] The consensus of many was that Fall had ruined the banquet and jeopardized his political future by the way he had addressed the president, wrote Gordon Owen.[66] However, Taft, known as a good-natured man, maintained his equilibrium. That night he resumed his travels.

Traveling with Taft to the International Border

When midnight came, the presidential train departed for El Paso to keep an appointment, a meeting with Porfirio Diaz, the president of the Republic of Mexico. It was going to be a singular event, the first time the president of either country had made a state visit to the other. Charles Harris and Louis R. Sadler called it "...the first presidential summit in U.S. history."[67] The meeting had a practical purpose. The distinguished-looking, silver-haired Diaz had ruled Mexico for close to thirty years by then. He was friendly to the extensive U.S. business interests in his country, but in 1909 Mexico was on the very brink of revolution. There would be much for the two presidents to discuss.

President Taft invited New Mexicans to join him on the night train to the border. They included Territorial Governor George Curry, recent Santa Fe Mayor Thomas B. Catron, and Republican Party leader Holm O. Bursum.[68] Bursum, at forty-two, was the youngest of the three. Meanwhile, El Paso and Ciudad Juarez were rushing to put the finishing touches on the protocols and heavy military and civilian security for the presidents' visit. Thousands of troops from each country assembled to protect Taft and Diaz.[69] The military presence was not overdone. The Secret Service had uncovered a Chicago-based anarchist plot to assassinate both presidents at the border.[70]

A hundred thousand people from around the region gathered in El Paso to greet President Taft on the morning of October 16. He and his entourage were treated to the glorious output of two cities.[71] El Paso, worried that Cd. Juarez might host the more lavish reception, had draped yards of bunting, amassed walls of fresh roses amid greenery, and showcased thousands of school children singing "My Country, 'Tis of Thee" in San Jacinto Plaza. With bells ringing and cannons ready to fire, male dignitaries assembled, all in the prescribed dress of Prince Albert coats, white ties, gray trousers, and silk hats. On both sides of the border, bands played one another's national anthem.

As the hour of the summit approached, border-state governors of both republics converged near the bridge over the Rio Grande.[72] The U.S. secretary of war, the Texas governor, and El Paso's mayor proceeded to the international line on the bridge. At the appointed moment, President Porfirio Diaz arrived with great ceremony in a horse-drawn carriage trimmed in gold. After elaborate greetings, the U.S. officials escorted Diaz across the river to Taft. When the presidents' meeting in El Paso ended, another ceremony unfolded in Cd. Juarez.

The summit had happened without incident; history had been made, and Holm Bursum was there to see it all. What stirring moments they must have been for him, a first-generation American. He remained an effective emissary for New Mexico in the months ahead. Soon statehood, so long denied, was within reach. On June 20, 1910, the territorial leaders again found themselves with William H. Taft. On that occasion, Bursum and his colleagues were in Washington, DC to witness a bill signing that at last brought their territory into the Union.[73] The men returned home with a big task ahead of them, building a state government.

1910: Crafting the Constitution

In 1910, with statehood imminent, the New Mexico Constitutional Convention met. One hundred delegates gathered: seventy-one Republicans, twenty-eight Democrats, and one Socialist. The more than thirty delegates at the convention who were of Hispanic heritage all were Republicans.[74] They constituted close to half of their party's delegation.

The convention got to work on a constitution that could attract the vote of New Mexicans. It also had to win the approval of Congress and the conservative President Taft. The Republicans took leadership at the proceedings. Attorney Charles Spiess of San Miguel County chaired the convention, and Holm Bursum headed his party's majority caucus; thus, the GOP had a strong hand in the election of convention officers, the formation of committees, and the drafting of operating rules.[75] Others of Bursum's and Spiess's party emerged as leaders as well. They were from many parts of New Mexico: Solomon Luna of Los Lunas, Charles Springer of Raton, Thomas Catron of Mesilla and Santa Fe, and Albert Bacon Fall of Three Rivers in Otero County. According to political scientist Dorothy Cline, the men were "master politicians—tough, fearless, colorful, and domineering."[76]

The constitutional convention limited the power of state government in both the executive and legislative branches. The framers set up a divided executive. It meant that the governor would not have full authority to administer the state but would share it with eight other elected executives, who could be from either party. All executives, including the attorney general, treasurer, auditor, and secretary of state, would run for office individually and have separate lines of control. As for the legislature, it was limited to sessions of sixty days. The constitution also ensured that corporations could operate with fewer restrictions in New Mexico than in some other states. Bursum pushed for the business-friendly provisions. The state, rich in mineral resources and suitable for agriculture, still needed a more diverse economy to flourish. It must be one that could draw capital investment, he reasoned.[77]

The constitution advanced civil rights. Almost a decade before the U.S. would assure women's right to vote, New Mexico extended a limited franchise. It was less than advocates of women's suffrage wanted, but it was a start. Democrat Reuben Heflin of San Juan County introduced a provision giving women the vote in school board elections. Among its supporters were Holm Bursum and Solomon Luna.[78]

Other measures protected the rights of people of different heritages. In the early twentieth century, some parts of the U.S. were passing racial segregation laws. New Mexico's leaders did not want such laws in their state. In one instance, *The Santa Fe New Mexican* reported, Hispanic delegates helped defeat a public-school segregation provision that would have discriminated against Black students.[79] The delegates also wanted to forestall discriminatory actions against Hispanic people. As Sanchez, Spude, and Gomez wrote,

> [T]he most striking part of the constitution concerned the territory's Hispanic citizens. In light of existing and expanding segregation laws and discriminatory practices against African Americans, Hispanic lawmakers pushed to protect their rights and traditions. In public schools, they protected Spanish-speaking students from segregation. Also, they sought to preserve the citizenship rights awarded under the Treaty of Guadalupe Hidalgo. They ensured that voters could not

be disenfranchised because of their religion, race, color, or ability to use English. Equally important to Hispanics was a clause that made it nearly impossible to amend the constitution. Future changes to the document required a three-quarter majority in the legislature. Republican Party boss Solomon Luna proved to be crucial to the passage of these proposals. It is said he had but "to raise a finger or an eye brow" to influence delegates' votes.[80]

Some considered Luna to be a major shaper of the constitution. In 1911, the people approved the New Mexico Constitution by a vote of 31,742 to 13,309.[81] It was another success for Bursum as his party's leader. More than fifty years into the future, his grandson Holm III would use provisions in the constitution to hold a referendum on an electoral matter and would learn firsthand the complicated steps it takes to repeal a law. Meanwhile, in 1911, Republicans' defense of the document as originally written may have cost them their first gubernatorial election, the one in which the first Holm Bursum was a candidate.

1911: Running in the First Election after Statehood

In 1911, with statehood near, people were excited about the upcoming elections. Both parties had tickets to create, and the GOP chose Holm Olaf Bursum to run for governor. His political prominence gave him great credibility with one of his cousins, a young man named Conrad Hilton, who was thinking about his own role in public life.

Hilton, the future hotelier, was in his early twenties. He already had spent eleven years working in his father's businesses, he noted in his memoir. Once at his father's behest, he had even managed the singing career of his sister and her two friends. Hilton, an impresario at twenty, found it challenging to attract large audiences during the trio's New Mexico tour. When he and the singers reached Albuquerque in the summer of 1907, Hilton met William Keleher, a twenty-one-year-old journalist. Keleher gave him valuable promotional advice and even served as the trio's press agent for a bit. The encounter gave Hilton a "lasting affection for Will Keleher," he said.[82] The two young men launched a friendship that would see them through their spectacular career changes, and their extended families would continue to make connections through the generations.

First, however, Conrad Hilton needed to establish his independence, to find an identity apart from his father's. "Wasn't it time I formulated a dream of my own?" he asked himself in 1911.[83] He made a plan and talked it over with his mother. A deeply-religious woman, Mary Hilton referred him to Socorro's old San Miguel Catholic Church to pray. He went. "From there I walked around to talk to Olaf," Hilton said, recalling his meeting with his Bursum cousin:

> Now I wanted a boost. Republican-wise things were popping across the nation. With our constitution accepted and our birthdate into the family of states officially set for January, 1912, Olaf planned to resign his smaller honors and go for the Big Plum—the governorship. Teddy Roosevelt, after four years of political retirement, had swung into action with a falsetto roar: "My hat is in the ring." So was mine, I told Olaf—in a minor way, of course. "I would like to run for the state legislature," I said.[84]

Bursum approved. Young Conrad Hilton entered the campaign and won a seat in the New Mexico Legislature. In a strange turn, Holm Bursum, who was predicted to be the state's first governor, lost his race. He was defeated, probably for reasons related to the constitution that he had helped craft. It is an irony explored in Hamm's *The Bursums of New Mexico*.[85]

Serving in His Middle Years: A Second Gubernatorial Race and a U.S. Senate Seat

In 1916, Holm Bursum ran for governor again. Let us check in on the era. Woodrow Wilson had defeated incumbent President William H. Taft four years earlier and was running for reelection. The world was fighting the Great War, and a terrible flu pandemic was waiting in the wings. That fall, however, the United States, not yet in combat, still enjoyed peace and health. In New Mexico, people were getting ready to elect a U.S. senator for the first time. When the state joined the Union, its senators had been chosen by the legislature, as the U.S. Constitution stipulated. In 1913, however, the Seventeenth Amendment had given the voters in all states the right to elect their senators directly. Democracy was expanding, and New Mexicans were excited about their new franchise. As for women's right to vote, the U.S. had not yet passed the Nineteenth Amendment, but that time was coming too. It was in the air, and women envisioned becoming full partners in the political process. Adelina (Nina) Otero Warren, a relative of Solomon Luna, was helping to lead the suffragist movement in New Mexico and soon would go on to win the Republican nomination to run for Congress.[86] On the threshold of such change, Holm Bursum launched his second gubernatorial campaign.

Press reports by Guthrie Smith[87] captured the flavor of the 1916 election in a politically exciting state. In September, the Republican ticket headed to Mora County, an expanse of high grasslands and mountains northeast of Santa Fe. The people of the county had been attending political meetings all week and now awaited the arrival of the top candidates: Frank A. Hubbell, vying for a U.S. Senate seat; Congressman Benigno C. Hernandez, up for reelection, and Holm O. Bursum, running for governor. A parade was about to begin. Automobiles, horse-drawn conveyances, and a hundred mounted men, all with U.S. flags, lined up for half a mile, Smith wrote. Men, women, and children flocked to the procession, the little ones carrying baskets of flowers. When Hubbell, Hernandez, and Bursum arrived to head the cortege, the children showered them with blossoms until their car was filled. The final rally, according to the older attendees, was unparalleled in the county. It lasted until nearly midnight. Many women were present, an indicator of New Mexico's intense interest in public affairs, said the reporter.

In late October, at a campaign stop in Raton near the Colorado line, Hubbell, Hernandez, and Bursum faced great odds, Guthrie Smith noted.[88] For starters, the town was staunchly Democratic. Furthermore, it had been raining all day, and for those willing to venture out that night, there were other attractions, a boxing match and a movie featuring a star actress. Still, the GOP candidates packed a lecture hall and delivered their speeches in Spanish. During the Raton stop, part of Bursum's pledge was to invest in New Mexico's schools and roads.

Bursum traveled far and wide in his big state that fall, meeting voters, communicating bilingually. By early November, he was in southern New Mexico, drawing record crowds. In Dona Ana County, near the border with Mexico, supporters celebrated him with a torchlight procession. A Deming headline declared, "Bursum's Campaign for Governor Now Becoming Like a Triumphal March." A Lordsburg paper predicted the governorship soon would be his.[89]

November 7, however, turned out to be profoundly disappointing for the Republicans. Woodrow Wilson won his second term, and in New Mexico, Frank Hubbell, B. C. Hernandez, and Holm Bursum all lost their elections. Bursum's defeat was by only a slim margin.[90]

In the sometimes baffling way of politics, B. C. Hernandez retrieved his congressional seat two years later. Then, a new twist in the story sent Holm Bursum to the U.S. Senate. He succeeded Albert Fall, the man who had brought a good bit of political theatre to the Alvarado Hotel during President Taft's visit years before. Far from having ruined his career that evening, Fall ascended—right into the Senate. In 1921, when President Warren G. Harding invited Fall to become secretary of the Department of the Interior, he accepted. His joining the cabinet meant leaving the Senate, which gave New Mexico Governor Merritt Mechem the task of appointing his successor.[91] Mechem chose Bursum. Fall tried to prevent the appointment, but Mechem refused to back down. He had the unanimous support of the GOP executive committee. Soon Bursum was off to Washington. A short time later, the new senator won the seat in his own right. Up for reelection in 1926, however, Bursum lost his race.

By then fifty-nine, Holm Bursum had been in the public realm for over thirty years, and he still had nearly three decades of life ahead of him. He retired from electoral pursuits and began to restore his personal finances.[92] He had not been the sort of politician who enriched himself while in office. In fact, his time in public service had not been good for his economic well-being. He decided to go home to Socorro County and rebuild his ranching business. His return to New Mexico also would give him proximity, in the years ahead, to his grandchildren, including his namesake, Holm Olaf Bursum III.

Lulu Moore Bursum
Organizing Women for Political Action in 1928

As Holm O. Bursum retired from public life, Lulu Moore Bursum was stepping beyond her role as an official's spouse into organizational prominence of her own. In the winter of 1928, she joined New Mexico's First Lady Maurine Dillon to honor Florence Pullman Lowden, the former first lady of Illinois. It was another political occasion at the Alvarado Hotel, a tea hosted by the Republican Women's Club of Bernalillo County that drew 350 guests. The *Albuquerque Journal* described the scene: "In the huge fireplace of the lounge logs cheerily crackled and reflected darting shadows that played about floor standards, wicker baskets and silver vases that held a profusion of red carnations...."[93]

Lulu Bursum, part of the receiving line, was "...exceedingly attractive in a gown of flesh colored georgette beaded with irridescent [sic] beads and designed with a bow of amethyst shade as a contrasting note," the reporter wrote.[94] We read of the velvets, brocades, and Spanish shawls on display, of the scalloped hemlines, the brilliants, and the pearls. Young women in pastel dresses served tea and little cakes and ices to the guests. We read about the red cathedral candles on the table and the potted hyacinths set about. The images are beautiful, but missing is any hint of the topics that animated the conversations that day. There was much of substance to discuss. Not long before, women had won the right to vote in the U.S., and Lulu Bursum and her colleagues were about to launch a political education program for New Mexico's women.

That summer, Lulu Bursum's political activity was in the news again. She served on the board of governors of the State Council of Republican Women and was a vice president on the executive committee.[95] The council planned a School of Politics, a way for women to explore their new roles in public life. The organizers prepared a curriculum, booked experts to staff the school, arranged financing and publicity, and invited two thousand participants. Sessions would operate throughout the state. Being part of a social auxiliary to a male-dominated party no longer was enough for women like Bursum. As her grandson would do in the 1960s, she was organizing a demographic within her party to a higher level of political activity.

Serving as a Regent for New Mexico A&M, 1935-1940

In 1935, Lulu Bursum's public work intensified, but she could not have anticipated its course. Governor Clyde Tingley appointed her to the Board of Regents of the New Mexico College of Agriculture and Mechanical Arts (A&M). Located in Las Cruces, A&M was the state's land grant institution, and three Democrats and two Republicans made up its board. Bursum was one of the few women to serve as an A&M regent up to that time and the only woman during her tenure. Her service spanned the administrations of two Democratic governors, and she would be on board to help solve problems as the college entered very rough waters.

As Bursum took her seat at the regents' table, she began to witness the troubles bubbling up at A&M. It involved a seriously ill college president, a subsequent turnover in the position, and a board chairman who seemed to step too far into the administrative void. As Professor Simon Kropp chronicled in his history of the institution, problems ranged from financial distress and slow growth to rumors of political interference in the daily operation of the college.[96] Governor Tingley acknowledged the problems, but, according to concerned locals, they did not abate.

In 1938, the board of regents hired a new president, Hugh M. Milton II. He had an impressive resume.[97] At forty-one, he was a veteran of World War I, an engineer, and an academic. From the family of British poet John Milton, Hugh Milton himself was known as an eloquent writer. In just a few years, he would be called back into military service as World War II broke out. He would serve with distinction in the Pacific theater and then join the Eisenhower administration, becoming undersecretary of the U.S. Army.

As Milton began his tenure as president in 1938, New Mexico A&M continued to struggle, for reasons, it appeared, beyond his control. Allegations of political meddling in the college's day-to-day financial operations persisted and appeared linked to one of the regents.[98] Concerns in Las Cruces grew, and in 1939 the college's accrediting body, North Central Association, began to take note.

Amid simmering troubles that year, New Mexico A&M celebrated its Golden Jubilee in style. The new governor, John E. Miles, was among the dignitaries, and U.S. Attorney General Frank Murphy gave the commencement address. Soon to be a Supreme Court justice, Murphy traveled to Las Cruces in the company of a Justice Department colleague, a rising young figure in the nation—J. Edgar Hoover of the Federal Bureau of Investigation.

The day after the jubilee, a surprise announcement circulated through the state. New Mexico A&M regents Lulu Bursum and Arthur Starr resigned from the board.[99] People took note, but Governor Miles did not want the pair to leave and did not act on their resignations. When Miles later reappointed virtually the entire Tingley board, Bursum kept on serving, but she grew more troubled about college matters that remained unaddressed. She was not alone. Others agreed that—for most of a decade—the institution had been controlled by people tied to a "local-state political machine."[100]

In April 1940, problems at New Mexico A&M crescendoed.

North Central Association released its investigation report, and it rocked the stakeholders.[101] Much was good at A&M, North Central said, from academic standards and administration to Las Crucens' confidence in four of its regents. It was the structure of the board that presented problems, however. With its short, non-staggered terms, the body lacked continuity and was destabilized by an external influence that seemed linked to the fifth regent. He, the long-serving board chair, offered to resign, but it was not enough. North Central removed A&M from its accreditation roster. The news prompted Miles to rethink board membership, and he decided to appoint new regents.

An Associated Press reporter caught up with Regent Bursum in Albuquerque. She no longer was inclined to relinquish her position, she revealed. "If I felt that my resigning would bring the college back to the accredited list," she said, "I would resign at once. I have worked hard as a member, have been faithful to the institution, and have helped it out of some of its problems."[102] Leaving voluntarily did not seem justified, but she would resign if so requested.

Soon Bursum's resignation was requested. On April 15, she issued a statement. "Had the numerous protests from Las Cruces citizens against the appointment of 'an aggressive Democratic machine politician' to control locally the destinies of the college been heeded by Governor Miles," she said, "in all probability the college would not have been taken off the North Central recognition list."[103] Bursum appreciated North Central's actions and commended three board members: William Starr, M. P. Hernandez, and Henry Opgenorth. She credited the governor with improvements but noted "...an intense politically-minded situation, whereby utilization of educational institutional boards had become recognized as legitimate spoils of the victor."[104] She thought highly of the new regents, referring to them all as "very fine men."

After she had spoken, Lulu Bursum resigned. She was leaving board service, but she expressed pride in the college and pledged ongoing support to it. By attempting to resign in 1938, she and Arthur Starr had possessed the courage to call attention to the problems facing A&M. Dutifully, they had continued serving as requested, remaining until the troubles they identified finally had to be addressed. She could take satisfaction in that.

Miles moved forward.[105] He complimented Bursum for what he termed her sincere, conscientious work, regretting, he said, being compelled by developments to replace the board. Then he turned his attention to his new regents. They included William A. Keleher, by then an Albuquerque attorney. Two other attorneys, a newspaperman, and a rancher completed the appointments. People's optimism about the college rose. They saw the new board as nonpartisan and out of reach of the local political machine. Under Keleher's leadership, the work to restore New Mexico A&M to the company of accredited institutions began.

In one of those unanticipated developments in family history, Lulu Bursum and one of the new regents whom she had praised in 1940 would have more in common than service to New Mexico A&M. She and William Keleher would not live long enough to celebrate a union of their families, but it took place in 2000 when Bursum's great-grandson Michael and Keleher's granddaughter Loretta married. The young people had met in 1994 as students at New Mexico State University,[106] the school once known as A&M. Lori Keleher returned to the institution in 2008 to join the faculty in the Department of Philosophy.

Returning to Party Leadership, 1941

Lulu Bursum had a new public role in the 1940s when Chairman J. Benson Newell named her to the GOP State Executive Committee.[107] She had worked to develop the women's branch of the party; now, she was part of the overall leadership. Serving with her was Manuel Lujan, Santa Fe's ex-mayor and part of the politically-talented Lujans of New Mexico. Members of his extended family are in both parties and have served in all branches of government. One day, Lujan's son, Manuel, Jr., would begin his long tenure in the U.S. Congress. He would be elected in 1968, after a very long drought for the GOP, a time when almost no candidates of their party won high offices in New Mexico. Lulu Bursum's grandson, Holm III, and his young Republican colleagues would help stage the political resurgence that sent Lujan, Jr. to Washington.

Endings

Many decades after his childhood sojourn in Colorado, the first Holm Bursum returned to the state. Seeking treatment for a long illness, he lived in Colorado Springs, the city where his mother had died en route to New Mexico. He was there until his own death in 1953 at eighty-six. When Bursum first arrived in the Rocky Mountain West at the age of eleven, no one could have imagined the role he would play in the region's politics and governance. He chose the Grand Old Party early and stayed faithful to it, from his young years as a Colt into his elder statesman period. He remained a passionate Republican to the end, Holm Bursum III said.

Lulu Bursum remained in Socorro until she died in 1963, also at the age of eighty-six. She missed by two years seeing her husband inducted into the Hall of Great Westerners in the National Cowboy and Western Heritage Museum in Oklahoma City.[108] It happened on June 27, 1965. Among Bursum's fellow inductees that day were Meriwether Lewis and William Clark. More than two hundred individuals have been so honored at the museum, including prominent Western figures Sacajawea of the Shoshone people and Chief Joseph of the Nez Perce. Also included are artists Frederic Remington and Charles Russell; writers Willa Cather, Zane Grey, and Tom Lea, and the former U.S. Supreme Court justice, Sandra Day O'Connor. Perhaps most moving for Holm O. Bursum would have been to find his name and story among those of fellow New Mexicans such as novelist Eugene Manlove Rhodes and his dear friend and fellow leader in the statehood movement, Solomon Luna.

Holm and Lulu Bursum had come to New Mexico when it was a territory with a rich and diverse past, and they worked to make it a state. Their lives as political organizers and public servants also established a family tradition. The next generations of Holm Bursums would accompany their party and state through new phases of history. Facing notable political and governance challenges, each Bursum would find his particular way to serve.

3

Democratic Dominance: One-Party Rule in the 1930s and 1940s

In any one-party state, conditions become stagnant.
   —Frederick C. Irion, Professor of Government, University of New Mexico, 1963[109]

When Holm Bursum III and the Young Republicans set out to help restore New Mexico's two-party system in the 1960s, they faced daunting political odds. Their work is best appreciated when we consider the context in which they grew up. It was a more than a two-decade period when Republicans found themselves unsuccessful at the ballot box and essentially sidelined from state government. The achievements and disadvantages of long-term, single-party rule tell a story worth reviewing. The account is enhanced by the people who acted on the political stage of those times and shared their memories, particularly William A. Keleher and Fabian Chavez, Jr.

William A. Keleher's *Memoirs* is rich with vignettes of the governors of the 1930s and '40s. The young journalist who befriended Conrad Hilton and reported on President Taft's 1909 visit to Albuquerque had become a distinguished attorney and public service-minded individual. Six Democratic governors—from Arthur Seligman to Thomas Mabry—appointed him to the State Board of Finance.[110] It was a select group with broad fiscal authority, a "little legislature," some called it. One of three appointed members, Keleher served with the state auditor and the governor. It was a position that gave him an excellent vantage point for his commentary.

Fabian Chavez, Jr. was another participant/observer whose insights enliven the story of twentieth-century New Mexico politics. Chavez offered his political perspective to his biographer David Roybal, starting with his years as a Santa Fe Young Democrat in the 1940s. He began serving in the state legislature in the '50s. By 1961, he had risen to be Senate majority leader. Two great New Mexicans of opposite parties went on record about Chavez.[111] Democratic Governor Bruce King stated that Chavez—a liberal—got along well with conservatives and pushed for good government. Republican Governor Edwin L. Mechem, who almost always had an opposition-majority legislature, appreciated Chavez's deep understanding of state government and benefitted from his bipartisan approach to leadership.

Yet another informant was longtime New Mexico newspaperman Will Harrison, who provided contemporaneous commentary. He had the look of his time—the sleek dark hair and trim mustache of a Thomas E. Dewey or an Ernie Kovacs. He had a talent for finding the intriguing small stories inside the bigger story and telling them with wit and detail. For followers of the state's political twists and turns, his observations were a must.

Viewing One-Party Governance

From the 1930s through 1950, New Mexico operated under the governance of one party. Democrats won virtually all statewide and congressional offices as well as a majority of state legislative seats. It had not always been that way. Early in the twentieth century, the Republicans had been the dominant party—but not exclusively.[112] In the first eighteen years of statehood, the Democrats were quite competitive. When New Mexico entered the Union in 1912, it was with a Democratic governor and Republican majorities in both houses of the legislature. Over the next years, the GOP held a legislative advantage by maintaining control of the Senate, but the House was different. In two of nine sessions, Democrats won the majority. As for the governorship, in eight elections from 1912 to 1928, the voters chose Democrats four times and Republicans four times. Democrats won the high-profile offices of secretary of state and attorney general more often than Republicans. Two robust parties had started out to share in the new state's governance, but the bipartisan give-and-take soon was to be over.

In the 1930s, as the Great Depression settled over the country, politics began to shift in New Mexico. The election of Franklin D. Roosevelt to the presidency in 1932 helped boost the state's Democratic Party to nearly exclusive power. Roosevelt's economic recovery programs meant work for people who needed it, and in New Mexico, the process of job distribution became tied to one party. Democrats quickly started to enjoy virtually 100% success at the polls in statewide races and most legislative ones. Fabian Chavez, Jr. was a boy when Roosevelt first won the White House, and he savored the memory of the long span of the New Deal years that extended into his young adulthood. "I had a mind-set that, God, the Democratic Party is undefeatable," Chavez said. "I had grown up with nothing but Democratic governors. Democratic congressmen. FDR had four terms."[113]

Clyde Tingley, Governor, 1935-1939

Necessary changes occurred during the Democrats' decades in power. Clyde Tingley, governor from 1935 to 1939, served New Mexico at a critical time. He took political risks to solve the government's financial crises, and he reformed New Mexico's election law on candidate selection. The reform created a controversy that threads through our story, eventually involving Holm Bursum III in the 1960s.

The dapper Clyde Tingley, broad-faced and of blocky build, had a determined nature. He grew up in Ohio in modest circumstances, but his wife Carrie Wooster Tingley came from affluence. They settled in New Mexico for her health, and there he in his well-tailored suits and she in her stylish hats graced public life with their concern for others.

William Keleher knew Clyde Tingley well and, in fact, wrote the new governor's inaugural speech. In his view, Tingley was the most highly qualified of the six governors in whose administrations he served. Keleher pointed out that Tingley was not as well-educated as some, nor was he "an original idea man."[114] His great talent was his ability to evaluate others' ideas, interpret them politically, and rapidly operationalize those of promise. Skillfully, Tingley confronted problems during the Depression, one of the most urgent being funds for education.

Saving Schools, Creating Jobs, and Expanding Health Care

New Mexico's public school finances had reached an alarming state, recalled Keleher. In some districts, money to pay teachers had run out. Tingley listened to the Finance Board's recommendation that he institute a sales tax.[115] It was not a common tax at the time, Keleher noted, but Tingley worked with the legislature to levy it despite the political risks involved. The sales tax would continue to support education through the years, but such funding for schools would remain a dicey factor in elections, as we shall see in 1962.

Clyde Tingley also thought about jobs. The federal government had funded public works projects to provide employment, and Tingley wanted a big share of the money for New Mexico. Twenty-three times he boarded trains to Washington, DC in earnest pursuit of monies, said Keleher.[116] With the help of Senator Dennis Chavez, the governor succeeded. When compared to other Americans, New Mexicans per capita ranked fifth in the amount of funds received. The state also secured the highest level of funding per capita for education.[117]

On his trips, the governor had more than jobs in mind. Having become friendly with President Roosevelt, he told him about a project dear to New Mexico's first lady, a hospital for children.[118] Free consultations and federal funds materialized to match what the Tingleys raised. From their efforts, the Carrie Tingley Hospital in Hot Springs opened in 1937.

Leading a Direct Primary Reform

In the political realm, Clyde Tingley had particularly great success. He expanded citizen franchise through electoral reform. He was following the trend toward greater democratization in the twentieth century. In 1916, Americans had their first opportunity to elect their U.S. senators directly rather than through their state legislatures, and in 1920, women nationwide secured the right to vote. By 1938, most states also had some type of primary election to give citizens the right to choose their parties' candidates for office. New Mexico was one of only four states with no such primary.[119] Instead, party conventions chose the candidates, a system that allowed powerful insiders to dominate the selections.

Governor Tingley wanted a system in which no intermediary stood between the citizens and their parties' nominees. He called a special session of the legislature in 1938 to pass a law creating a direct primary. It was a controversial move. The first Holm Bursum, by then an elder statesman, was queried about the question of the day. "The people are privileged to obtain the kind of electorate nominating system for public officers they desire," he said.[120] He recommended that any direct primary law be submitted to the citizens in a referendum to assure that the reform was one they wanted, not merely a ploy to give a political entity a short-term advantage.

In the end, Tingley's reform prevailed. The legislature passed the direct primary bill, but the reform was not an easy one to keep. It weaves in and out of our story for decades. Before long, the primary would be compromised, and a quarter of a century after it first appeared in New Mexico, Holm Bursum III and the Young Republicans would lead an effort to revive it. They would use the referendum process as Bursum's grandfather had advised in 1938.

Building a Political Machine

Clyde Tingley could take credit for many accomplishments during his governorship, one of the greatest being his use of federal resources to rescue New Mexico economically. To succeed, he had to show political strength in the state and in Washington. It meant turning out the vote for the Democratic ticket, and from the 1930s into the '40s, that ticket was headed every four years by Franklin D. Roosevelt. To secure more funds for the state's economic recovery, both Governor Tingley and Senator Chavez wanted to build a political machine with loyal supporters, said Suzanne Stamatov, and "[t]hey appointed faithful followers to key positions that facilitated their goals."[121] She noted that, according to Will Harrison, Tingley kept tight control of state jobs, not only in Santa Fe but in state institutions such as colleges and hospitals. Lulu Bursum, as a regent for a state college in the 1930s, could attest to what machine politics looked like in higher education.

The matter of jobs affected party registrations in New Mexico. Holm Bursum III recalled his grandfather's comments about the political impact of economic recovery in the 1930s. Many rank-and-file Republicans began to leave the party then and register as Democrats to pursue federally-funded employment. "They had no work; they needed jobs," the younger Bursum said. "You couldn't blame them." In the 1960s, he, as a new political organizer, made an effort to win some of those Democrats and their progeny back to the GOP.

Political machines have their drawbacks, leveraging great power as they do through party discipline and a system of rewards. Not only do they have an advantage over the party out of power, but they also tend to tamp down the aspirations of people within their own ranks who challenge their methods. Even then, there are ways to use party power for the good. In New Mexico, political and social advances took place during the Democratic decades.[122] A striking example was Georgia Lee Lusk, who made progress for women in public life. In Lea County, Lusk ranched, raised children, and taught school. Later, she served as state superintendent of public instruction, helping to normalize the idea of women as elected officials in the executive branch. In 1946, Lusk was elected to the U.S. Congress. She was New Mexico's first woman to serve in the House and the only woman from that state until Republican Heather Wilson won a seat fifty-two years later. Civil rights also advanced in the '40s. In 1949, Tibo J. Chavez, majority leader in the Senate, passed New Mexico's first fair employment legislation. Other developments, however, were not as heartening.

Confronting the Downside of One-Party Rule

During one-party rule, some statehouse officials drifted toward unethical practices. One that caught people's attention was the "deadhead" matter. Deadheads were the political operatives on the state payroll who did party tasks, not government work. Another was the Democratic Party's taking a percent of state employees' salaries for its treasury. Yet another was cronyism in state contracting. All were causing concern in the party and beyond.

In the 1940s, Clyde Tingley wanted to return to the state government and reform it. In fact, he had not wanted to give up his gubernatorial post.[123] However, term limits stood in the way of his running again, so in 1938, he set out to amend the state constitution. He asked John E. Miles, Dennis Chavez, and other party leaders to help. They had demurred, and when Miles became his successor, Tingley responded. He made Governor Miles' Inauguration Day more than memorable by locking up the executive mansion and taking the key with him.

John E. Miles, from a hardworking, homesteader background, had built a remarkable political career. He was a good governor in William Keleher's view "...despite the constant pressure of old political cronies to whom he tried his best to be loyal."[124] The pressure from those colleagues may have helped exacerbate the problems of machine politics in the state, especially in political appointments. In 1940, when Governor Miles was up for reelection, Clyde Tingley decided to challenge him in the Democratic primary. Tingley, having waited out a term, was eligible to run again. He pledged to rid the government of the deadhead problem.[125]

Despite Tingley's opposition, Miles won the Democratic primary and went on to his second term as governor. In 1942, however, his administration faced a different kind of challenge, a legal one. A grand jury looked at the deadhead situation during an inquiry into the practices of several officials in the Miles administration. According to an Associated Press (AP) report, the grand jurors claimed that the governor "...had forced on department heads for 'purely political reasons,' employees who perform no service and cost the state some $150,000 a year."[126] Another of the findings, according to the AP report, concerned the purchase of highway equipment in no-bid contracts amounting to $1,660,735. Sixty-seven percent of the funds were spent with one company.

The governor himself was not indicted, but six other officials were. One was J. O. Gallegos, New Mexico's state revenue commissioner and simultaneously Socorro's mayor. In Commissioner Gallegos' case, the alleged irregularities on his expense accounts pertained to his claims of having been in Socorro on official business for an extended time—every day for a year. The matter of the indictments remained unresolved. It was wartime, and New Mexico lacked resources to process all cases. Even District Judge David Chavez, who would have heard the cases, was called into military service. He was in uniform on the day that he received the indictment report and dismissed the grand jury.[127] For the indicted, the presumption of innocence prevailed. J.O. Gallegos continued in his dual state and local roles, and before long, he would face an electoral challenge from Holm O. Bursum, Jr.

As one party became powerful enough to monopolize all state offices, practices developed that went beyond those of any single official. They carried over from one administration to another, becoming systemic. One statehouse problem that began to surface was the employee salary levy matter. For a levy to operate, people employed by the state government were pressured into making political contributions. In New Mexico, it meant that some state employees could be induced to give a small portion of their salaries to the treasury of the party in power.

Still another sore spot was the state government's regulation of the liquor sales industry. At the time, the state regulator had the power to issue and cancel liquor licenses without reporting to an oversight board. Occasionally ethical boundaries were pushed. In 1950, for example, regulator Tom Montoya drew criticism for sending out five hundred postcards to liquor dealers soliciting help for his office-seeking brother. He defended himself. The cards went only to dealers whom he considered his friends, he said, not to the entire roster. Nonetheless, the mailing produced a minor ruckus and an editorial, which called attention to the subtle coercion that the postcards represented.[128]

The state's insurance contracting raised yet more questions: conflict of interest and questionable purchasing practices.[129] In 1950, the *Carlsbad Current-Argus* noted that the state had spent most of its nearly $500,000 expenditures—a few million in today's currency—on insurance from four vendors. All were Democratic businessmen who simultaneously held government or party positions. One was Victor Salazar, who had multiple high-level roles in New Mexico. At the same time that he was contracting with the government as a private insurance company owner, he also served as the state's revenue commissioner and the Democratic Party treasurer. Another top insurance contractor was Clinton P. Anderson, a United States senator. Anderson, a South Dakota native, had moved to New Mexico for health reasons and had become one of its most successful leaders. He had served in President Harry Truman's cabinet as secretary of the U.S. Department of Agriculture and had presided over Rotary International. His business and political power hardly could be overestimated.

A rougher aspect of the long-term one-party rule was illegal gambling in New Mexico. William A. Keleher, in his *Memoir*, recalled the 1940s proliferation of gaming operations at the hands of an out-of-state syndicate.[130] Apparently, the crime organization had made serious incursions into New Mexico, illegally placing roulette wheels, slot machines, and other devices around the state. Expansion plans were in the works, according to Keleher. Giving a percentage of their proceeds to politicians was part of the deal. Some claimed that the state police knew of the violations but would not act, even when citizens offered to provide the documents for legal proceedings, Keleher noted.

More recently, Paula Moore has written about the gambling corruption in New Mexico in the '40s. In her inquiry into the unexplained death of a young woman in 1949, she found a story fraught with unlawful gaming and political payoffs. Moore published her findings in 2008 in *Cricket in the Web: The 1949 Unsolved Murder that Unraveled Politics in*

New Mexico.[131] It explores the intricate interplay of power, misdeed, and cover-up in the tragic demise of Ovida (Cricket) Coogler, an 18-year-old Las Crucen who socialized with state and local government officials.

The Coogler case was a chilling episode in an era of machine politics in New Mexico, a symptom of the broader misuse of governmental power. The case caught people's attention in the late 1940s and helped open the door to the idea of moving back toward a two-party system.

4

Republican Persistence: Cracks in the One-Party System

The Republican Party in New Mexico is not dead yet. Emphatically not.
—Reginaldo Espinosa, Chair, State Young Republican Association, 1948[132]

The Republican Party's comeback in mid-twentieth-century New Mexico would take years of patience, fortitude, and wit. In the 1930s and '40s, it meant working up slates of candidates in election after election, realizing that the party was not likely to take a single state or congressional office and few other ones. It meant being serious about running but having a sense of humor in defeat. In Albuquerque, a lunch club of former GOP candidates began to meet regularly to talk politics and amuse one another over their common circumstance: having lost a race to a Democrat. Calling themselves the OBs, enough of them stayed ready to step up and help their party try again as new elections needed their candidacies. Their eventual resurgence, they knew, was going to require the wisdom of the seniors and the energy of youth.

Keeping the Young Wing Aloft

Just as party elders stayed active, the younger generation of Republicans persisted too. The young wing of the Republican Party had a rich and lively history in New Mexico. It dated back to the late nineteenth century—to the Colts of the first Holm Bursum's time. At least by 1902, more formal young Republican groups made the news and then seemed to surge in 1916.[133] In 1902, the *Roswell Register* reported on a Young Men's Lincoln Club, which promised to engage in the "political battle" of an upcoming election. In 1910, a Young Republican club in Raton invited men as young as sixteen to join "the party of progress," according to *The Spanish American*. Six years later, Thomas Hughes of Albuquerque, with the blessing of the Republican National Committee, began to organize Young Men's Republican Clubs in New Mexico. In September of 1916, newspapers reported vividly on membership applications pouring in and clerks striving to keep up with the paperwork. From north to south, young men organized in Colfax, San Miguel, Bernalillo, and Dona Ana counties. Santa Fe's club had 145 members. More were to come. Ralph E. Twitchell led the new group. In his fifties, he was not precisely a young Republican himself, but as an attorney and public servant, he lent weight to the effort.

For a network of politically active young people to persist, the organizing and reorganizing had to go on year after year. In January 1920, a Young Republican League met in Santa Fe and discussed a statewide expansion. Anticipating women's suffrage, the group decided to omit "Men" from its title. When women got the right to vote, people in New Mexico went into action. In one case, Republican women in Bernalillo County allied with Young Republican men to ensure that both groups would have candidates on the ballot. The collaboration was heartening—full of zest, strategy, and the wisdom of women and youth. It is worth a pause to discover the details.

In 1926, the Bernalillo County GOP prepared for its nominating convention. Party leaders, to improve election prospects, began negotiating a partnership with independent Democrats. The Republican Women's Club and the Young Men's Republican Club became alert to the possibility that, during the upcoming talks, the nominations promised their groups could be on the chopping block. They joined forces to insist on their share of candidacies. They wanted women nominated for a state legislative seat and two county offices, and they wanted Henry Sandoval, a Young Republican, nominated for county assessor. Gilbert Espinosa, himself a part of the young wing, was appointed to the county party's resolutions committee. He helped author a declaration that included a statement for the ages:

> Whenever a political party perpetuates its same leader, and for any reason whatsoever, excludes the younger element or any element from its ranks, and council, we believe that it is certain to drift away from the principles upon which it was founded and alienate itself from the support of the general public.[134]

In the face of such advocacy, the Bernalillo County Republicans worked out their ticket.[135] Just before the election, they rallied at the armory, marching there in a parade that stretched for nearly a mile. Future Governor Richard C. Dillon and former Governor Octaviano A. Larrazolo led the procession. Young Republicans had organized the event, which surpassed earlier such demonstrations, according to the press. The county GOP ticket swept the elections on November 2, 1926, and women were on the ballot.

Facing a Downturn

Having a vibrant young presence in the Republican Party during the early statehood years was not surprising. The party competed well at the polls then, and its role in governance was robust. In the 1930s and '40s, however, the story changed. It must have been challenging to maintain a young Republican wing during the Democratic flourishing in the Roosevelt and Truman era. Despite the difficulties they faced, the young women and men of the GOP carried on. YR clubs began popping up in places like Curry and Rio Arriba counties, Grants, Gallup, and Las Cruces. By 1944, the YRs planned to have a club in every county, and President James Chacon pledged to do his part.[136] The leadership already showed geographic diversity. Chacon's colleagues were men and women from clubs in counties as far-flung as Rio Arriba in the north, Eddy in the south, and Torrance and Guadalupe in between.

Four years later, the national Republican Party took a great blow, and it affected the New Mexico party as well. In 1948, the GOP presidential candidate, Thomas E. Dewey, had seemed to be on an easy stroll to the White House, according to political forecasters, but Harry Truman beat him decisively. Down-ballot Republican candidates in New Mexico had similar disheartening outcomes. The Democrats took all executive and congressional offices, as had become the norm, and in the state legislature, the GOP minority lost even a few more seats.

Republican leaders gathered for a post-election meeting. State Senator Sidney Gottlieb of Cubero, just defeated, declared that they were at a wake. "The Republican party as such is dead—it is a thing of the past," he said. He could not imagine its resuscitation and proposed a new party, a new name.[137] The young wing responded. Reginaldo Espinosa, chair of the state

Young Republicans, had just won his election to the New Mexico Senate. To him, prospects did not look so dim. "The Republican party in New Mexico is not dead yet," he said. "Emphatically not." He acknowledged problems but predicted, "...with the co-operation of the youth of this state, we shall bring back the Republican party."[138]

To an extent, Espinosa was right. In 1950, the Young Republicans organized the Ballot Box Brigade. They registered voters, got them to the polls, trained election officials, and pushed for accurate ballot counting. "Once we get the voter in the front door, Espinosa cautioned, we don't want his vote to be lost out the back door."[139] Youthful enthusiasm helped drive the political process. That year, Edwin L. Mechem won his landmark election, the first GOP governor elected in a generation and, at thirty-eight, the youngest. Before his quantum leap, another young Republican, Holm O. Bursum, Jr., ran a politically significant race in Socorro. His 1948 win caught the state's attention, but he had succeeded even before then.

Introducing Holm O. Bursum, Jr.: Taking on the Machine

Holm O. Bursum, Jr., born in 1908, followed his parents in a life of ranching and public service. Growing up, he had enjoyed the usual play of youth, he recalled, but he had a serious bent as well. In an interview with Martina Franklin, he told the story of his life.[140] As a student at Socorro's high school, Bursum had earned enough credits to graduate at midterm in 1923. Soon after, he went east to join his father, who was serving in the U.S. Senate. Bursum, Jr., still only fifteen, enrolled at Central High School, a beautiful red brick building in the Columbia Heights district of Washington, DC. In the spring of 1924, Central was the site of young Bursum's second high school graduation. Thus he was an alumnus of the same institution that had graduated J. Edgar Hoover about a decade earlier.

Bursum explored the nation's capital, he told Franklin, enjoying the Smithsonian and visiting the new Lincoln Memorial, dedicated just two years before. He also spent time among staffers in the U.S. House of Representatives. One day, he had gone over to the Senate Office Building and found an investigation of the Teapot Dome Scandal in progress. The scandal, of course, featured his fellow New Mexican, Secretary of the Interior Albert Bacon Fall, a man who had presented a challenge or two to his father over the years.

Holm Bursum, Jr. continued his account with his return to the Southwest. He worked for a few months for a business in El Paso. Then, he attended junior college at New Mexico Military Institute (NMMI), completing his studies and graduating from there at a record age of seventeen. He went on to a Citizens' Military Training Camp in Arizona in pursuit of a commission in the Officers Reserve Corps. The course, authorized by the National Defense Act of 1920, was scheduled for one month each summer for four years. On his usual fast track, Bursum finished his training in one summer on-site and with a few subsequent correspondence courses. His NMMI credits had counted too. He worked in Nogales for a time and in 1927, enrolled at the University of New Mexico (UNM) in Albuquerque, where he studied business and played football. He graduated in 1929 and went east again—this time to the Ivy League, studying for a year at the University of Pennsylvania law school.

In the spring of 1930, Holm Bursum, Jr. returned to Socorro for good. He was home to help with the ranch. His father expressed no objection to his leaving law school, he told his interviewer Martina Franklin. The Depression had hit, and in 1929, livestock prices had tumbled to the point that sheep and cattle were nearly worthless, he said. The elder Bursum had not completely recovered financially after years of public service, and his son's work came in handy. Not long after returning home, Holm, Jr. met a lovely young woman. Elizabeth (Betty) Puckett, from Ada, Oklahoma, had come to teach in Socorro's high school. The two married in 1933, and Betty Bursum became a beloved figure in Socorro and beyond. The Bursums started their family and soon became active as a couple in the Republican Party.

Serving the County

In 1940, Holm Bursum, Jr., thirty-two, won election to the Socorro County Board of Commissioners. His fellow candidates, Gregorio U. Sanchez and James Sanchez, also were in their thirties. The young commission must have seemed like a fresh start for a county government that was in financial distress, as it turned out. According to the *Albuquerque Journal*, "...[T]he general fund for the fiscal year which had six months to run had been spent by the outgoing administration, and the salary fund with six months to go was overdrawn."[141] The situation was complicated by poor tax collections in the county and an overspent bond on the building of a new courthouse. The county was unable to pay its salaries or meet other obligations, and the new commissioners set to work to solve the problems they had inherited.

The *Journal* covered Bursum's summer trip to Santa Fe to avert a crisis. The commissioner was there to arrange for a transfer of other county funds to cover the needs on an emergency basis. In the article's photograph, Bursum, Jr. looked much like his famous father. He had posed formally in a suit and tie, his broad-brimmed fedora tilted just so. Not all that long ago, the reporter noted, the young man had been playing football for the University of New Mexico.

As commission chair, Bursum pledged to get the county's income and expenditures under control. "We are going to work and sweat this thing out," he said. "…[T]here is no reason why Socorro County should always be on the verge of financial collapse."[142] The press picked up on Bursum's word choices, titling his effort "the Work and Sweat Drive." The plan called for the county to sell off superfluous equipment, look for bargains, close down expense accounts, and hire a person to be both a purchasing agent and county manager. Bursum gave examples of the economizing efforts. The officials were finding cheaper prices on items from typewriter ribbons to coal shipments. When local vendors offered better deals than out-of-state ones, the county bought locally. The commission looked at old purchasing agreements, and, where they could, they settled with creditors, saving the county hundreds of dollars. Furthermore, Bursum said, they were willing to disappoint people who wanted favors. Political expediency was not a driving force for them.

Caesar Sebastian, the comptroller in Governor John Miles' administration, was impressed. "This new bunch is practicing economy in every way possible and with good luck in getting taxes in the county should be on a current cash basis within a year," he said.[143] The *Journal* gave Bursum the last word on the Work and Sweat Drive: "This is not good politics according to the old standards," Bursum remarked, "but I've got a hunch the people are going to like it."

Running for State and City Office: The Defeats

Three years later, Holm Bursum, Jr. branched out politically. In April 1944, he challenged incumbent Mayor J. O. Gallegos. The affable

Gallegos, running for his fifth term, was a strong opponent.[144] While serving as mayor, he also had been the state revenue commissioner in the Miles administration and was based partly in Albuquerque. His indictment by a Santa Fe grand jury two years before had not hurt him politically. At the polls, his townspeople showed their appreciation of him and his administration. Gallegos won his mayoral race with fifty-nine percent of the vote.

The Bursums took time for other political activities that spring. Holm, Jr. had a second race coming up. He had entered the Republican primary as a candidate for New Mexico's public lands commissioner, one of the nine elected positions in the divided executive branch. Betty Bursum's work was with the Socorro Republican Women's Committee. She helped organize an event for Carroll E. Gunderson, a state legislator from Grants who was seeking the GOP nomination for governor. People from throughout the county gathered to hear him.

Gunderson's thoughts in Socorro that May 11 evening were on agricultural development in the Middle Rio Grande Valley, but he also commented on the national scene.[145] He expressed his party's concerns that Franklin D. Roosevelt was wielding his power in all three branches of government. Congress seemed under the control of the executive, Gunderson said, and passed the president's legislation without much debate or change. Roosevelt extended his power even in the judicial branch, he continued. The president was appointing enough justices of his own ideology to compromise the Supreme Court's independence. Finally, FDR was running for his fourth term, thereby upsetting precedent and exceeding the two-term limit that George Washington had advised. For many Republicans, the federal system of checks and balances seemed to be in trouble.

Concerns such as Gunderson's animated political talk at many levels—from candidates' debates to conversations around family dinner tables. In the Bursum household, a ten-year-old named Holm III was learning that having a political philosophy and knowing the issues of the day were natural and important.

In June 1944, Holm Bursum, Jr. lost his primary race for the nomination to run for public land commissioner. He came in second of three candidates, defeated by Richard C. Dillon, but the ex-governor had little chance at the ballot box in November. Republicans won no statewide races that year. Bursum, Jr. was still young. He soon would change careers, and he would run for public office again.

Running Again: A Mayoral Race with Broad Implications

In 1947, Bursum joined other investors to establish a community bank for Socorro, and by the end of the year, he was its president. Ranching had become a lesser pursuit, and banking had become his profession. A few months later, he re-entered electoral politics. It was 1948, the year when Reginaldo Espinosa declared that young people would reinvigorate the Republican Party, and Bursum, who had just turned forty, was running a second time for mayor.

Socorro's mayor of twelve years, J. O. Gallegos, decided not to campaign for another term. However, he was endorsing Bursum's opponent, City Councilor R. A. Bangerter. The Democrats had been in power in Santa Fe for such an extended time, and given Mayor Gallegos' long years in a state government post, Bursum was, in a way, running against a machine. People around the state had their eyes on Socorro to see how the election would turn out.[146]

On April 6, 1948, Holm Bursum, Jr. made the news. He won his mayoral race with sixty-four percent of the vote.[147] An Associated Press report circulated through New Mexico, stating that he and his ticket had swept all city offices. Republicans A. B. Baca, G. L. Benavides, Herbert Falkner, Harold Olsen, and Moise Zamora won their races to serve on the city council with Bursum. In a year otherwise not good for their party, Bursum and his fellow candidates had done well. The new mayor promised monthly public financial reporting. It was a kind of transparency that had been lacking in earlier administrations, the *Socorro Chieftain* editorialized, but it was required by law and deserved by the people.[148]

Bursum's mayoral election in 1948 was an early sign of the cracks that began to show in one-party rule in New Mexico. Young Democrat Fabian Chavez, Jr., running his own campaign in Santa Fe County that year, saw the changes coming too. He called the ensuing years the Democratic Party's *hara-kiri* period. It was a time of factionalizing and some unfortunate governance decisions, he reflected.[149] The 1950s were going to be different for both parties.

Taking a Step Backward: Weakening the Direct Primary

Before long, the debate on the direct primary versus the convention nominating system popped up again in New Mexico. Clyde Tingley's reform empowering citizens to nominate their parties' candidates fizzled. It had lasted only a decade. In 1949, the Democratic-majority legislature passed a bill that must have made the former governor wince. It weakened the direct primary by instituting a pre-primary convention. The new system meant that potential candidates had to secure at least twenty-five percent of delegate votes at their parties' conventions before they could advance to the primary elections.[150] It was not as tightly-controlled and exclusionary as the old convention system, but it did give party bosses more opportunity to be gatekeepers of the nomination process. Citizen franchise was diminished.

New Mexicans of both parties, dismayed by the assault on a democratic reform, pushed back. They found leaders in Democrat Dennis Chavez, Jr., the son of the U.S. senator, and in W. C. Oestreich. The men organized a petition drive with two objectives: first, to suspend enactment of the pre-primary law immediately and second, to take the question of repealing the law to the voters in a referendum.[151]

Petitioning entailed getting the signatures of citizens throughout the state. It meant taking on several Democratic Party leaders in the process. Chavez and Oestreich met serious opposition and even threats, they reported. As a protective measure, they arranged for an armored vehicle to transport the petitions to Santa Fe for filing. Governor Thomas Mabry, of their own party, ribbed them over their concerns, saying publicly:

> Might I offer you a fully-equipped, well-trained State Police escort? You know there have been no marauding Indians along this road for many generations now, and I am sure that Bernalillo, Algodones or Santa Fe politicians you fear might molest you, would never make such a daylight attack with armed policemen nearby.[152]

Chavez and Oestreich replied with ironical gratitude for the governor's offer and then turned serious about the intimidating tactics that state employees had used against referendum workers. The petitioners would be hiring an armored truck after all. Ultimately the effort to suspend the law succeeded. It meant two changes, the first being that the party conventions would not nominate candidates for the primary in 1950. Instead, Democratic and Republican voters would choose their parties' candidates directly at the ballot box. The second change meant that a referendum to repeal the pre-primary law would be on the ballot that fall.

Though Democrats in power had weakened the direct primary, some high-profile party members wanted to restore it. In addition to Dennis Chavez, Jr., there was Attorney General Joe L. Martinez. He was an impressive young public servant who declared that his reelection was less important than the referendum's success. The people, he argued, had been partially disenfranchised, all to keep a political machine intact.[153] Notable State Representative Calvin Horn was just as firm. The pre-primary system was "not democratic," he stated.[154]

The repeal of a law through a referendum is a long, complicated process in New Mexico, and, in 1950, it failed. The pre-primary law, suspended that year, went back into effect for the 1952 and 1954 elections. After that, however, the legislature took action, scuttling the pre-primary convention. New Mexico returned to the direct primary from 1956 through 1962. Then in 1963, a great political maneuver would take place, and the pre-primary system would return. That year, the Young Republican Association, under Holm Bursum's leadership, would undertake a drive to restore the nominating process to the people.

Making Waves: Mechem vs. Miles in the 1950 Campaign

For some time, people had viewed state government with resignation. Serious ethical problems—deadheads on the state payroll, salary levies, cronyism in contracting, politicization of the state police force, and unethical liquor regulation—had not abated on their own. By midcentury, however, New Mexico voters seemed to see a way out. They were ready to confront the disadvantages of long-term, one-party rule. The Democrats in control of state government, "...had become suspect, to put it very mildly," wrote Howard J. McMurray.[155] McMurray, a University of New Mexico professor, was himself a Democrat. He had been a U.S. congressman from Wisconsin and had run for the U.S. Senate in 1946, but Republican Joseph McCarthy, soon to be notorious for his anti-communist tactics, beat him.

The Democrats' electoral fortune in New Mexico across two decades did not mean that their party was unified or that all agreed on a code of ethics. Factions formed and fought bitter primary battles over governance ideas. The liberal and reform-minded found leadership in Senator Dennis Chavez, states R. David Myers, while more moderate groups rallied to John E. Miles and Clinton P. Anderson.[156]

John E. Miles, a popular party veteran, had a great following. Born in Tennessee, Miles homesteaded in eastern New Mexico and built a political base there. With his dark hair combed straight back, his light eyes compelling, Miles had an impressive appearance and exuded self-confidence. He was a good campaigner, an approachable official who appealed to voters across ethnic, geographical, and ideological divides. He had won the governorship twice and held other high posts. He even served a term as a U.S. representative, during which he shared an office with fellow freshman John F. Kennedy. Miles was a consistent winner.

In 1950, John E. Miles entered his party's primary to run once more for governor. His most daunting opponent was David Chavez, a former state and federal judge and Senator Dennis Chavez's younger brother. Chavez was the very judge who in 1942 had received the grand jury report indicting several officials in the Miles administration. In the 1950 primary race, Chavez campaigned against the deadhead practice associated with then-Governor Miles,[157] but Miles won the nomination. Senator Chavez was not pleased about his brother's defeat. Later it would show.

That year something unusual was happening on the other side of the political divide in New Mexico. Edwin L. Mechem, a young attorney, took on the governor's race for the GOP, and the outcome was going to astonish people. Mechem was a big, handsome, quiet man with an amazing memory for people and a dry sense of humor. He was the son of a district judge and the nephew of a governor. In 1946, he also had been the surprise winner—by fourteen votes—of a state legislative seat.[158] He was the only one of his party elected in Dona Ana County that year. In dry times for the GOP, it was statewide news.

Senior Republicans could see that Mechem had the potential to be a prominent politician, but he resisted it. Both he and his friend Holm O. Bursum, Jr. had shown promise in their breakthrough elections in the 1940s. Furthermore, public service was in their family traditions, with their close relatives having held high government office. Party elders approached the young men to consider the gubernatorial race. For two decades, those very elders had done their part to keep Republicans on the ballot by running in futile races. Now they looked to the younger generation. Mechem and Bursum flipped a coin. The loser was going to have to run for governor, Bursum's son remembered, and the loser was Mechem.

Republicans' expectations for winning the governorship in 1950 were not high. The powerful John E. Miles was too formidable an opponent. Mechem's candidacy was simply to serve as a place keeper on the ballot and to organize the party at the county level for future elections. Mechem signed on to the plan, with no illusion that he would go to Santa Fe.[159] For six months, he traveled throughout New Mexico. From summer into fall, he stopped in towns, villages, and rural residences, sharing his ideas for government reform. Fabian Chavez, Jr. remembered that the appealing young candidate came across as someone with an unblemished record.[160] His good government ideas were resonating with people, and some Democrats began to consider voting across party lines.

One example of a crossover voter was Orville Pattison of Curry County in the solidly Democratic eastside of New Mexico. Orville's son Hoyt Pattison recalled the story of his family's political evolution.[161] The Pattisons' history in the state was similar to that of others of the time. In 1912, the family came from Indiana to Artesia, New Mexico, hoping that the dry climate would be good for the health of one of its members. Later, they homesteaded north of Clovis. As Republicans, they soon realized that to fit in with the politics of the county and state, they needed to register as Democrats. In the summer of 1950, however, Hoyt Pattison noticed that his parents' party affiliation began to shift. Home from his studies at New Mexico A&M, he remembered seeing his father in the living room of their adobe farmhouse talking with a young man. That man was Ed Mechem, Republican candidate for governor.

Mechem was out in the summer heat, driving the highways and farm roads of the state, working hard to organize the Republican Party for future elections, and not yet imagining that he was going to win that very year. "Ed Mechem made a very favorable impression," Pattison said.[162] "He was a sincere and solidly conservative person." By then, the Democrats statewide had earned a reputation for corruption in governance, Pattison continued, and Mechem had come along to change that. He "...saw the future of correcting the wrongs in New Mexico government." Pattison's family was part of the electorate that opened the way for a two-party system again in the state.

Senator Dennis Chavez, watching the election from his position of power within the Democratic Party, seemed not entirely opposed to a Mechem victory. Subtly, the senator began to speak and act in ways that may have helped the young Republican. Chavez, of course, had criticized John Miles when he ran against his brother David during the primary. Then, in the general election, the senator called out the deadhead problem. Five days before voters went to the polls, Chavez gave a strikingly candid interview. In it, he named four men prominent in the Bernalillo County

Democratic Party. They were on the public payroll—in some cases the state payroll—Chavez said, but they were not earning all that they were paid. "Barnacles and leeches," he called them.[163]

On November 7, Edwin L. Mechem won the governor's race. It shocked him and rocked the opposition, giving Senator Dennis Chavez's reform ideas new relevance. Chavez had warned the Democrats that they could not continue their less desirable practices in the long term, or the voters would react. The election results had made his point, he concluded.[164] He believed the Cricket Coogler case, illegal gambling, liquor regulation problems, and officials' ties to oil and gas corporations played into his party's loss of governorship. He mentioned again the need to remove deadheads from the statehouse.

Although the astonishing Republican victory did not completely end one-party dominance, Mechem's gubernatorial performance led to three reelections for him. He became known fondly as Big Ed and Honest Ed. Political scientist Frederick Irion thought the people voted for Mechem because he brought reforms to the state government that rectified other administrations' excesses.[165] The Republican's services were not always called upon though, Irion noted. Of his six gubernatorial races, Mechem lost two. When the voters did elect him, they did not make it easy for him to implement his reforms. In his four wins, only one other Republican won a statewide race with him. More often, Mechem went to Santa Fe as the lone Republican in the elected executive branch, the eight other officials being Democrats. Even the lieutenant governors in three of Mechem's four administrations were from the opposition party. In his work with the legislature, he faced Democratic control in both chambers in all sessions except 1953-1954, when house Republicans had a majority of one. Nevertheless, Mechem found a way to bring a higher ethical standard to governance—through executive action and bipartisanship with the Democrats who would work with him.

As important as Mechem's wins were, the GOP needed to expand its success to other candidates and other offices to be part of an enduring two-party system. One way was to develop the younger wing of the party. Mechem knew that, and he knew a young man who already was engaged in that work, Holm O. Bursum III.

5

Holm O. Bursum III: Growing Up in the GOP

...I got involved in politics when I worked with Gov. Ed Mechem to revitalize the...Young Republican wing of our party.
—Holm O. Bursum III[166]

While New Mexico dealt with the Great Depression and its political after-effects, the grandsons of Holm Olaf Bursum were growing up on the family ranch in Socorro County. Holm III and his younger brother Michael lived in enviable circumstances with loving parents, a vast and spectacular space to roam, multi-generations of family close by, and a grounding in the Presbyterian Church. Although their home was modest and money was scarce during the Depression, they had compensations. They had a good education, hard physical work to master, and a second language to learn at an age when it came easily. They also had a legacy, a remarkable connection to the history and government of New Mexico.

The third-generation Holm Bursum had much to live up to. He was named for his grandfather Holm Olaf Bursum, but the appendage "the Third" did not really fit. There was a little twist in the story. The young man's father, Holm Bursum, Jr., explained the matter.[167] It started with his own name, Bursum, Jr. said. His middle initial "O" did not stand for "Olaf" as his father's did but for "Otto," a tribute to his grandfather Frank Otto Bursum, who had died so young in Iowa. Despite the differences in his and his father's names, the second Holm Bursum took on the designation of "Junior." It became permanent as it migrated to legal documents. Holm, Jr. pointed out that his son's name technically should not have a "III" with it, but people began referring to them as "...Jr. and the 3rd instead of Big

Holm and Little Holm so they got us all fouled up. Nobody knows who we are anymore," he observed wryly.

Name complications aside, people did, of course, know who the Bursums were. Holm III remembered his upbringing in and around Socorro as a good one, but in his early school years, he found himself living two counties over. Children who grew up on ranches in the West's great spaces sometimes had to leave home for their education. In Holm Bursum's case, he lived with his grandmother Hester Puckett in Roswell in 1941-42 when he was in the first grade. Traveling from the Bursum ranch house to Roswell in Chaves County was not a simple matter in those days. It was a three-hour trip that entailed rattling over gravel roads a large part of the way. The small boy went on his own, riding in an old stretch vehicle with a driver/owner who made the trip routinely as a commercial venture.

How might the seven-year-old have felt about crossing rough desert and mountain terrain and getting home for brief visits only every six to eight weeks? "I didn't have a choice," Bursum responded with a smile, setting the matter aside as one not worth poring over. It was fine living with his grandmother, he said. He made friends that he reconnected with when he returned to Roswell for the seventh grade. Holm Bursum was learning independence, mobility, and a knack for building relationships for the long term. They were qualities that would serve him later as a state political organizer.

Encountering History: The Shaking Earth and Pancakes with a Future President

During World War II, the U.S. government took some of the rangeland in central New Mexico for weapons testing, asking the ranchers to voluntarily vacate for a time. That time, as Ron Hamm chronicled, turned out to be permanent.[168] As part of the war effort, the Bursums gave up a good portion of their ranch and moved into Socorro, where Holm III had the novel experience of going to school close to home.

From the time he was eight, Holm Bursum III worked on the family ranch. When he was not in school, he was out on the rangeland, often staying in the bunkhouse. One summer day, at the age of ten, he came closer than most Americans to witnessing a major historical event of the era.[169] Very early on the morning of July 16, 1945, the young Bursum was asleep when an intense shaking of the bunkhouse and a brilliant flash of light roused him. The still-drowsy child could only marvel at such a showy and violent sunrise and imagine that an earthquake was rattling the land. Later, he would realize that he had been present at the explosion of the world's first atomic bomb. It had been detonated sixteen miles from where he slept, on the ground that would come to be known as Trinity Site.

A little over two years before, scientists, military personnel, technicians, and others had gathered secretly in New Mexico's northern highlands. At Los Alamos, they created the most powerful bomb the world had yet seen. The public knew nothing of the weapon until its detonation that July morning south of Socorro in 1945. Even then, its sound, light, and motion were attributed to a relatively conventional cause. "...[A]n Albuquerque radio station broadcast a news bulletin at noon that an ammunition dump had exploded near Alamogordo. This prearranged news release...meant that all had gone well," wrote Jon Hunner.[170] While those back in Los Alamos understood the coded broadcast, most New Mexicans did not immediately learn what had transpired in their state. The following month it became clearer when the United States dropped two atomic bombs on Japan, hastening the end of World War II.

As a teenager, Bursum was intrigued by the blast that had occurred almost in his backyard. One day, he and his friends went by horseback to see what remained of the detonation site. They came upon a depression in the ground, its sand and other materials having been turned into glassy green trinitite. It made a wonderful surface for an exciting game, Bursum recalled in 2018. "We would get our horses into a run and get up on the trinitite with the horses going full speed," he said. "...[W]e would suck up on the reins, and the horses would kind of squat or sit down and go sliding across the trinitite. I think the horses enjoyed it as much as we did."

Another adolescent adventure brought Bursum to the ranch house of Lyndon B. Johnson, the majority whip of the U.S. Senate. In the summer of 1952, Senator Johnson had just purchased cattle from a New Mexico rancher. Holm Bursum, Jr., part-owner of a trucking company, was contracted to deliver the shipment to Johnson's Texas ranch on the Pedernales River, according to Ron Hamm. Bursum assigned his eighteen-year-old son Holm III to accompany his business partner on the long drive from Socorro County to central Texas. They made it in one stretch, calling on Johnson before dawn. The future president of the United States, with the help of his staff, treated the drivers to a pancake breakfast—but not before he had laughed over a note that Holm Bursum, Jr. had sent along for his son to deliver. Written on the first Holm O. Bursum's old Senate stationery, the message said, "This is what happens to the grandsons of U.S. senators. They end up being truck drivers."[171]

After his brief visit with Lyndon Johnson, the young Bursum began to have his doubts about the Texas senator's authenticity as a cowboy. It was something about the way he tucked the legs of his pants inside his boots, he told his biographer Ron Hamm.[172] On the other hand, there was no doubt about Holm's genuineness as a young man of the Southwestern range. He spoke with humor about his almost organic connection to the land. Instead of having the blue eyes of his father and grandfather, he said, his were brown like the desert he grew up in. He knew how to speak Spanish, ride a horse, work cattle, manage sheep, grade roads, fix fences, and more. He also had decided that ranching was going to be his life.

Building Skills and Learning Politics

When his father was elected to the county commission in 1940, Holm Bursum III was a boy of six. By the time he was thirteen, his dad was Socorro's mayor. He saw his father work hard as a rancher and banker and then go down to a local government building to give his time to the needs of the city or county. His grandmother and mother, too, were busy at the work of public service. Along the way, he learned of his grandfather's historic pursuits. Specific plans for his own political life may not have been formed in his youth, but his family had taught him civic engagement. Their path soon was to be his. The youngest Holm Bursum was about to take his own first steps in politics as a student on a university campus.

In the fall of 1952, not long after he visited the Johnson ranch on the Pedernales, Holm Bursum III went to college. His choice was New Mexico A&M in Las Cruces. Later known as New Mexico State University, it was the land grant school that his grandmother Lulu Bursum had served as a regent more than a decade before. From 1952 to 1956, Bursum studied at A&M. It was a hundred fifty miles down the Rio Grande from Socorro, on a road that made for an easy ride compared to his schoolboy travels to Roswell.

During Lulu Bursum's service as a regent, New Mexico A&M had taken on big building projects. By her grandson's time, the campus offered a mix of architectural designs, including a few utilitarian WPA (Works Progress Administration) buildings of the Depression era. The most striking style, however, tended toward imposing sand-colored structures with red-tiled roofs. Bursum and his fellow students passed from building to building along walkways well shaded from the desert sun, their routes embellished by ornamental fish ponds, splashing fountains, and a bell tower to ring out the hours. At the west end, where Bursum gravitated, the barns, corrals, and fields of the College of Agriculture gave a rural feel to the place. To the east was the best sight of all, the jagged backdrop of the Organ Mountains. In shades of blue, gray, rose, and purple, their granite pinnacles changed as they absorbed the light throughout the day.

Bursum, an animal husbandry major, had a notable presence on campus. He was preparing himself for a career in ranching and, through the Reserve Officers Training Corps, for a commission in the U.S. Air Force. He had grown tall, lean, and handsome, with warm brown eyes under dark brows, a strong jaw, and a sweet, disarming smile. He looked at home in any dress, whether he was in jeans and a cowboy hat, a suit and tie, or the crisp uniform of a military cadet. Most important, he was a contributor. The gregarious young man joined several organizations.[173] Some reflected his major: the Ag Club, the Block and Bridle Club, and the wool judging team. Others involved military training. He was the cadet captain and executive officer of his Air Force ROTC squadron. His campus residence association elected him president. He joined a fraternity. Campus government caught his interest, and he won a seat on the student commission and became the junior class vice president. Not surprising given his background, he also involved himself in partisan politics. He joined the college Young Republican Club.

In 1954, the A&M Young Republicans got ready to campaign for their party's ticket. Bursum's interest in the race was both partisan and personal. His father ran in the primary that year, campaigning to be the GOP nominee for governor. Governor Edwin Mechem had reached term limits, and Bursum, Jr., who had flipped a coin with him in the 1950 race, seemed like his natural successor in 1954. The Socorro Republican's political philosophy and ethics harmonized with Mechem's, and the voters in two prior elections had appreciated those very qualities.

In February, Holm III had traveled to Santa Fe to join his parents at the state GOP convention. Because the direct-primary reform of Clyde Tingley was no longer in effect in 1954, the pre-primary convention delegates were going to decide whether or not Holm Bursum, Jr. would progress to the primary ballot. Having his photogenic family—Betty, Holm III, and Michael—at the convention had to have been an asset. A press photographer covering the event caught the moment when Holm III stood near his mother, leaning toward her as if to hand her a sheaf of papers. Betty Bursum, it seems, had been pressed into service as a convention page, perhaps such an atypical role for a candidate's wife that it warranted a picture in the newspaper.[174] Smiling, she was taking her assignment good-naturedly. The photograph captured an attractive image of mother and son, similar in their dark hair and striking angular features.

At the convention, the family got to see Holm Bursum, Jr. and one other candidate win party support to run for the gubernatorial nomination in the primary. Bursum got 662.5 votes; his closest competitor, Alvin Stockton, got 521.5.[175] Stockton, in his early forties, ranched in Colfax County. He had been speaker of the New Mexico House of Representatives in 1952 when the Republicans had a rare and slim majority—by one vote. Stockton appealed to a particular group of Republicans, some of whom had broken to an extent with party leader Edwin Mechem. Mechem stayed scrupulously neutral in the race, but his supporters favored Bursum.

May came and with it, the primary. Many expected Holm Bursum, Jr. to prevail, but he fell behind. Alvin Stockton won 14,320 to 12,537.[176] The men exchanged messages.[177] Bursum wired congratulations to his opponent, and in a public statement, referred to Stockton as a fine man. Bursum also thanked the people of Socorro County for the overwhelming support he had received from them. He had won in several other counties, including Dona Ana, where his college-student son had been on his team. Stockton, in turn, complimented Bursum for having run a clean campaign and been an upstanding candidate. With the formalities of the election over, Holm Bursum, Jr. resumed his municipal work. He had been reelected as Socorro's mayor just the month before.

As Holm III prepared to return to college in the fall, he wanted to speak to his father about an important matter. He wondered about committing as a Young Republican to campaign for Alvin Stockton in the general election. The primary results had made the issue a sensitive one for the young man. The elder Bursum had no problem advising his son to put personal feelings aside and support the GOP candidate. For the young man, it was a lesson about party unity. He went to work for the Republican ticket.

In the general election, Alvin Stockton was unable to build on Edwin Mechem's breakthrough victories for the GOP. His Democratic opponent, John F. Simms, Jr., won the race, and the governorship returned to the opposing party for a term. The gubernatorial primary vote represented an unfortunate rift among Republicans, Holm Bursum III reflected many years later. Mechem had delivered the party major victories in 1950 and '52. By 1954, however, a faction resisted building on those successes. New Mexico's GOP, so clearly in the minority, had won a significant office only recently. At such a tender stage of party renewal, more unity and harmony among Republicans might have given them better results at the polls. As a young man, Bursum began to ponder that notion.

As Holm Bursum, Jr. carried on in elective office locally, Betty Bursum had her public roles as well. In the first half of the 1950s, she had been elected as a vice president of the Federated Republican Women's Clubs of New Mexico and served as a member of the Socorro Municipal School Board.[178] As an elected school board member, she gave her sons a model of a woman in public office. Women had been voting for over three decades, but, restricted by attitude and custom, they still did not have a full array of elective and appointive offices open to them. Education-related public service was an exception, and Betty Bursum, like Nina Otero Warren, Georgia Lee Lusk, and Lulu Bursum before her, took her opportunity to serve where it existed.

Losing a Son and Brother

On a summer day in 1955, the Bursum family faced a tragedy that would stay with them all their lives. The younger son Michael died in a work accident.[179] He was sixteen and up early one morning to take on an assignment in his father's trucking partnership. He was operating as instructed when a cable he was holding became, by accident, a conduit for a deadly electric current. It was a horrifying moment, an irreversible action with unintended consequences on the part of the man supervising the work. The grief that Michael's death generated lodged irrevocably in Holm Bursum and his parents and brought sorrow to their community.

Finding His Life Partner: Lieutenant Bursum Meets Earle Powell

In 1956, near the first anniversary of his brother's death, Holm Bursum III graduated from New Mexico A&M. He entered the U.S. Air Force as a second lieutenant. Stationed in Texas and Kansas with the Strategic Air Command, he trained to be a pilot, bombardier, and navigator. He served for three years, achieving the rank of captain. During his time in the Air Force, he met a young woman named Earle Bounds Powell. She was studying at the University of New Mexico. Bursum's cousin Earl Puckett and his wife knew her and thought she and Holm should meet. The young woman agreed to a date—but "for coffee only," she stipulated.

Earle Powell captivated Holm Bursum. She was well educated, sophisticated, and witty. She was independent, outgoing, and fun, and she was stunning. From a family who ranched in West Texas and New Mexico, she, like Bursum and other children of ranchers, spent part of her school years away from home.[180] She attended El Paso's Radford School for Girls. The school's alumnae included another ranch child, Sandra Day O'Connor, a justice of the U. S. Supreme Court. During Earle's time in El Paso, she took a turn as a princess at the Sun Bowl festivities. For her post-secondary education, she went east. She studied at Sullins College in Virginia and the Tobe-Coburn School for Fashion Careers in Manhattan. Before and after her New York studies, the young woman worked on a degree at the University of New Mexico (UNM).

After her Manhattan adventure, Earle Powell moved to Midland, Texas,[181] where she established a close relationship with her mother's friend Anne Ingrahm and worked at Murphy's Department Store. It was an exciting time. Young professionals were flooding into Midland to work in the booming oil industry of the Permian Basin, and, in the newly-cosmopolitan little city, social life was abundant. Soon, however, Earle returned to the University of New Mexico to complete her bachelor's degree in education and history, taking time to reign as the queen of the UNM Engineers Ball in 1956.[182]

From the airbases where he was stationed, Holm Bursum began to rent small planes and fly to Albuquerque to see Earle Powell.[183] Their coffee-only date progressed. On December 27, 1958, she, in white taffeta, Chantilly lace, and pearls, married Bursum at St. Andrews Episcopal Church in Roswell. She joined him in Kansas as he completed his military service at Forbes Air Force Base near Topeka.

In the summer of 1959, the young couple returned to New Mexico and settled in Albuquerque. Holm was going into banking, not ranching as he had planned. At least two factors changed the direction of his life. First, the part of the Bursum ranch that the federal government needed for weapons development during the war had become a permanent part of the White Sands Missile Range. Second, the productivity of the land that remained to the family had been compromised by a drought that began in the late 1940s and persisted well into the '50s. The Bursums had had to sell off their sheep in 1954. After that, they tried to run cattle on a reduced range. Under the circumstances, earning a good livelihood through ranching was not promising for a young couple. Bursum's new plan was to join his father in banking in Socorro, but first, he took a position at Albuquerque National Bank to learn the business. He also joined the local Young Republican Club. Soon he would be at work on the campaign of Edwin L. Mechem, who was running for his fourth term as governor.

Bursum discovered that while he had been away, an ambitious young Republican had moved to New Mexico: David F. Cargo of Michigan. The two men soon would meet. They had different political philosophies and notably different leadership styles, and, for a short time, they would vie over their separate visions for the Young Republicans. As it turned out, each man had particular skills that New Mexico needed on its way back to a two-party system.

6

1959–1960: Early Young Republican Revitalization

Eight Young Republicans attended a state convention in Albuquerque and elected nine state officers.
—Will Harrison, Political Columnist, 1959[184]

As 1960 approached, the Republican Party could look back one hundred years to its first presidential triumph, the election of Abraham Lincoln. His victory had been a brilliant start for a party only six years old, and the success continued. Of the fifteen individuals who served as the U.S. president between 1861 and 1933, twelve were Republicans. In the campaign of 1932, however, Franklin D. Roosevelt realigned the political system for several election cycles, winning the White House and making Democratic Party presidential candidates unbeatable for twenty years. The Republican resurgence in the 1950s came through the person of Dwight D. Eisenhower, a war hero and, until he ran for office, a nonpartisan figure.

As Eisenhower's second term was ending, two well-matched young candidates for the 1960 presidential election had emerged: Richard M. Nixon and John F. Kennedy, both in their forties. They were Navy veterans who had served in the Pacific theater in World War II. In their post-war years, they were colleagues in the U.S. House of Representatives. Each came from a populous coastal state, Kennedy in the East, Nixon in the West. In the 1950s, both moved on to the Senate, and Richard Nixon became the U.S. vice president shortly after that.

In the summer of 1960, their nominating conventions behind them, Nixon and Kennedy launched vigorous campaigns for the White House. It was the first year that presidential candidates faced each other in televised debates. It also was the first year that Hawaii and Alaska, newly-admitted states, participated in electing a president. Richard Nixon pledged to campaign in all fifty states. It was a promise he kept despite hospitalization for an injury that cut nearly two weeks off his campaign time. Theodore H. White, a journalist who covered the 1960 pursuit of the presidency, described "the barbarism of American electioneering." A trained athlete would have found it exhausting, he said. He noted that media organizations knew the hardships of the campaign trail and switched out the reporters who accompanied Kennedy and Nixon so as not to wear them out. "[Y]et the principals themselves," White wrote, "...were never spared, never rested, were never permitted those moments of quiet thought, that, somehow, should accompany an attempt at so great and responsible an office."[185]

Holm Bursum III, watching Richard Nixon throughout the hard campaign, appreciated his willingness to travel to every state to support candidates all up and down the GOP ticket. It engendered Bursum's lifelong admiration of the man, whom he would one day meet. His personal library, he said years later, included many works on Richard Nixon.

Electing Edwin L. Mechem Again

While the riveting national campaign was gearing up, Edwin L. Mechem in New Mexico was running for his fourth term as governor—or at least Republicans hoped he would be their candidate. For him, it would be a comeback race against an incumbent governor. Mechem had won the gubernatorial office in 1950, 1952, and 1956, but in 1958, he lost the election. It had been quite a surprise. He had been defeated by a one-term state representative from Portales, John Burroughs. Mechem had been rather cheerful about his loss. He had wanted to resume his private life, and after Burroughs' inauguration on January 1, 1959, Mechem returned to his hometown of Las Cruces to practice law. He had hardly unpacked when the Republican Party came knocking on his door, pressuring him to run again in 1960.

Part of the pressure came from the Bernalillo County Young Republicans (YRs). In a resolution, they "urged" Mechem to consider the race but specified that they were not endorsing him, thereby preserving their policy of not championing candidates before a primary.[186] One of the members of the club was state Young Republican President David Cargo. As a newcomer to New Mexico, he quickly had caught himself up on the political scene. He had learned that Mechem was 'the' candidate to draft for any statewide campaign, but the ex-governor was not yet saying yes to another run.

As the deadline for filing candidacies approached, Cargo grew worried and seemed to be losing patience.[187] The young man, who leaned left as a Republican, probably would have preferred to support a candidate of his own philosophy, and one seemed to be on the horizon. A little momentum was growing in the party for State Senator Richard Pousma of Gallup. Cargo, careful not to endorse anyone officially, nonetheless, had praised Pousma as a positive element in the GOP.[188] The political chatter was that Cargo could deliver the Young Republicans' support for him. Pousma, however, did not board the bandwagon that was being outfitted on his behalf. If Mechem decided to run, he said, he would defer to the former governor. Cargo adapted quickly. Capitulating to the particularities of New Mexico politics, he soon joined the voices urging Mechem back into the public realm.

Introducing David Francis Cargo

David F. Cargo would become a prominent figure in New Mexico in the 1960s, and the story of his start in the state GOP was one that he himself found amusing. Of boyish countenance and signature dark-rimmed glasses, Cargo had moved from Michigan to Albuquerque in the late 1950s to practice law. He had been active in college Young Republican organizations in the Midwest, and within months of his arrival in Albuquerque, he got in touch with the New Mexico Young Republican Association. In the summer of 1959, Cargo attended the state convention. There, as he told it, he found himself elected the association's president. It happened at the Hilton Hotel in Albuquerque, and he remembered the occasion with humor:

> Joe Pino, who was trying to get elected as the Young Republican National Committeeman, nominated me to be the organization's president. It was seconded by Tom Clear. I campaigned vigorously and was elected State Chairman of the Young Republicans. I have to say, though, that the campaign really wasn't that vigorous. The convention's attendance was a grand total of seven! And, they weren't that well organized.[189]

The young wing of the GOP, stalwart through the 1930s and '40s, apparently had gone into a slump. Political columnist Will Harrison reinforced Cargo's account of the YR gathering in 1959 with his usual sardonic observation: "Eight Young Republicans attended a state convention in Albuquerque and elected nine state officers. It's typical of the 'young' movement in both parties in New Mexico, big front and no substance."[190]

As the YR president, Cargo began to strengthen clubs in the north, especially in Santa Fe, Taos, and Rio Arriba counties. His leadership style was bold, colorful, and even a little brash. Although he stood at the party's junior level and was new to New Mexico, he had no qualms about diving into public commentary and advising party elders through memorable statements to the media. In one case, Cargo chastised the Republicans for their failure to elect more state executives. Mechem, as governor, had always gone to Santa Fe as the sole Republican among a host of Democrats, Cargo had learned. Everyone else—the lieutenant governor, the secretary of state, the attorney general, and others—had been of the opposite party. Enough, Cargo said. He called on the GOP to cease "breeding a defeatist complex" and stage a lively primary to bring in a new guard of candidates. He invited positive thinkers to rush to file their candidacies ahead of the party's "retread McKinley-ites and office secretaries."[191] His audacious remarks made the news. "The press loved David Cargo," Holm Bursum III remarked.

Democratic Senator Dennis Chavez had his eye on Cargo and his liberal tendencies. The senator and the young attorney from Michigan had gotten to know one another through mutual acquaintances. Chavez sometimes took Cargo on his strolls through downtown Albuquerque. Here and there, the senator dropped in at restaurants and other establishments to shake hands and chat with his delighted constituents, Cargo recounted. He enjoyed the outings, and Chavez took note. Predicting that the young newcomer would do well in New Mexico politics, the senator invited him to come over to the Democratic Party. "I had great respect for Chavez," Cargo said, "but I had to tell him, 'Unfortunately, Senator, I'm a Republican and I want to remain one.' He laughed and we shook hands."[192]

Moving into Leadership: Holm O. Bursum III and the State Young Republican Association

While Cargo was acting as a spur to his party's senior wing, Holm Bursum III re-established himself in New Mexico. The young Albuquerque banker, his military service completed, was ready for political action. Shortly after he joined the Bernalillo County Young Republican Club, he took a leadership role. In November 1959, with sixty-five members present, officers were elected: Ray Tabet, chairman; Holm Bursum III and Dennis Cordova, vice chairmen; Victor Ortega, secretary; Mrs. Bill Gonzales, treasurer, and Robert Salazar, Tom Garcia, and Betty Walker, members of the executive board.[193]

Bursum loved bringing new people into the Young Republican world, and among his first recruits was the woman he had just married. Earle Powell Bursum, who had grown up in a West Texas family of Democrats, came to embrace the GOP wholeheartedly, but initially, an exchange was involved. In a charming and deft move, she made a deal with her husband. She, a Democrat, would join his Republican Party. In return, he—a Presbyterian—would agree that their children would be brought up in her denomination as Episcopalians. It was an arrangement that Bursum liked to remember, one that had worked out well, he concluded.

By the summer of 1960, Holm Bursum had moved up to the chairmanship of the local YR club. He also took on a bigger role, one suited to a young banker. Early in 1960, David Cargo appointed him treasurer and finance director of the New Mexico Young Republican Association.[194] Bursum was making connections and coming up with new ideas about how young people could operate within the Republican Party. Before long, his and Cargo's differing visions for the YRs would lead to a brief contest and a striking change of direction, but for a time, they worked together.

Reviewing the Roots of the Mechem-Burroughs Rematch

In the fall of 1960, the Young Republican State Central Committee met to plan for the upcoming election. Ed Mechem, once again, finally had been persuaded to be the GOP's candidate. It would be his fifth campaign for the governorship. He had run four times in the 1950s, winning three of the races. The back story of his 1960 race had its intricacies, which invites a brief review of gubernatorial politics at the time.

Edwin L. Mechem, after two terms in the governor's office in the early 1950s, never expected to occupy it again. His successor, Democratic Governor John F. Simms, Jr., was doing a good job, Mechem thought. Simms faced reelection in 1956, and it should have been a smooth run. Instead, controversy about his welfare policies formed like a cloud over his prospects. Many in both parties considered the policies harsh, and the ensuing conflict was a disaster for Democrats, said Fabian Chavez, Jr. It was part of what he called their *hara-kiri* years.[195] Another Chavez, Senator Dennis Chavez, was watching developments in the Simms administration. For the second time, he appeared to look favorably on a Mechem candidacy.

Mechem did not want to oppose Simms in 1956. The two young men had been friends across party lines since their days in the state legislature. Furthermore, Mechem was enjoying his private law work and resisted committing to another race for governor. In the end, however, the pressure from his party—and indirectly from Senator Chavez—sent Mechem back into the fray.[196] Mechem won, but two years later, he lost to John Burroughs of Portales, a personable Texas native with waves of silver hair and a friendly smile.

The Democrats took up a few of the less-desirable practices from the one-party past. Fabian Chavez, Jr., by then a state senator, saw the conflicts of interest that arose in the Burroughs administration. In one case, political colleagues of Burroughs appeared to be taking advantage of their proximity to power. They created an asphalt company to do business with the State Highway Department and its contractors, Chavez said. Similarly, Harold 'Fats' Leonard, Burroughs' appointee to the State Highway Commission, had sold equipment to the Highway Department and its contractors.[197]

Another type of problem was party fundraising in the state government. Governor Mechem had stopped the practice, but in 1959 the Democratic Party resumed assessing state employees one percent of their salaries for its treasury. At first, Governor Burroughs defended the practice as a way to raise needed funds. His heart may not have been in it, however. Five months into his term, after public pushback, Burroughs announced that state employees' salaries no longer would be tapped for political purposes.[198] He added that he actually had not liked the levy, considering it a hardship for workers.

The levy system was gone, but party patronage practices had resurfaced. The press covered the rather egregious developments.[199] Shortly after Burroughs took office, his department heads met with State Democratic Party Chairman Seaborn Collins. Collins had an announcement. Statehouse employees, he said, were to fill out cards on which they recorded their county precinct numbers as well as their wives' maiden names and party registrations. The cards were to be signed by employees' Democratic county precinct chairmen as a kind of reference and stored at state party headquarters. State employees in Santa Fe had even more stringent party-loyalty requirements, according to journalist Tony Hillerman. They had to pledge money and volunteer time to Democratic campaigns, a rule attributed to a local party official. The systems created anxiety among some state workers.

Practices such as party endorsements for state jobs and salary levies no longer played well with many New Mexicans. In 1960, Ed Mechem, who had been turned out of office two years earlier by the voters, was looking like an attractive alternative to the Burroughs administration. Mechem just had to contrast his style of governance with the incumbent's. Richard Cheney, a Young Republican of Curry County at the time, remembers how his aunt regarded the gubernatorial campaign. A cartoonist, she showed Governor Burroughs sitting atop a stack of documents, stating that he was running on his record. Challenger Mechem was scaling the document pile and remarking, "I'm running on your record too."[200]

The Young Republicans got ready to work for the Mechem election, giving them a chance to build capacity as strategists and organizers. First, they set up a Truth Squad. Each member was assigned to research one agency in the Burroughs administration and to prepare to counter any information coming from it that appeared inaccurate. Second, Holm Bursum and others approached the senior GOP to offer the Young Republicans as partners in a robust campaign.[201]

Making a Political Breakthrough in Eastern New Mexico: Hoyt Pattison and a GOP Ticket

Meanwhile, in Curry County in the expansive agricultural lands of eastern New Mexico, another step toward two-party politics had just been taken. Hoyt Pattison, the college student of 1950 whose family had transitioned from the Democratic Party to the GOP, was by then a young married man with children. He had established himself as a farmer, rancher, and businessman, and he and his wife Joy Pattison joined in local Republican activities.

In 1960, Hoyt Pattison decided to collaborate with Clovis attorney Esther Smith to make a change for the GOP in their region.[202] They approached Curry County's most famous Republican, William H. Duckworth, to run for state senator. A retired drugstore owner in Clovis, Duckworth was a distinguished elder in the party. From 1921 to 1923, he had served as the lieutenant governor in the administration of Merritt C. Mechem, New Mexico's fifth governor. Duckworth was well-regarded. His business in a Democratic community never seemed to suffer because of his Republican affiliation, Pattison observed.

Nearly forty years after he had held a state office, Duckworth agreed to enter the 1960 campaign. However, he had one condition. There must be a full slate of Republican candidates; he would not run alone.[203] Pattison, Smith, and others went to work. Coming up with several GOP candidacies was a challenge in eastern New Mexico at the time, but by the filing deadline, a complete ticket had materialized. Republicans were running for sheriff, county assessor, county commissioner, and more. Pattison himself became a candidate for a New Mexico House seat, and his stepmother Luciester Pattison filed for one of ten positions on the State School Board of Education.[204]

In times when women candidates for any office were scarce, Luciester Pattison offered voters strong credentials for a state school board position: a master's degree in education, years of teaching, and leadership in political and ecumenical organizations. In Hoyt Pattison, she also had a testimonial to her character. She had been Pattison's stepmother since he was nine, a strict and caring parent to him and his siblings and half-sibling. The children did not always appreciate her efforts at the time, Hoyt Pattison recalled with a smile, but he was deeply grateful to her for making him the person he grew to be.[205] For Luciester and Hoyt Pattison to hold places on the Republican ticket of 1960 meant a great deal in their family's history, and in a larger sense, it was part of the evolution of the Republican Party in eastern New Mexico.

Assessing the 1960 General Election

In the fall general election, Vice President Richard M. Nixon lost the presidency to Senator John F. Kennedy in an excruciatingly close race. Kennedy won the popular vote by less than one percentage point.[206] His electoral college vote margin, however, was much more comfortable: 303 to 219. Political analysts have discussed how the election might have gone differently. Only a few votes in five states had made the outcome close. "If twelve thousand people in Illinois, Nevada, New Mexico, Hawaii, and Missouri had voted Republican instead of Democratic," wrote John A. Farrell, "Nixon would have been president."[207] It was that close. A more common focus has been on Kennedy's slim margin of victory in Illinois and his larger but possibly contestable margin in Texas. A few vote tallies in the two states were disputed based on allegations of local officials' dishonest counts. It left some people wondering if even the Electoral College victory, thus the presidency, actually might have been Nixon's. No definite answers materialized. Perhaps the greater point to be taken from the 1960 election is that the voters were all but evenly split over which candidate they wanted in the White House.

For Republicans, the outcome at the top of the ticket was disheartening, but it was a good year for down-ballot Republicans across the country. Nixon's fifty-state campaign strategy had worked in that respect. In New Mexico, results most decidedly were mixed, however. In the presidential race, the state did not end up in the Nixon column, but the vote was close. Kennedy won the mostly Democratic state by a slim 2,294-vote margin.[208] In congressional races, the New Mexico GOP made no progress at all. Likewise, in state legislative ones, control of both houses remained with the Democrats. Nonetheless, there were victories to celebrate. Edwin L. Mechem won his fourth gubernatorial term, albeit by a narrow margin.

On the east side of the state, Curry County Republicans made the news. The political experiment launched by Hoyt Pattison, Esther Smith, and their colleagues paid off. One of their candidates claimed a victory. The people elected the venerable William H. Duckworth to the New Mexico Senate. Duckworth was the first Republican to win an office in Curry County, Hoyt Pattison remarked,[209] and soon, he would become the Senate minority whip. Pattison lost his race to the incumbent State Representative Frank Foster. Although Pattison would not be joining Duckworth in Santa Fe that January, he was looking to the future.

The lieutenant governor's race produced the greatest surprise of all. Tom Bolack, a Republican of Farmington, defeated Joseph A. Montoya, a Democrat of Albuquerque. For the first time since 1928, New Mexico voters elected two Republicans to the executive branch. Finally, Mechem would have a lieutenant governor of his own party. The size of the win, however, tempered GOP elation. It was by fewer than three hundred votes,[210] a number that invited a second look. Joseph A. Montoya (not to be mistaken for his fellow Democrat U.S. Representative Joseph M. Montoya) contested the election. The grounds he used were unexpected. He filed a case in state district court seeking to disqualify the franchise of a category of people: American Indians residing on federally-designated reservations. It became a voting rights issue, and the outcome would not be known for a year. While voters on reservations and the rivals at the heart of the case held their breath, one of the latter moved forward. Lt. Governor-Elect Tom Bolack had a suit to pick out and travel arrangements to make for his inauguration in Santa Fe.

Holm Bursum III could see progress in the election of 1960. With Nixon's campaign having helped Republicans throughout the country, the party picked up twenty seats in the U.S. House of Representatives, giving them a forty percent share of the vote.[211] Republicans also had done well in state legislative races around the country. Although victories in New Mexico had been few, they were significant, and the Young Republicans had helped secure them. Bursum wanted to keep the young-wing momentum going. He wanted to partner with those who had won elections and connect with promising candidates for the future. Edwin L. Mechem, Tom Bolack, and Hoyt Pattison were on his list.

Territory Senator, Holm Bursum, Socorro, New Mexico, Date: 1900–1910. Courtesy of the Palace of Governors Photo Archives (NMHM/DCA),

Holm O. Bursum III. Courtesy of the Bursum family.

Earle Powell Bursum and Holm Bursum III. Courtesy of the Bursum family.

Ex-Governor John E. Miles, Lieutenant-Governor Tom Bolack, Governor Edwin L. Mechem, U.S. Rep. Joseph Montoya, first, seventh, ninth, and eleventh from left, respectively. Second Lady Alice Bolack, First Lady Dorothy Mechem, and Della Montoya, sixth, eighth, and tenth from left, respectively. Persons Known-Mechem, n.d. (Prob. 1961 or 1962). New Mexico Department of Tourism Photograph Collection, Image 2311, Courtesy of State Archives of New Mexico, 1205 Camino Carlos Rey, Santa Fe, New Mexico 87507.

State Representative David F. Cargo (Bernalillo County), District Judge Caswell S. Neal (Carlsbad), and Assistant Attorney General Boston Witt, 1963. Opening trial in Santa Fe for reapportionment suit brought by Cargo to increase the numbers of representatives for Bernalillo County. Courtesy of Palace of the Governors Photo Archives (NMHM/DCA), Negative Number: 029219.

Michael Bursum U.S. Representative Joe Skeen, and Holm Bursum III, 1996.
Courtesy of the Bursum Family.

Holm Bursum III, U.S. Senator Pete V. Domenici, and Michael Bursum, 1996.
Courtesy of the Bursum Family.

Holm Bursum III with daughters (L-R) Elizabeth Spencer and Julia Bursum Arnold and grandchildren Ben Spencer, Jr.; Caroline Spencer, and Anne Spencer, at the Bursum ranch, 2002 They are standing in front of the ruins of the ranch house.
Courtesy of the Bursum family.

Earle and Holm Bursum, 50th Anniversary. Courtesy of the Bursum family.

Holm Bursum III with his children (L-R): Julia Bursum Arnold, Holm Bursum III, Michael Bursum, Holm O. Bursum IV (Cuatro), and Elizabeth Spencer.
Photo: Tony Gambino Photography.

7

1961: Young Republican Leaders in the State and Nation

In our campaigns, no matter how hard fought they may be, no matter how close the election may turn out to be, those who lose accept the verdict, and support those who win.

—Richard M. Nixon, Vice President of the United States, An address to the U.S. Congress on January 6, 1961[212]

As the new year arrived, many Republicans still felt distressed over the close presidential race. On Election Night just two months earlier, Richard Nixon had watched his vote margin dwindle in crucial states. Around midnight, he had stepped up to the podium at the Ambassador Hotel in Los Angeles to concede provisionally to John Kennedy. Nixon's supporters in the room were crushed. The next morning, when Minnesota was called for Kennedy, the outcome finally was clear. Nixon sent a formal concession and congratulations to the new president-elect. That ritualized bit of electoral politics was difficult enough, but an even more poignant acknowledgment of his defeat awaited him in January.

On January 6, 1961, Vice President Nixon and Speaker of the House Sam Rayburn presided over a Joint Session of the U.S. Congress as the Electoral College votes for the presidency were counted. Shortly thereafter, Nixon remarked that he was the first vice president in a century to announce his opponent's victory before Congress. Then, in the American tradition of the peaceful transfer of power, he addressed the president, vice president, and Congress, saying, "...you all work in a cause that is greater than any man's ambition, greater than any party. It is the cause of freedom, of justice, and peace for all mankind. It is in that spirit that I now declare that John F. Kennedy has been elected President of the United States...."[213]

Earlier, Nixon had closed the chapter on allegations of fraudulent voting in Illinois and Texas. Right after the election, journalist Earl Mazo had begun investigating possible irregularities in the two states, but Nixon asked that no more be done. The U.S. and the Soviet Union were engaged in the Cold War, and at that vulnerable time, Nixon pondered the broad implications of an untidy transition between administrations. "...[N]o one steals the presidency of the United States," he told Mazo a month before the electoral vote-counting ceremony. "Our country cannot afford the agony of a constitutional crisis."[214] Thus, with vision and some grace, Richard Nixon moved on. In just a few months, Holm Bursum III would find himself in a banquet hall in Minneapolis, listening to the former vice president address a national gathering of Young Republicans.

Despite their party's loss of the presidency, the Young Republicans in New Mexico were going to have a good year. In Santa Fe, they had a governor and—almost miraculously—a lieutenant governor ready to champion them. Nationally, the party was finding its place in a decade dominated by the Kennedy and Johnson administrations. It was an interesting time to be Republican. Passionate intraparty confrontations over political philosophy and factional control soon were to flare up, and as the GOP struggled and changed, it would have to recover from two successive presidential defeats. Bursum was about to take a journey through that decade with a national Young Republican leader named Leonard J. Nadasdy. They would become friends for life, and in the early years, they would serve as the loyal opposition until the day in 1968 when they elected a president from their party. Meanwhile, with midterm elections coming up in a year, the New Mexico GOP had work to do. For the young wing, it was time to plan a YR state convention and elect officers.

Redirecting the New Mexico Young Republican Association
Competing Conventions

When Holm O. Bursum III decided to run for the presidency of the young wing of his party, he did so with a deep feeling for New Mexico and its Republican traditions. His grandfather and father had run in elections when young Republican leaders like Thomas Hughes, James Chacon, and Reginaldo Espinosa were organizing the new generations. Bursum saw an opportunity to work with his peers in the 1960s and to plan a Young Republican revitalization.

David Cargo still held the presidency of the New Mexico Young

Republican (YR) Association in 1961. He saw the New Mexico GOP's future in Bernalillo, Santa Fe, Taos, and Dona Ana counties, areas he called urban.[215] He focused mostly on the northern counties and pushed club development there. Two factors characterized his YR years. He remained noticeably to the left of most Republicans in his new state, and he had not let up on sparring with GOP elders. In the unusual pairing of David Cargo and the New Mexico Republican Party, a smooth working relationship between the young and senior wings had yet to be achieved. Meanwhile, Holm Bursum III in Bernalillo County grew stronger as a leader. He represented change, and his vision for the YRs began to generate statewide interest.

Cargo perhaps was focusing on his plans to run for public office and may not have been tracking the new trend in the Young Republican Association. Given what was to transpire in April and May, it appeared he had stepped back from the YRs a bit. That spring, the executive committee met, apparently with Cargo not in attendance. The committee set the date of a state convention, May 6, in Albuquerque. Frances Marron Lee, New Mexico's GOP National Committeewoman, was invited to give a major address. Lee's relationship with New Mexico was richly historic. Her father Owen Marron, a Democrat and Albuquerque mayor, had worked for statehood alongside the first Holm Bursum. Frances, however, had become a Republican. She and her husband Floyd Lee were ranchers whose vintage adobe home was the inspiration for a setting in Willa Cather's *Death Comes for the Archbishop*.[216] Lee knew the intricacies of state history and politics. She would be decisive in helping the YRs move in a new direction.

When David Cargo learned of the convention plans, he grew concerned. Tensions between his group and the new-movement people became front-page stories in the *Albuquerque Journal*.[217] Cargo's group changed the convention date to July to avoid a schedule conflict for Frances Lee. They pointed out that the senior party was gathering on May 6 in Ruidoso and that the national committeewoman could not attend meetings in two such widespread cities on the same day. The other YRs remained firm, however, calling on Cargo to convene the May convention. Cargo declined, but days later, he changed his mind. His decision seemed linked to Lee's. She had accepted the YRs' invitation to address their May convention, stating unequivocally that she would be in Albuquerque on the 6th.

One of Cargo's associates, however, was not pleased with the new plans and the emerging group within the YRs. Young Republican National Committeeman Joe Pino commented on the "country club" element in the state organization and called the highly-anticipated May meeting a "rump convention." He promised to take the matter to the Young Republican National Federation (YRNF). The YRNF had the power to invalidate the proceedings, he stated.[218] Holm Bursum chose not to respond to Pino through the media. Airing intraparty divisions in the newspapers was not his inclination, he said, reflecting years later on the incident. A public squabble would have made it harder to bring factions together for the GOP's ultimate purpose: to build up the whole party, win elections, and help govern the state.

Electing Holm O. Bursum III

On May 6, 1961, one hundred fifty Young Republicans gathered at the Alvarado Hotel in Albuquerque for their state convention.[219] Over half of the delegates were from Bursum's Bernalillo County club. It was a phenomenal turnout, given that in 1959 only eight people had shown up for the event. Political writer Will Harrison had needled the YRs about their low attendance then, but no numbers jokes flowed from his pen in 1961.

On schedule, David Cargo opened the convention, and by acclamation, the delegates elected Holm Bursum III as their new president. A strong team took office with him: Robert Dorr, executive secretary; George Stapp, treasurer; Emma Gonzales, recording secretary, and Patty Springer, corresponding secretary. Vice presidents by region were Julio Garcia, Dave Lucero, and Tony Sanchez. Ted Bishop served as vice president for the university clubs. Elected to the executive committee were Leonard DeYoung, Benny McKeel, and Lany Keith. Fred Mossman became the new national committeeman to the Young Republican National Federation, defeating David Cargo for the post.

Bursum addressed the convention. Stressing unity and decorum, he called on Young Republicans to reclaim their place "on the front pages again but only in the areas I have described." He "...called for harmony with [the] state's senior party, with 'no more diametrically opposed conditions.'"[220]

Then National Committeewoman Frances Lee spoke. She essentially had given her blessing to the change in the direction of the Young Republicans when she chose to honor her commitment to the May convention. To the young people, she offered a bright picture of GOP progress nationwide, pointing to the seats gained in Congress and in state legislatures. "...[H]alf of Americans believe as you do," she said.[221]

Despite Joe Pino's plan to take his grievance to the YR National Federation, no actions of the May 6 convention were invalidated. In fact, no concerns were evident at higher party levels. A YRNF official and national senior party people had traveled to Albuquerque to speak at the convention.[222] New Mexico's Young Republican revitalization had been launched with the blessings of many.

David Cargo moved on from the Young Republicans and launched his entry into electoral politics. The following year he would run a race in Bernalillo County and win a seat in the New Mexico House of Representatives. He also took on a weighty project for the next several years. He worked to create equitable, population-based districts in New Mexico for both state legislative and U.S. congressional seats. The changes he helped make are monuments on the state's road back to a two-party system, as the latter part of the story reveals.

Meanwhile, Holm Bursum III, twenty-six years old, had achieved quite a political victory. Fresh from his election as Young Republican state president, he was about to use his deep knowledge of New Mexico to connect with political talent in places where others might not have looked for it. He was going to move beyond Cargo's urban areas to support an emerging Republican presence in the high plains and deserts of the eastern and southern counties. The Democratic Party had dominated the region for decades, but Bursum saw new possibilities.

First, Bursum attended the Young Republican National Federation (YRNF) convention in Minnesota. There, in his grandfather's tradition, he would try his hand at organizing bloc votes at a political convention. Young leaders at the national level noticed him. One of them, Leonard J. Nadasdy, became a lifelong friend.

Warm and polished, Len Nadasdy was a distinguished-looking, dark-haired young man, who worked as the manager for employee communications at General Mills. When he and Holm Bursum met, Nadasdy was running to be chairman of the Young Republican National Federation. The two young men had much in common. Both had grown up in rural states, with fathers who were mayors of small cities. Both their fathers were in the wool-growing industry, Bursum's as a sheep rancher and Nadasdy's as the head of a large wool growers' cooperative. Most important of all, the young men had been raised as dyed-in-the-wool Republicans. Their political educations had begun at home around the dinner table.

Electing Leonard Nadasdy: *"...[W]e are going places."*[223]

Leonard J. Nadasdy dedicated himself to the Young Republican National Federation for a decade and a half. In 2018, the last full year of his life, he took the time to write his reflections for the Bursum story. Nadasdy's unpublished memoir takes us through critical years in the evolution of the GOP's young wing. In the 1960s, that wing would help prompt a change in the direction of the entire Republican Party.

Len Nadasdy began his great adventure in politics as a six-year-old in Brookings, South Dakota. One day in 1936, he came home with a Roosevelt-for-President button pinned to his shirt.[224] His parents quickly clarified his party affiliation for him, exchanging the FDR button for an Alf Landon one. In 1944, Nadasdy, then a teen, campaigned in his town for presidential candidate Thomas E. Dewey. Nadasdy had admired Dewey as a New York prosecutor tough on racketeering and other organized crime. Dewey had gone on to the governorship of New York, and during his presidential run, he touted his administration as one both progressive and solvent. He supported social programs and other government interventions within the constraints of good fiscal practice. His liberalism appealed well enough to Republicans of the 1940s, but it would become less attractive to the party with time.

1944 was a hard year, as it turned out, for any Republican to oppose the incumbent president. Franklin D. Roosevelt had built political strength over twelve years in office, putting social safety nets in place at home and executing a successful wartime strategy abroad. FDR beat Dewey, but Dewey came back four years later, this time with a very different opponent. Vice President Harry Truman had stepped into the presidency after Roosevelt's death in 1945. Three years later, however, he seemed vulnerable to defeat. Polling favored Dewey.

Nadasdy, then at the University of Minnesota, was excited about a Dewey win. His father, though, was not so sure. Dewey's vagueness about campaign issues bothered the elder Nadasdy, but the consensus of others was that, after sixteen years, a Republican was headed to the White House. On Election Night, Len Nadasdy was ready for a win. The campus GOP had scheduled festivities for later in the evening, but early vote counts suggested that the election might not go as predicted. Truman had taken a lead that was holding. As the hours passed, Dewey's prospects dimmed beyond hope. Len's father's trepidations had been warranted. At midnight, the young Nadasdy went to bed with nothing to celebrate.

The next morning, in a lecture hall, Nadasdy watched his professor's notes flutter to the floor and remembered his opening words. "Forget everything I told you about politics ...," Dr. Asher Christiansen began. "History was written yesterday, and we must re-evaluate political science." It would take time to analyze the election that contradicted "historical precedence and political polling," Christiansen concluded.

Nadasdy, for one, was ready to keep exploring the complexities of politics. The end of the 1940s was an exciting time for it. Soldiers home from World War II began to invigorate political life, he said. Wanting more say in public policy, the young veterans gravitated to the major parties. The Young Republican (YR) organization became a training ground for new politicians, according to political writer Theodore White. Several national YR chairmen finished their terms and then went right into public office, some winning seats in Congress. Their Democratic counterparts, on the other hand, tended to go directly into electoral office, "...without having bothered with junior-league politics," White noted.[225]

Len Nadasdy learned a great deal in the junior league. In 1949, he went to his first Young Republican National Federation (YRNF) convention. He was hooked. The YRNF was a heady place to be, refreshed as it was by the activism of young war veterans and ready for the post-Roosevelt era. Nadasdy, at nineteen, was younger than most delegates. He remembered working his way through the convention hall, looking for fellow acolytes of Thomas E. Dewey. His search brought him into a warm, enduring friendship with the New York delegation. He learned how candidates for the YRNF chairmanship won elections. He saw how ideological and regional blocs played into YR leadership contests. He saw how a YRNF candidate's allegiance to a particular GOP presidential hopeful could affect his or her acceptability to the various blocs, and he learned how to maneuver among them all.

At the next YRNF convention in 1951, excitement about the upcoming U.S. presidential election was high. Senator Robert Taft of Ohio seemed destined for the GOP nomination. Taft, a conservative, was no stranger to the White House, having lived there when his father, William Howard Taft, was president. The Young Republicans who supported Taft slated their candidate for YRNF chairman. The New York YRs, being anti-Taft, had an opposing candidate. Nadasdy helped his New York friends elect their man.

By then chair of the Minnesota Young Republicans, Nadasdy also got an appointment to the YRNF executive committee. His new visibility brought him into the rapidly-evolving world of one of the most skillful political organizers of the mid-20th century. The impressive individual was F. Clifton White, a young man who would affect party organizations throughout the nation. In New Mexico, Holm Bursum III would encounter White's brilliant strategies and blunt tactics as they played out in his state's party in the mid-1960s.

Clifton White, a decorated war veteran, lectured in political science at prestigious schools like Cornell. Then, he moved into more direct political work. Pleasant, known for his jaunty bowties, he had a gift for turning socio-political trends into campaign action. He understood Young Republican power, and by harnessing it, he took increasingly significant roles in the presidential races of the 1950s and '60s. Theodore White called Clifton White "...a technician of politics—one of the finest in America."[226]

Early on, Clif White was part of the Dewey organization in New York and, through that relationship, had many YR contacts. He was about to use them to great effect in the 1952 campaign for the GOP presidential nomination. He was going to help defeat the conservative Robert Taft by allying with another element of the party—one that was drawn to the less politically-defined General Dwight D. Eisenhower and his wartime achievements. White was going to be of considerable help to the general.

While an uncertain Eisenhower was pondering the idea of running for president, Clifton White made a move. In 1951, he invited Nadasdy and other select YRs to a meeting in Chicago. At a press conference, he named them as state directors of the youth movement for Eisenhower. White's bold claim was quite a stretch. "At the time, none of us had any kind of organization," Nadasdy said, adding that "White handled the meeting with great success." Using aspirational strategies and nudging reluctant candidates toward a presidential nomination were to become Clifton White's stock in trade. His work to prompt Eisenhower's candidacy was practice for him. In another decade, his political moves would be masterful.

White's recruit Len Nadasdy practiced his own organizing skills back at the University of Minnesota in the fall of 1951. Working with the

YMCA, he staged a mock nominating convention on campus, arranging for a band, a Pennsylvania congressman at the podium, and press coverage. Eisenhower won on the first ballot, earning Nadasdy an invitation to work on the general's actual nomination at the Republican National Convention in Chicago in 1952.

In July 1952, Len Nadasdy joined the exciting movement for a new era in the GOP. Young volunteers for Ike flooded into Chicago ahead of the Republican National Convention. They camped out in the warehouses of companies sympathetic to Eisenhower. From there, the young people went to airports and train stations to greet the arriving state delegations. They served coffee, offered campaign buttons, pinned on corsages, and arranged transportation to hotels. Through daily newsletters, they updated the delegates on Eisenhower's momentum. They staged seemingly spontaneous rallies infused with their enthusiasm. They engaged in youthful antics too. A steam roller was parked near the convention hall to symbolize Taft supporters' tactics. Axes were wielded by the young to break padlocks on side doors in protest of Taft-controlled access to the convention.

During balloting for the presidential nomination, Nadasdy's Minnesota gave up its votes for favorite-son Harold Stassen and put Eisenhower over the top. Young people, exultant, flooded the aisles. "Hoarse but happy" is how Nadasdy described himself in the moment of victory. The effort that the youth had lavished on Ike brought rewards at the convention. In November, Eisenhower went on to win the presidency in an electoral-college landslide.

Len Nadasdy finally could be euphoric over a presidential victory on Election Night, but it was not as he would have scripted it. He should have been at party headquarters, cheering with fellow campaigners. Instead, he was stuck in a tent, listening to a radio in Virginia's snowy mountains. Nadasdy was at an Army training camp. The Korean War was raging, and after the GOP convention, Nadasdy had reported for a Reserve Officers Training Course. By December, he was at Fort Jay in New York. There he, a young lieutenant, received a hand-inscribed invitation to the inauguration of Dwight D. Eisenhower. With Army orders and expense funds in his pocket, Nadasdy traveled to Washington for the historic occasion.

President Eisenhower began to appoint people to high government and party posts, but one man overlooked in the distribution was F. Clifton White. White's exclusion would have repercussions as he found new allies in the GOP. Nadasdy thought White was not committed to an ideology except as a tool in campaigning. Power was his objective, so, seemingly rebuffed by the liberal/moderate wing of the party, he moved to the conservative one. He formed a YR group in the late-1950s that Nadasdy and others referred to as the Syndicate. White and the Syndicate proceeded to amass power.

Len Nadasdy became a YRNF regional coordinator in 1955. In 1957, he saw White and the Syndicate elect John Ashbrook, a future congressman, as national chair. In 1959, Nadasdy and his allies came back to elect Ned Cushing. Although Nadasdy did not foresee it, in two years, he himself would become YRNF chairman. Holm Bursum III of New Mexico would help him win.

Strategizing in Minnesota: The YRNF National Convention of 1961

The Minnesota Young Republicans had won their bid to host the 1961 YRNF convention in Minneapolis in June. Nadasdy was working hard on logistics when pressure mounted for him to run for the national chairmanship. Reluctant and busy, he took some time to decide.

Eventually, Nadasdy went on the road, visiting YR regional conferences and testing his platform. He promoted a national organization that recognized the variety in Republican perspectives, one that was open to "all ideas within the scope of good government policy," he said. He proposed that the Young Republicans observe boundaries in their relationship with the senior wing, not endorsing a candidate for the U.S. presidency until the GOP had nominated one. Despite F. Clifton White's plans to the contrary, Nadasdy did not want the YRNF to become a presidential primary candidate's campaign tool. Another of Nadasdy's planks was to reach out to state YR associations. He wanted to strengthen the whole Young Republican infrastructure by building a national team of field organizers to work in the states. A third plank addressed the development of local YR clubs. He created a model built on good programming for club meetings and political education for members. He envisioned Young Republicans across the nation, educated and trained, canvassing in their communities, meeting voters, and hearing their concerns.

It was getting to be exciting—the thought of leading the Young Republican National Federation that had drawn him in when he was nineteen and taught him much. Nadasdy found that his ideas had appeal. His campaign took off, with endorsements coming in from many regions of the country. Of course, the New York delegation supported him, but one important group, the Californians, had deferred their decision. They had received him well but left him in suspense as to their endorsement. Even without them, Nadasdy counted fifteen delegations in his camp.

F. Clifton White's group put forth their candidate, Robert Hughes, state treasurer of Indiana. Like Nadasdy, Hughes won good support early in the process. Sixteen delegations, including Texas and Illinois, were on board with him. The contest was on.

The convention started on June 22, bringing three thousand Young Republicans to the Radisson Hotel in Minneapolis. An opening reception took place at the White Bear Lake Yacht Club near St. Paul. It was a fetching summer scene—a dazzling white, multi-story clubhouse set against the blue of the lake and the green of a golf course. With lush woods on the horizon, the resort had a vintage aura and romantic appeal. F. Scott and Zelda Fitzgerald had cavorted there in the 1920s, and later the yacht club turned up as a setting in a Fitzgerald novel.[227] Holm Bursum III and his New Mexico delegation soon were part of the scene.

Len Nadasdy, both a convention host and candidate, was at the clubhouse to greet the arriving YRs. He was still wondering how the California delegation would vote in the chairmanship race. Then, the Golden State bus pulled up, and he heard the notes of "California Here We Come" drift through the open windows. Watching in pleasant surprise, he saw each delegate step out into the summer evening wearing a Nadasdy button.

Meanwhile, others were showing support for Nadasdy in a less dulcet manner. Holm Bursum appreciated Nadasdy's platform. It was similar to the one he had run on in his state election a few weeks before. He and his delegation had votes to cast for Nadasdy, but, being from a small state, they did not have many. They needed augmentation, and Bursum had a plan. The Four Corners states could come in for Nadasdy as a bloc. Bursum approached New Mexico's neighbors in the region: Arizona, Utah, and Colorado. Later, he worked farther afield with Wisconsin's Peter Kohler of the Kohler plumbing products family. Bursum had his bloc, and he remained friends for life with some of those he met as he organized.

While Bursum strategized regionally, Len Nadasdy visited the remaining uncommitted delegations. As the voting finally got underway, Bursum waited until the critical moment when a bloc of support would make the difference. The Four Corners' vote came in with a touch of drama, and it put Nadasdy over. From there, he won even more votes. The move had been classic Bursum. He was a talented organizer, a constructive actor. He had a modest, low-key communication style, but no one could mistake his commitment to an ideology and a plan of action. He was creating a kind of political organizing that worked.

In the end, Nadasdy won his election by two hundred votes. His running mate for co-chairwoman, Jean McKee, lost, however. A staffer for the liberal Republican Senator Jacob Javits of New York, McKee was a high-quality candidate, Nadasdy thought. Her defeat disappointed him. The new co-chairwoman was Patricia Miller Hutar of Illinois. At thirty, she had come up through the ranks from precinct and ward leadership to a national YR position. Slim and dark-haired, in a tailored dress, she had the presence of a serious politician with a touch of glamour. Patricia Hutar was an up-and-coming national Republican leader.

As the convention proceeded, one speaker high on the agenda was Richard M. Nixon.[228] Amplifying the theme of unity, he called for party harmony and warned his young audience that extremism was developing in parts of their organization. He implored them not to drive out good people because they did not gravitate to positions on the political edge.[229] The Republican Party had room for a wide variety of views, Nixon said. The differences within the GOP, he said, were fewer than the differences between their party and the Democrats.

Senator Barry Goldwater of Arizona also was in Minneapolis in 1961. He was just three years away from his presidential campaign, although he had not yet committed to run. In fact, he was not even close to such a decision, but F. Clifton White had plans for him. Holm Bursum also recognized Goldwater's growing prominence in the party. The two men met at the convention, and Bursum asked for Goldwater's endorsement of New Mexico's 1962 ticket.[230]

Bursum had used his time well. When he left Minnesota, he had a pledge of support from Barry Goldwater and new friendships with Len Nadasdy and others. At a national level, Bursum had caught people's attention with his organizing skills. One person in particular who noticed his work was Patricia Hutar. In another two years, as Hutar's star in the GOP was rising, Bursum would receive a most unexpected and potentially life-changing call from her.

The convention in the Twin Cities wound down. Strategist Clif White assessed his wins and losses within the Young Republican power structure. His candidate for chairman had not prevailed against Leonard Nadasdy, but Patricia Hutar had defeated Nadasdy's running mate. Soon, Hutar would be working with White, who already was strategizing for the 1963 YRNF convention. He could envision that assembly, and it would go down in party history.

Looking beyond the formal GOP, F. Clifton White saw a new kind of conservatism developing in the country.[231] It was not simply the traditional type that called for protections of individual freedoms closely tied to property rights, limits on federal government power, a balanced budget, free trade, and reticence about international entanglements. The new conservatism might have embraced several of those ideas, but there were others. As different groups gravitated to the movement, it became broad and challenging to define. The message came very close to the concerns that some voters grappled with in their daily lives. It had become deeply personal, incorporating people's hopes and trepidations as they coped with the socio-economic and cultural shifts taking place in the United States in the 1960s. The movement also included threads of a growing mistrust of government institutions.

Clifton White grasped the strands of the new conservatism. He thought they could lead to winning the White House. In October of 1961, he was going to hold a private meeting in a Chicago hotel room. With a carefully selected group, Patricia Hutar among them, Clif White was about to launch a movement to nominate Barry Goldwater for the presidency. Soon after, he would pitch the plan to Goldwater himself. Goldwater, according to writer Theodore White, was "...indifferent—but amused."[232] From late 1961 into 1962—without Goldwater's endorsement of his work and before the senator ever agreed to run—Clifton White divided the United States into nine regions. Through meticulous research and thoughtful strategy, he began developing state delegations of pro-Goldwater people for the 1964 Republican National Convention. As he had done for Eisenhower, White recruited young people in the states to be part of the advance guard. His organizing would play out in consequential ways in many places, among them New Mexico.

Chartering Clubs under a New Constitution and Launching a "Re-Register Republican" Drive.

Holm Bursum came home from the YRNF convention fired up

and ready to expand the New Mexico Young Republican Association. Not confining himself to the Rio Grande corridor that ran from Taos through Albuquerque to Las Cruces, Bursum went statewide. He organized at a good pace. From July into December, an average of one club per month came into the association under a new constitution. The chartering schedule of Young Republican clubs[233] reflected the geographic scope of the expansion, from Albuquerque to the international borderland, from the eastern plains to the northwest corner:

July: Bernalillo County, President William A. Gardner.
July: Dona Ana County, President Dave Lucero.
August: Guadalupe County, President Lorenzo Delgado.
September: Santa Fe County, President Julio Garcia.
November, Curry County, President Hoyt Pattison.
December, San Juan County.

The chartering of the Curry County club under the new constitution was especially notable. President Hoyt Pattison was one of the young political talents supported during the time of YR revitalization, and within two years, his accomplishments would win national Young Republican recognition.

Holm Bursum worked with the senior party to achieve the reach that he did. Frances Marron Lee helped. Although her father had been a prominent Democrat, Lee could not have been more dedicated to the GOP. Her public service was extensive.[234] In 1935, Governor Clyde Tingley appointed her to the University of New Mexico Board of Regents, and she served until 1947. She also chaired school boards in two counties. In 1953, President Dwight Eisenhower appointed her to the Inter-American Commission for Women. She traveled internationally, working for the civic education of women in North and South America. Her fluency in Spanish was an asset. In 1959, Lee began thirteen years as New Mexico's GOP national committeewoman. When she decided to support Holm Bursum and his efforts to revitalize the young wing, she had given him a great gift. Bursum knew its value. In part through Lee, he made contacts with senior party people throughout the state. One such prominent Republican was Fanny Bliss in Clovis.

Fanny Bliss whole-heartedly supported the Young Republicans in Curry County, where Hoyt Pattison, Esther Smith, and others already were actively organizing. Reflecting on that time, Bursum remembered Bliss fondly. She was a powerhouse, a career woman with interests in childhood education and civic engagement. She operated a kindergarten in Clovis and was president of the New Mexico Federation of Republican Women. Her party connections were impressive; she had even had tea with First Lady Mamie Eisenhower in the White House.[235]

"Fanny Bliss was our den mother," Bursum remembered fondly. He had considered her quite a party elder then, he said. Looking back as a man in his eighties, he acknowledged with a chuckle that Bliss probably had been only in her fifties at the time. Regardless of which age perspective he was coming from, Bursum had a great heart for intergenerational party work and respect for people like Fanny Bliss and Frances Lee who walked the path ahead of him.

The YR Association treasury had little money for organizing, Bursum recalled. The young leaders, new in their careers, had limited resources themselves. They made do. After work and on the weekends, they got in their cars and set out. Sometimes, they found lodging with family or friends. Often, fellow officer John Mitchell, who worked at Sandia Laboratory, was on those trips.[236] A Minnesota native, Mitchell was new to New Mexico. One benefit of his travels with Bursum was getting to know the state, seeing its diversity in terrain and climate. In San Juan County on club business one winter, the young men stayed with Bursum's uncle. Mitchell had been telling his hosts about the heavy snows he had known in Minnesota. The next day, he remembered in amusement, they found themselves snowbound on the high Colorado Plateau of northwestern New Mexico, unable to get back to Albuquerque for a day and a half.

As the Young Republican leaders traveled from club to club, they made every chartering ceremony a standout event with a dinner and a guest speaker. Bursum welcomed the new clubs by arranging for senior-party luminaries—Governor Ed Mechem, Lt. Governor Tom Bolack, or State Party Chairman Joe Skeen—to address the young people. Sometimes a YR leader from another state was on the agenda, and almost always, a large delegation from Albuquerque came along with Bursum to salute the new clubs. Having Albuquerque contingents join in on the celebrations made an important point. Often in statewide organizations, Albuquerque serves as the hub. It means that the organizational traffic flow usually is from other parts of the state into its largest city. Under Bursum's leadership, the Albuquerque YRs journeyed out. They traveled far and wide in New Mexico—to the benefit of all.

The celebratory events around the state usually were paired with executive committee meetings where Young Republican leaders conducted association business and networked. The YRs took positions on the major issues of the day and disseminated their work. In July 1961, for example, they published their concerns about Soviet aggression in Germany. They urged the United States to resist the U.S.S.R.'s actions,[237] but later that summer, the Berlin Wall went up. The YRs were engaged at all levels of public life. It was a dynamic scene.

In 1961, the YRs also launched a "Re-register Republican" drive. Through a mailing, they invited Democrats with conservative outlooks to consider changing parties. Early on, they saw favorable comments from about a third of those who responded, Bursum told the press.[238] The concern that the YRs expressed in their letter was a Cold War one. They were the generation that reached adulthood in the decade after World War II. It was the Atomic Era, and the Bomb was more than a distant reality for young New Mexicans. As a teen, Holm Bursum III literally had glided across the trinitite left by the explosion of the first nuclear weapon. As he and his peers matured, they had seen the United States' wartime ally, the Soviet Union, become a rival in the nuclear arms race. It was an unsettling time—not just because of the destructive potential of atomic bombs but also because of competing ideologies.

In 1959, Soviet Premier Nikita Khrushchev had spoken about societal evolution in a way that many Americans found threatening. The voluble Russian leader declared that, in the natural course of human affairs, communism would replace capitalism.[239] The United States, Khrushchev believed, would not be exempt. Americans in both parties in the 1950s and '60s denounced Soviet communism. Some resisted their own government's liberal programs, seeing them as incremental steps to the kind of centralized economy that Khrushchev championed. People also were on guard about Russian aggression as the Soviets made moves in Europe and Cuba. The U.S. democratic and capitalist systems seemed in jeopardy. The Young Republicans thought it might be the time to invite Democrats who shared their concerns into their party.

Mick Wilson, head of New Mexico's Young Democrats, predicted that few of his party actually would re-register as Republicans. Social justice was not the same as socialism, he argued. He added that even the well-off in his party accepted their "obligations to the rest of society."[240] Bursum, looking back after several decades, did not remember whether the drive had produced many registration changes. Recalling it with a smile, he put it in the category of "we tried everything." Regardless of the outcome, the two young party leaders had referenced an enduring question: how to address socio-economic challenges in the United States and make progress. They did not agree on how the federal government and free enterprise should play their respective roles in solving the problems, but their dialog was a good one.

Making Politics More Inclusive: A Speech and a Court Decision

In the fall, Patricia Hutar came to Albuquerque. On November 9, the Young Republican National Federation's co-chairwoman headlined a fundraiser at the Western Skies Hotel. Holm Bursum served as master of ceremonies for the evening, and National Committeewoman Frances Lee and Bernalillo County Club President William A. Gardner were on the agenda.

The Western Skies Hotel was just the venue for such a gathering. New, modern, touted as New Mexico's largest hotel, it had expanses of glass, a sleek, elegant design, and mountains as a backdrop. It was the type of place that could host a president, and a few months later, John F. Kennedy would stay there on his visits to the national laboratories at Sandia and Los Alamos.[241] To no one's surprise at the Young Republican event, Kennedy's name came up. He was finishing his first year in office, and Republicans were concerned about the size of the federal budget and a U.S. foreign policy that did not seem to be a match for Soviet aggression.

Patricia Hutar addressed the Young Republicans, delivering a conservative message that fit the times.[242] She saw dangers to freedom in the U.S. from two directions. One, coming from abroad, was communism. The other was internal: apathy and lack of initiative. She reminded her audience that President Kennedy had called for people to make sacrifices for their country in light of the global situation. Republicans were ready, she declared—ready to cut federal spending—but the Democrats would not support a leaner budget. She gave the YRs a charge. Keep political engagement high, she urged, even in years with no elections. Work to interest young adults in partisan politics, and find young candidates to run for office.

When Frances Lee[243] came to the podium, she must have been pleased to see the seventy-five fresh young faces in front of her. Lee was sixty years old in 1961, a trim, fashionable woman. She had seen great political change in New Mexico. She was a child when her father, O. N. Marron, joined Holm Bursum's grandfather at the Alvarado Hotel in 1909 to plead the cause of statehood before William Howard Taft. They had succeeded in bringing New Mexico into the United States over the objections of those who found the territory too foreign. What seemed alien to some, Lee celebrated. She grew up knowing cultural diversity and was bilingual in English and Spanish. She had graduated from the University of California at Berkeley and returned home to use her education in public service. Half a century after New Mexico finally had been admitted to the Union, Lee spoke about another kind of inclusion—women in state and national political life. She called for a deeper and broader engagement of women in party work and government.

At mid-century, the U.S. did see women in party positions and in elective office but with limitations. For example, the Young Republican National Federation had a co-chairwoman, but a man always held the top position. Likewise, the number of women elected to high government positions was strikingly low.[244] In 1961, only two women served in the U.S. Senate: Margaret Chase Smith, a Republican of Maine, and Maurine Neuberger, a Democrat of Oregon. Only eighteen women served in the more than 400-member House of Representatives. No woman yet had been appointed to the U.S. Supreme Court. No woman yet had been chosen by either major party to run for president or vice president, and only two women had served as governors of their states. Frances Lee foresaw change. She and Patricia Hutar were two party leaders a generation apart who invited young women to achieve alongside them. They had allies among the men in the party, one of them being Holm Bursum, whose support for women seeking office would be life-long.

As the Young Republicans enjoyed their banquet that night in November, an undercurrent of excitement was moving through the political world in New Mexico. Just the day before, Lieutenant Governor Tom Bolack had received important news. The case that Joseph A. Montoya had brought in state district court against Bolack's election had been decided. Montoya had argued that the election should be invalidated, in part, because voters on the Navajo Reservation had contributed to Bolack's win. People living on federally-controlled reservations, Montoya contended, should not be eligible to vote in state elections. Judge John B. McManus, in an important affirmation of voting rights, rejected Montoya's claim.[245] Montoya decided to appeal the case to the New Mexico Supreme Court, but Bolack, at least for the moment, could enjoy a court victory that confirmed his electoral one. Voters of Native heritages on reservation lands had an even more profound reason to celebrate.

Tom Bolack's retention of his office would become very consequential a year later. Meanwhile, a new development was unfolding, the sort that makes New Mexico politics utterly absorbing. It had to do with the strategizing of one man—Congressman Joseph M. Montoya—in his rise to higher office. It resulted in a plan that took into account the fragile health of New Mexico's aging U.S. senators. The culmination of events would give Holm Bursum III a weighty topic to discuss with Richard Nixon during a quiet moment at a meeting in Washington, DC late in 1962.

1961 had been a whirl of activity for Holm Bursum III at all levels of party organizing, from local and state to national. The hours involved and the miles traveled happened at a time when he was establishing himself in his banking career. He and his wife also had started their family with the births of two children, Holm IV and Elizabeth. Bursum's political organizing as his consuming leisure-time pursuit was a gift to the two-party system, and he was just getting started.

8

1962: Local Organizing and Midterm Surprises

The state or national [Republican] organizations can raise all the money they want to, but it isn't doing any good if we don't have strength on the local level.
—Edwin L. Mechem, December 8, 1961[246]

Most of Holm Bursum's organizing for the Young Republicans (YRs) happened in 1962. It was midterm-election time for the Kennedy administration, and surprises were in store for the fall. One was a global crisis; another was a triumph in Curry County, and the third led to an abrupt change of course for two titans of New Mexico politics. The year started simply enough as the YRs resumed their organizing at the county level. Bursum was learning from the party's best, Edwin L. Mechem. Mechem often stopped in Albuquerque to pick up his protégé to attend events with him. It must have been a pleasure for the governor to associate with the composed young man who had grown up knowing party leaders and respecting their feats to keep the GOP alive. He was the right partner for Mechem in 1962. As Hamm noted, "Holm offered youthful vigor, enthusiasm, and organizational skills; Mechem provided star power."[247]

Mechem indeed possessed the luster of a great man, but Holm Bursum III was developing star power too. Sharply dressed in suit and tie, he was the young professional from Albuquerque who drew a good audience when he arrived in a community. Rebuilding a party from low registration numbers—especially attracting a new generation—takes a particular approach. Bursum had one. He was relaxed and cordial, but he had purpose. In his talks on principles and platforms, he presented Republicanism in a way that his audiences found modern and appealing. He inspired young people to come together and get to work. In a conversation about his organizing success in the 1960s, Bursum downplayed it. "You know how it is," he said, his eyes crinkling at the corners. "If you're from out of town, you're the expert."

Organizing and Running on the Eastside

The Young Republicans started a full-fledged organizational push in January of 1962. National leader Len Nadasdy had pledged to provide field organizers to state associations, and soon Jerry Roe, the YRNF executive secretary, was en route to New Mexico.[248] Holm Bursum took Roe to the eastern part of the state, a region similar in landscape, climate, and politics to West Texas. The young men worked their way from the agricultural communities in east-central New Mexico southward to the oil towns. In Clovis, Bursum and Roe met with Young Republicans from Curry, Roosevelt, Guadalupe, and De Baca counties. They also attended a regional meeting in Artesia, conferring with YRs from Eddy, Chaves, and Lea counties.

Bursum had been following Edwin Mechem's approach to party organizing in 1950—assuming that the Democratic counties on the eastside were open to political change. He and Roe ended their tour in Alamogordo at the Desert Aire. Meeting with Chair John Price, they celebrated the Otero County YR Club's new charter. Governor Mechem himself flew in for the event, along with Lieutenant-Governor Tom Bolack and state GOP Chair Joe Skeen. The excitement in the banquet room had to have been remarkable. There they were, the top party leaders: Mechem, the polished and seasoned political celebrity; Bolack, the hero of the impossibly close lieutenant-governor race; Skeen, the high-spirited young leader of the senior wing, and the newest and freshest of them all, Roe and Bursum, Young Republican stars.

The next month, Bursum and state YR treasurer John P. Mitchell were off to Washington, DC for leadership training with the Young Republican National Federation. Bursum checked in with Len Nadasdy, whom he would bring to New Mexico in the fall. He also renewed ties with Barry Goldwater, already a front runner for the presidential nomination.[249]

At home, Bursum welcomed two new clubs. In April, he celebrated with the Chaves County Young Republicans in Roswell. Carlsbad chartered next under the leadership of Tom Nord.[250] It was the second club in Eddy County, a remarkable party success in that region. The number of clubs under the new charter grew to twelve. At the state convention in Las Cruces that May, the arriving delegations showed how much geographic range the YRs had achieved. New university-based clubs also were coming on board.[251] Soon Highlands' and Eastern New Mexico's clubs would join those of the University of New Mexico and New Mexico State.

As the Young Republicans organized for their party's campaign in 1962, some considered running for state legislative seats. In Albuquerque, John Mitchell, William Gardner, David Cargo, and other high-profile YRs decided to try for the New Mexico House. To run in Bernalillo County was a daunting prospect for Republicans. The Democrats had a firm hold on the seats, and since candidates ran at large in the populous county, winning as a member of a minority party was difficult. Although the outlook was not favorable, just having Republican candidates on the ballot showed their faith in the two-party system. Mitchell credited Holm Bursum with encouraging him to enter electoral politics. "He was a good leader," Mitchell remembered. "He got us involved and running for public office."[252]

In eastern New Mexico, Hoyt Pattison had decided to make his second run for the state legislature. Ted Waldhauser, a Minnesota transplant known as the Cowboy Mayor of Clovis,[253] was watching. Mayor Waldhauser saw that Republican Pattison and attorney David Norvell, a Democrat, both wanted to run for a House seat. Waldhauser, himself a Democrat, was tall, brusque, and influential, Pattison said. He had become a successful rancher, farmer, and cattle feeder in Curry County, and he understood his region. He realized that Pattison and Norvell had the potential to become rivals in the election—and to be good legislators. He did not want the young men to oppose one another.

The mayor counseled Pattison to run for a different at-large position than Norvell. Pattison listened and made an appointment with Norvell to discuss how they would file their candidacies. Waldhauser got his wish. Norvell decided to file for position two. He would take on an incumbent in the Democratic primary, Frank Foster, the person who had defeated Pattison in 1960. Pattison would run for position one against Albert Matlock, a Democrat who had been a state legislator before. Pattison would have had a formidable opponent regardless of which race he entered. Party registration was 7:1 in the Democrats' favor that year, he recalled.[254] At least he and Norvell would not vie for the same seat.

All the Republican state legislative candidates knew the odds. In

1962, the House of Representatives had sixty-six seats, and Democrats held fifty-nine of them. Time would tell if the GOP could make inroads into that overwhelming majority. Meanwhile, Holm Bursum III and the YRs continued working with the senior party on the campaign.

Preparing for the General Election: the Impacts of a State Crisis and an International Event

1962 was the year of midterms for John F. Kennedy's administration, and in New Mexico, it was time to elect a governor. Incumbent Edwin L. Mechem was seeking his fifth term. His Democratic opponent, House speaker Jack Campbell, got ready to challenge him.

The race was a tough one, its central issue the state's finances. Four years earlier, when Mechem lost to John Burroughs, the state had a seven million dollar surplus. But when Mechem returned to the governor's office in 1961, the surplus had been spent down, he said.[255] Compounding the problem was the fact that the state legislature did not have enough revenue to meet budget obligations.[256] New Mexico faced a ten million dollar deficit, putting public schools at risk of inadequate funding. The school crisis did not rise to the one Governor Clyde Tingley confronted during the Great Depression, but it was serious enough. Governor Mechem proposed a one-cent gross receipts tax increase, a temporary hike until the state's finances stabilized. Campbell argued that the deficit was a fraction of what Mechem claimed and campaigned on no tax increases.[257] Mechem, in his frank conversation with the voters, had put his reelection at risk.

Campaigning as the Young Republicans

The Young Republicans jumped into the campaign. It is hard to overemphasize the commitment they needed to organize as they did that year, driving long hours on rough roads and spending time carved out of family life. They faced daunting electoral odds and had little money. What they did have abundantly was senior-party endorsement, camaraderie among themselves, and a belief that their state would be better with a robust two-party system.

As the campaign's temperature rose to match the summer heat, Holm Bursum and his team got busier. He and Robert Dorr and John Bulkley visited Young Republican clubs throughout the 121,000 square miles of

New Mexico. They strategized with local YRs around small-town restaurant tables and similar venues. Together, they planned for the ultimate outcome: good voter turnout for their candidates in November.

Occasionally, in a pleasant change from their long drives, the YRs flew with State Senator Joe Skeen. Skeen, who owned a plane, was a big, friendly Hondo Valley rancher in his mid-thirties. As state chair of the GOP, he was a good link between its senior and young wings. His conversations with his YR passengers were lively. He had a passion for three things: fiscally responsible state government, economic development through industry, and a strong two-party system. Young people, he knew, were the key to making the GOP competitive again, and he was pleased to see how quickly YR clubs were forming. As he pointed out, "If you don't start raising them young, you don't have anything to pick at harvest time."[258]

Toward the end of summer, Bursum and his colleagues traveled to eastern New Mexico. He had not abandoned his idea that the Republican Party could grow in the region's Democratic counties. He had begun the year in those counties with his and Jerry Roe's January tour, and when he returned in August, he had an equally intense itinerary: [259]

> A Saturday seven a.m. breakfast meeting in Santa Rosa on old Route 66 east of Albuquerque.
> An 11 a.m. lunch meeting in Clovis on the High Plains near Texas.
> A 4 p.m. meeting in Carlsbad, in the Chihuahuan Desert in the southeast.
> A seven p.m. meeting in Artesia, thirty-six miles north of Carlsbad.
> A Sunday nine a.m. breakfast meeting in Roswell, on the plains forty miles north of Artesia.
> A noon lunch meeting in Tinnie west of Roswell, in the foothills of the Sacramentos.

The next weekend, Bursum and his team started again, heading south to county seats near the international border.[260] On Saturday, they visited Alamogordo for a nine a.m. meeting and headed 130 miles west for a two p.m. in Deming. Then, they turned back east to Las Cruces for a six p.m. meeting. On Sunday, they were 150 miles north, in Bursum's hometown of Socorro, to help start a new club. As with most weekend itineraries, the organizers returned to Albuquerque on Sunday evening, their cars dusty, windshields splattered with insects, and the tread on their tires a little thinner. On Monday mornings, they were back at their regular jobs.

Although their schedules were taxing, there is good evidence to suggest that Holm Bursum found ways to keep the travel light-hearted and full of merriment. Retired state legislator Don Tripp recalled a similar political trip in the 1970s.[261] Bursum had gathered up a crew of still-young Republicans to travel the state and campaign for Joe Skeen for governor. "It was fun," Tripp said, "because Holm Bursum made it fun." Their time on the campaign trail even entailed "riding mechanical bulls in Roswell," he remarked dryly, as if such capers were a standard part of gubernatorial barnstorming.

In September, another Young Republican club chartered, in San Miguel County in the northern highlands.[262] Chair Benjamin Coca worked with Hilario Montano, the county's senior party leader, to host an event. They invited people from two counties and featured candidates in state and local races. Among those running was Coca himself, candidate for county school superintendent. He also launched a drive to register new voters and those wanting to change party affiliation. His club could have written a guide on young political action at the local level: build the voting base, collaborate with the senior party, fundraise, and run for office.

In October, counting down to Election Day, Holm Bursum welcomed Len Nadasdy to the state.[263] The Young Republican National Federation leader had promised to campaign for Republican congressional candidates, and he was hard at work in 1962. He helped new U.S. Representative Bob Dole of Kansas in his reelection and made early connections with a young George H. W. Bush in Texas. In New Mexico, Nadasdy spoke at a luncheon for the Bernalillo County YR and Teen Age Republican clubs at the Alvarado Hotel. John F. Kennedy's foreign policy was on his mind. He was concerned about the president's hesitation to act abroad, particularly as the Soviets built the Berlin Wall. Now that the wall had gone up, Nadasdy said, it would take serious military action to remove it. He also called for an expanded U.S. blockade of Cuba. After his Albuquerque speech, Nadasdy spent two days on the road with Bursum. They were going south and east—to Las Cruces, Carlsbad, Roswell, and Clovis. It was Bursum's third sweep through the east side that year, and Nadasdy was getting a close look at his organizing strategies in Democratic domains.

Facing the Cuban Missile Crisis

While the Young Republicans worked on the midterm election, an international emergency was developing: the Cuban Missile Crisis. It evolved as a Cold War standoff. In the 1950s, the United States had installed missiles in Turkey and other sites near the U.S.S.R. When the Soviets began installing nuclear weapons in Cuba in 1962, the U.S. reacted. Alarm spread through the population, even to children, who were not insulated from their parents' and teachers' sense of doom. Apprehension over the unfolding events would impact the midterm elections nationwide. Typically, the incumbent president has seen his party lose congressional seats at midterm, but John F. Kennedy's case was to be different. Facing off with Nikita Khrushchev in October, Kennedy convinced the Soviet leader to remove his country's missiles from Cuba. It was a diplomatic move that not only avoided armed conflict but won the president an election advantage. Kennedy already enjoyed a 61% approval rating. After the crisis, his rating rose to 74%.[264] His party would do well in congressional races in November, not losing many seats in the House and, in fact, gaining a few in the Senate.

Making the Most of Election Results

In New Mexico, Republicans' best bet for a win was in the governor's race, but Jack Campbell beat Ed Mechem. Political scientist Frederick Irion alluded to the anomaly of a Democrat running on a no-tax-increase pledge and a Republican calling for higher taxes. Irion also mentioned the budget shortfall. "The day after the election," he said, "Democratic estimates (rather quietly, of course) rose to Mechem's anticipated ten million dollar figure."[265]

Governor Campbell eventually acknowledged the size of the budget deficit and proposed a property-tax increase, but his plan stirred up opposition both inside and outside his party. Ultimately, he accepted a gross-receipts tax increase, doing so at Democratic legislators' urging. Speaker of the House Bruce King got the increase through,[266] and Campbell implemented it. The solution to the budget-deficit problem held some irony for the GOP.

For the Republicans in 1962, the governorship had been lost, but on the state legislative side, they began to make gains. Only two years after state Senator William H. Duckworth's breakthrough election in Curry County, Hoyt Pattison won his race for a House seat. He was the only Republican to win in the county that year. Clovis Mayor Waldhauser's advice not to oppose David Norvell had been sound. Both young men succeeded at the polls, became legislative leaders, and maintained a cordial relationship across party lines. "I always got along with Dave Norvell," Pattison said.[267] Later, Pattison's bipartisanship would produce significant results, bringing more legislative power to his party.

In Bernalillo County, Republicans David Cargo and Lawrence Prentice won two of nine at-large House seats. They were among the four new state representatives who boosted the Republican membership in the House from seven to eleven. John P. Mitchell, Holm Bursum's YR colleague, also ran well in Bernalillo County. Although he did not win, he made a good showing. If legislative districting had been a reality at that time, Mitchell speculated, he might have succeeded. Regardless of the outcome, he felt some satisfaction in his close race, especially since he was a first-time candidate.[268]

Another bright note for the party was the race for an at-large U.S. House seat. Jack Redman, a personable Albuquerque physician, had narrowed incumbent Congressman Joseph M. Montoya's margin of victory to 12,389 votes.[269] It was a slim edge for a Democrat in such a race. The GOP's organizing was keeping its candidates competitive and hopeful.

Replacing Dennis Chavez: Joe Montoya, the "Dead Senator" Bill, and Edwin Mechem

Edwin Mechem had lost his gubernatorial race and was looking forward to going home to Las Cruces in January, but his public service was about to be extended. On November 18, Senator Dennis Chavez died. It was an emotional time for New Mexico. The beloved Chavez had been part of governance since 1922. Democratic leaders had dreaded what had just come about—that Chavez, ill with cancer, would die while a Republican governor was in office. By state law, the governor had the duty to appoint a replacement until the next regular election. No special-election provisions existed for vacant U.S. Senate seats, as they did for House seats.

A year earlier, a group of Democratic legislators had tried to forestall what for their party would be a disadvantage: Governor Edwin L. Mechem's appointing Chavez's successor.

The legislators' actions involved a powerful force in twentieth-century New Mexico politics, Joseph M. Montoya. Montoya aspired to reach the United States Senate, where he would be only the third person of Hispanic heritage to serve New Mexico in that body. The other two had been Republican Octaviano Larrazolo, who served for three months in the late 1920s, and Democrat Dennis Chavez, whose terms ran from the 1930s into the 1960s.

Montoya, a master of politics, knew the intricacies of government and saw ways to facilitate his rise to the upper chamber. According to some political observers, what transpired shortly before and soon after Dennis Chavez's death relates to Montoya's quest for a Senate seat. It became a complicated matter, and to fully appreciate the developments, we review the remarkable career of the New Mexico political giant known as Little Joe Montoya.

Joseph M. Montoya Rising

Joseph M. Montoya's name was ubiquitous in New Mexico politics from the 1930s into the '70s. Montoya was from Pena Blanca, a farming community on beautiful river land south of Santa Fe. He grew up in a politically active, education-minded family whose roots in the area went back to the 1700s. His father served as sheriff of Sandoval County; his mother taught school, and he was a remarkable politician from the start.

Young and slight, Montoya took on the nickname Little Joe. Despite his youth, he was not to be underestimated. In 1936, while studying law at Georgetown University in Washington, DC, Montoya did something out of the ordinary for a twenty-one-year-old college student. He got himself elected to his state's legislature.[270] In 1939, at twenty-four, he became the majority leader of the New Mexico House of Representatives by acclamation.[271] It was another striking achievement. Democrats controlled more than three-quarters of the House seats at the time, giving them a large pool of members from which to choose a leader.

Montoya moved up. From 1940 to 1946, he served in the state Senate, rising to majority whip and judiciary committee chair positions.[272] In 1946, when he was just thirty-one, he gave up his Senate seat and won the lieutenant governor's race to serve in Thomas Mabry's administration. Mabry and Montoya won reelection in 1948.²⁷³ Since governors and lieutenant governors ran separately in those days, each candidate had to wage individual campaigns. Montoya was building political muscle early in life.

While Joseph Montoya served as Mabry's lieutenant governor, his brother Tom also worked in Santa Fe. Tom Montoya had become Governor Mabry's state liquor regulator, but controversy over his practices led the governor to dismiss him in 1950. Tom Montoya returned home, where soon he won a seat on the Sandoval County Commission.

As Tom Montoya rebuilt his political career at the local level, Joe Montoya was spending two years out of office. It was a rare interlude for the latter Montoya, the result of a failed primary election. If Joe Montoya came to dislike Governor Clyde Tingley's doing away with the old convention system, it probably stemmed from his unsettling primary experience in 1950. The problem started when he launched a campaign to oust U.S. Representative Antonio M. Fernandez. Montoya wanted to run for a seat in the U.S. House, and defeating Fernandez in the Democratic primary was the first step. Fernandez was highly regarded in their party, but Joseph M. Montoya, given his own remarkable standing, may have had a fair chance of beating him—until a certain Joseph A. Montoya also entered the primary race.

Some observers thought that Joseph A. did not intend to win the primary but simply to draw votes away from Joseph M. The move, perhaps, was adeptly designed to benefit Fernandez. Indeed, Fernandez won his party's nomination with 41,796 votes. Joseph M. Montoya garnered 37,660 votes, and Joseph A. Montoya got 10,679.²⁷⁴ The math was telling and could have led Joseph M. Montoya to imagine a different scenario if his near-namesake had not entered the primary. If the race had been structured through the old convention system, it most likely would not have included the second Montoya. The matter left Little Joe wary of the direct primary. More than a decade later, he would move to reinstate the pre-primary convention, and his actions would prompt Holm Bursum III and others to resist the change. Meanwhile, Montoya found another way to return to public office.

By 1952, Joseph M. Montoya had recouped. He won his state Senate seat again. Two years later, he won a third term as lieutenant governor, serving with Governor John F. Simms. When Montoya returned to the executive branch, he vacated his Senate seat, and the Sandoval County Commission met to fill it. The commissioners chose their own chair, Tom Montoya, for the post.[275] Once again, the brothers served together in Santa Fe. Joe, as lieutenant governor, presided over the Senate where Tom was a member. The popular and durable Montoyas were building political capital and expanding the boundaries of their power.

In 1956, Joe Montoya won his fourth race to be lieutenant governor, and Edwin L. Mechem won his third gubernatorial term. It was shaping up to be an odd administration: Big Ed, the Republican, with Little Joe, the Democrat. However, the morning after the election, a new office opened up, one particularly interesting to Montoya. His old primary opponent, Antonio Fernandez, had just been re-elected to Congress, but hours later, he died of a stroke. Montoya had failed to unseat Fernandez in 1950, but six years later, sad circumstances gave him the chance to run in a special election to serve out Fernandez's term.

In the special election, Joseph M. Montoya ran for the congressional seat against oilman Tom Bolack, an up-and-coming young GOP politico who had been mayor of Farmington. Montoya beat Bolack and kept getting reelected.[276] He built seniority in Congress and served on the House Appropriations Committee. His next goal was the U.S. Senate, where New Mexico's seats had been held for years by two powerful men, Clinton P. Anderson, then in his sixties, and Dennis Chavez, in his seventies. Both had serious illnesses.

Passing a Bill to Fill a Vacant U.S. Senate Seat

In 1961, Alfonso Montoya, another brother of Joseph M. Montoya, was serving in the New Mexico Senate. By that time, the deteriorating health of both U.S. senators was a concern, especially if either had to vacate his seat. The governor, of course, would appoint his replacement, and in 1961, the governor was Ed Mechem.

In case either Dennis Chavez or Clinton Anderson could not finish his term, certain Democrats wanted to be prepared. In the New Mexico House, Representative Mack Easley introduced legislation to authorize special elections for U.S. Senate vacancies.[277] Will Harrison called it the "Dead Senator bill." It would accomplish the group's objective—to foreclose on Republican Governor Edwin Mechem's ability to fill a Senate seat. Joe Montoya, still a U.S. representative at the time, could run in such a special election. If successful, he would have an incumbent's advantage in the next primary and in the general election.

The special-election bill passed both houses of the legislature; Mechem vetoed it, and Democratic Majority Leader Fabian Chavez, Jr. refused to push for an override.[278] In Chavez's view, crafting a bill that assumed a particular colleague's demise was objectionable. His position bitterly disappointed Senator Alfonso Montoya, who openly said so. The Montoya faction would need to regroup yet again.

Coping with the Death of Dennis Chavez and Making a Senatorial Appointment

Such was the situation when, on November 18, 1962, the news broke of the death of U.S. Senator Dennis Chavez. Chavez had been an institution in New Mexico, befriending many of both parties. His political comrades included Holm O. Bursum, Jr., with whom he had the pleasure of discussing public policy in fluent Spanish. Mechem had his own cross-partisan friendship with Chavez and refused to talk about a replacement for days.

Vice President Lyndon B. Johnson flew to New Mexico to speak at the senator's funeral. In a quiet moment, he talked with David Cargo, attempting to find out who would replace Chavez.[279] The press speculated about a successor as well and raised several possibilities.[280] Would it be Holm O. Bursum, Jr., Socorro mayor and banker; Robert O. Anderson, Roswell oilman and philanthropist, or Junio Lopez, mayor of Las Vegas and recent congressional candidate? Other names came up: Jack Redman, the Albuquerque physician and good vote-getter, and Paul Larrazolo, a district judge and son of former U.S. Senator Octaviano Larrazolo.

Mechem did not share his deliberations publicly. Years later, he revealed that he had had a person set to go who ultimately declined the appointment.[281] Mechem would not identify the individual. Could he have approached Holm Bursum, Jr. at some point? Would Bursum have wanted to serve in the U.S. Senate as his father had? A year earlier, when both Dennis Chavez and Clinton Anderson had been hospitalized, Will Harrison mused over why Bursum, Jr. might be Mechem's choice should either senator retire. According to Harrison's source, it had to do with Mayor Bursum's 1940s breakthrough elections in Socorro and his years of good public service.[282] Holm Bursum III did not know if his father had been in talks with the governor about the vacancy, but he did say, "I think if my father had wanted the Senate seat, Ed Mechem would have appointed him."

Taking the Senate appointment had serious drawbacks for any Republican. Only two years remained in Chavez's term. It meant his successor immediately would have to build an organization and raise campaign funds for a hard race in 1964. Under the circumstances, no strong GOP prospects wanted the job, Mechem discovered.

As Mechem's term was ending with no appointment in sight, the Young Republicans joined thousands of New Mexicans of both parties to urge the governor himself to go to Washington. Mechem was reluctant for a host of reasons, not the least being that he—the young man who had set politics spinning at midcentury—had just turned fifty. He wanted to leave public life and rebuild his law practice, but his party had other ideas.

Holm Bursum III happened to attend a national leadership meeting when the senatorial appointment was still pending. "I saw Richard Nixon on the stage," he recalled. The former vice president was there, waiting for a conference session to begin. Bursum stepped onto the stage to join him. Nixon, hearing the young man was from New Mexico and knew Mechem, smiled and asked, "How is Big Ed?" The question gave Bursum his moment. He brought up the vacant Senate seat and efforts to persuade Governor Mechem to go to Washington. Nixon listened carefully and offered to see what he could do. People have speculated about who finally convinced Mechem to take the appointment. Their identity is a mystery, but to have heard from party leaders such as Nixon might well have influenced Mechem's decision.

On December 1, Edwin Mechem, with one month left in his term, resigned as governor. Lieutenant-Governor Tom Bolack, whose election had been affirmed by the New Mexico Supreme Court just six months before,[283] stepped up to replace him. Minutes later, Mechem accepted Governor Bolack's appointment of him to the U.S. Senate. If Bolack had not won his election in 1960 and if the courts had not upheld its validity, Mechem's appointment would not have happened. Within days, Mechem, whether he wished it or not, was en route to Congress.

One person who could not have been pleased to see Ed Mechem in Washington that December was Joe Montoya. What a bothersome set of circumstances for him. If Mechem had not vetoed the "Dead Senator bill," Montoya probably would have been the one on his way to the Senate.

Furthermore, if Tom Bolack, his old special-election opponent from 1956, had not won the lieutenant-governor post in 1960, Mechem would still be in Santa Fe, not in the halls of Congress. Montoya's only recourse was to run against Mechem in 1964, and if he could secure his party's nomination, he knew the odds were in his favor in the general election. Winning the nomination in a direct primary, however, was not always easy, as Montoya well knew.

Democratic primaries often drew throngs of candidates in Montoya's time because the stakes were high. Those contenders who won the primary races in June usually sailed through the general elections to victory in November. The real contest for Democrats then was not with Republicans but with each other. One way to reduce the primary competition was to funnel nominations through leaders at conventions, thereby weeding out frivolous candidates who were entering a race simply to block another's chance to win. The state legislature could reinstitute the pre-primary convention in 1963 simply by passing a bill, and Governor Jack Campbell could sign it. The demolition of the direct primary could happen very soon.

Ending the Year: A Party and a Visit with the New Governor

As 1962 was coming to an end, Holm Bursum arranged for a celebration. In Albuquerque, he hosted a post-election party for the local Teen Age Republican Club. He sponsored the club, and to thank the teens for their campaign work, he brought in popular candidate Dr. Jack Redman to cheer them on.[284] Decades later, Bursum pondered a question posed to him. How he had managed his many commitments? How had he stretched his time to work with the party's young and senior wings and with adolescents as well? In his mind, it had not been anything exceptional. His young energy, he implied, had made it a natural match, an easy task. "In 1962, I was only twenty-eight," he said with a smile, "and the teenagers weren't that far behind." The youth could see that their older siblings were having a good time in their YR clubs, and they wanted in on the fun, he assumed. He was glad to support them. That is how Bursum, as an organizer, saw politics. It needed to be intergenerational. It needed to be hard and serious work, but light-heartedness and fun were on the agenda too.

In December, Bursum and Young Republican leaders visited Tom

Bolack in Santa Fe. Time was ticking on Bolack's one-month governorship, and he had some wisdom to impart. He was keenly aware of his uniqueness, being only the second Republican elected to a state executive office in thirty-two years. His campaign for lieutenant governor had benefitted from party organizing.

Nationally in 1962, the Republican Party was just one decade out from the long years of the Roosevelt/Truman administrations. Governor Bolack knew the GOP's full comeback would depend in part on the work of its young wing. He made a point to welcome the new San Miguel County YRs and to praise all the Young Republicans for their work. They were bringing "...back the true American two-party system to the people of the country," he told them.[285] He offered the leaders practical advice for upcoming election cycles, pointing them to the Colorado Republican model. Through tight links among precinct, county, and state chairs, the Coloradoans had created direct connections between candidates and voters. It was bringing them good results at the ballot box.

In 1962, a two-party system seemed to be evolving in New Mexico. Despite President Kennedy's high approval ratings and the boost to his party in the midterms, more New Mexico Republicans won state legislative seats. Some of them came directly out of the Young Republican movement. Furthermore, the state had a GOP senator for the first time since 1935. Ed Mechem and Holm Bursum III had done the kind of local organizing that worked. Ron Hamm summed up their collaboration:

> Together they set out to breathe new life into the younger elements of the party. They crisscrossed the state by plane and automobile from Taos to Deming, from Hobbs to Silver City and a couple dozen cities and towns in between. Their efforts netted new Republican organizations in 25 communities, both large and small, and helped launch several successful political careers. They included longtime state Rep. Hoyt Pattison of Curry County; long-serving member of the New Mexico House of Representatives Dick Cheney from San Juan County; and Colin McMillan, first a state senator from Roswell and later assistant secretary of defense under Pres. George H. [W] Bush.[286]

9

1963: Tensions, Toil, and Tragedy

The YR Convention in 1963 was a turning point for American conservatives.
—M. Stanton Evans, Newspaper Editor.[287]

    1963 was an off-year for state and national elections. In Patricia Hutar's playbook, it was a year for development, for bringing more young people into the excitement of politics. In New Mexico, government reform was on the agenda for Young Republicans. The controversy over convention-controlled nominations versus the direct primary had been worming its way in and out of New Mexico politics for over two decades, and when it resurfaced early in 1963, Holm Bursum and the YRs acted. That fall, a second opportunity to promote good government came along during Albuquerque's city elections. By winter, a third substantial development made the front pages as David Cargo helped create a more representative state legislature. The work of young people in the party was complex and consequential.

    On the Young Republican National Federation front, a powerful movement was forming that would surge into the party's senior wing and affect presidential politics. That spring, prominent federation leaders made a striking overture to Holm Bursum. Had his response been different, it might have impacted a dramatic national gathering of the Young Republicans in San Francisco that summer. Then, in the eleventh month of 1963, a national tragedy struck. Its impact would affect political alignments for some time to come.

Passing a Pre-Primary Convention Bill in the State Legislature

Early in 1963, as expected, the New Mexico Legislature passed a bill to authorize pre-primary nominating conventions again. Governor Jack Campbell signed the bill into law. It did not surprise many that U.S. Representative Joseph M. Montoya's name was quietly associated with the change.[288] Montoya, who planned to challenge Edwin L. Mechem in the 1964 Senate race, did not want to spend his campaign resources in a crowded Democratic primary. With the new law in place, he could secure his party's nomination more easily and concentrate on the general election. All was going according to plan until an irritant appeared on the scene. Petitions to subject the pre-primary law to a referendum began circulating throughout New Mexico, compliments of the Young Republicans. Many Democrats were among those picking up their pens to add their names to the petitions.

Serving the Community and Building a Marriage

Political organizing and government reform consumed time, and Holm Bursum III learned to fit his Young Republican work into a life filled with many other commitments. As a young banker, he had professional and philanthropic affiliations that stretched beyond the workday. He served as an officer of the New Mexico Business and Manufacturing Association and helped organize New Mexico Heart Association and United Fund drives.[289] He operated from a supply of talent and energy, as well as from his family training and the quality of his partnership with Earle Bursum.

Earle prioritized her home life, but she had a community profile too. She had worked as a teacher for a time. She also volunteered with SOS (Sabin Oral Vaccine Sunday) Clinics and was active with a YWCA committee, the New Mexico Wool Growers Association, the Albuquerque Opera Guild, and St. Marks on the Mesa Episcopal Church.[290] At home, she and her husband were building a warm and trusting relationship. They had friendship along with the romantic and practical aspects of marriage. Public people in one sense, they were discreet and private as well. "We never talked out of school," Earle Bursum told biographer Ron Hamm, adding that she provided a supportive base for her husband.[291] She spoke of their years in Albuquerque when their children were very young. She had arranged the family schedule so that the children's end-of-day routines happened early, and they were off to their rooms to rest for the night. The young parents, reunited after the day apart, then had a quiet evening for two.

At times, the couple merged their work in the community. Earle was involved with the Opera Guild; Holm served as its treasurer. Holm was the head of the state Young Republican Association; Earle organized YR competitions and supervised the Teen Age Republican Club members in projects. In January of 1963, the Bursums took on a big community project as partners.[292] They launched the Bernalillo County March of Dimes and Mothers March campaigns. They had attended a regional planning meeting in Sacramento, California, and, once they were back home, they recruited six thousand volunteers to raise funds to promote maternal and infant health and the prevention of birth defects. One of their best ideas, Holm Bursum remembered, was to approach Albuquerque's Rich Richardson of Rich Ford. The dealership donated a new car for a March of Dimes raffle, boosting the fundraiser by thousands of dollars and providing one lucky ticket holder with a superb prize.

Another of the Bursums' joint projects was a personal one. *The Albuquerque Journal* featured it in a story.[293] Earle Bursum, a stylish woman trained in the fashion industry, turned her design interests to her house. It was on San Pablo Street in the city's northeast heights, and it became a canvas for her vision of color, texture, and artful contrasts. With paint, art, and accent pieces, she created a modern interior in off-white, with touches of persimmon, turquoise, olive, and black. Some pieces of furniture were finished in warm walnut; others were made of rattan. From travels with her husband in Western Asia and North Africa, she incorporated vintage brass and copper pieces into her more contemporary décor. Her husband helped her update hand-me-downs, making an accent table of a ceramic pot, a coffee table of a salvaged door, and lamps of recycled table legs. For their rec room, Earle bought a department store's old Formica-topped checkout counter at a bargain price and transformed it into a storage cabinet. It was a charming story of a young couple using thrift, imagination, and their own labor to create a vibrant setting for their family.

From the way Holm and Earle Bursum arranged their evenings to the surroundings they inhabited, they built a retreat for themselves in a busy existence. They created a buffer from the usual stresses of life and—given Holm's political mission—some that were not so usual.

Sailing the Mediterranean: A Telephone Call, a Layover, and a Decision

The Bursums took time in 1963 to accompany Earle's parents, Earl and Jane Powell, on a grand tour. For several weeks, they visited the Mediterranean world, sailing from Portugal to Greece and from Turkey to Morocco, with many stops in between. One day aboard *The Oslo Fjord*, Holm Bursum received a call from the United States. It was not common to receive a shipboard call in those days, he said. Having no idea what the summons to the phone was about, he soon heard Patricia Hutar's voice at the other end of the line. The co-chairwoman of the Young Republican National Federation was calling from Chicago. She and her colleagues urgently wanted to meet with him, she told him. Bursum agreed that, when he returned to the U.S., he would reroute his flight home through Chicago.

It meant something that Patricia Hutar had called Holm Bursum III with urgent business.

The young national leader had been building her political credentials since her early twenties.[294] In 1955, she was named the Outstanding Young Republican Woman in Illinois. In 1960, she served as the assistant director of her state's Nixon-Lodge presidential campaign. That year, she helped interview President Dwight D. Eisenhower on national television. With her dark hair and fashionable dress, she reminded some people of another new woman on the national political scene, Jacqueline Kennedy. The comparison caused her to fidget a moment as she considered her response, she said wryly. Her day job was with a Chicago public relations firm. She also had modeled in the fashion industry but played down that aspect of her career to shift the focus elsewhere. Politics was what she loved. F. Clifton White saw Hutar as a person of significance and brought her into his inner circle in the Draft Goldwater movement. In just another year, she would be the highest-ranking woman in the GOP, serving as assistant chairwoman with Dean Burch, head of the Republican National Committee.

Holm Bursum was well aware of Pat Hutar's standing in the Republican Party. When he returned to the United States from Europe, he flew on to Chicago. There at O'Hare International Airport, Hutar and her colleagues were waiting for him. They asked him a momentous question: Would he agree to run for the office of chairman of the Young Republican National Federation? Would he be willing to try to succeed Leonard Nadasdy? It was an enormously appealing invitation—to seek an office that in some cases propelled its holder onto a congressional seat or other high position. Those in on the discussion with Bursum that day knew just what was being asked of him. The campaign for the chairmanship would be tough. Hutar once described it this way:

> Running in a Young Republican campaign is almost like running in a national election. It's fought out every inch of the way. At the convention, you visit all the state meetings and caucuses; they spear you to the left and right and put you over the broiler. Then, of course, after the election, everyone works together.[295]

As Bursum considered his answer, he thought about the politics of his running. He knew that Nadasdy was backing another candidate, one who was the choice of his longtime New York allies. But Bursum and Nadasdy were close friends. Regardless of which candidate won, Nadasdy would be able to celebrate his successor. "It would have been a win either way for Len," Bursum reminisced. He considered the voting blocs and coalitions within the YRNF. Even without Nadasdy's direct support for Bursum, the chairman's regard for him was widely known. Running for the Hutar faction—with a subtle nod from Nadasdy—Bursum had a chance to win.

The decision to try for the chairmanship was not one for a jet-lagged young man to make on the spot, but Holm Bursum's answer came quickly. He would not run. Just twenty-eight and still new to the banking industry, he did not yet hold the kind of professional position that would give him time and financial resources to take on a national office in the Republican Party. "I was not a big shot at the bank where I worked," he said with a twinkle. "I was a little shot." He decided to remain as he was, to focus on his career and support his family. Even in retrospect, he had no regrets, no room for what-ifs.

Leonard Nadasdy had regrets, however. He had wanted Holm Bursum to succeed him, he revealed in an interview fifty-five years later. "I thought Holm would have run well," he said, looking back. The young New Mexican had organizational skills and a solid political philosophy. What would have made him a standout as a candidate, Nadasdy thought, was his exceptional warmth and friendliness.

Back in Albuquerque, Bursum got ready for the state Young Republican Association convention. He was running again for the presidency, and his reelection campaign was going to be several degrees less complex than the one that Pat Hutar had just proposed.

Running Again at the State YR Convention

On May 17, the New Mexico Young Republican Association's convention opened in Santa Fe. Senator Edwin L. Mechem addressed the delegates. He was fifty-one that year and had set the standard for an elected official. He earned his reputation for honesty and ethics in governance. It was good for young people to see how he regarded his constituents. He assumed that he and they had a mutual interest in public policy and the ability and willingness to grapple with complicated issues. One of his trademarks was to urge people to think critically. He called on them not to rely on others' presentations of important matters but to read the documents of government themselves to inform their opinions.

At the YR convention that spring, Mechem talked about a growing bureaucracy and an elitism that he saw taking hold in Washington.[296] The 1960 presidential election, he pointed out, had produced nearly a fifty-fifty split of votes for John Kennedy and Richard Nixon. Yet the Kennedy administration governed as if it had received a strong mandate, not taking into account the perspectives of half the nation, Mechem said.

Mechem also opposed President Kennedy's proposed tax cuts, deploring the budget deficit that would result. He turned to the question of disarmament. He was concerned that the United States would consider such a move during a time when the Soviet Union was militarily strong and aggressive. Mechem remarked that Kennedy, as a candidate, had not told voters he would embrace nuclear test ban proposals. Those proposals, Mechem thought, would be opposed by people such as Edward Teller of the Manhattan Project and David Lilienthal of the Atomic Energy Commission. Mechem warned of the activities of an Arms Control and Disarmament Agency. Authorized by Congress, the agency was working toward a treaty that would disarm the U.S. in three stages. Simultaneously, the police power of the United Nations would grow. Mechem remarked that disarmament agreements were difficult to enforce, citing the problems that Kennedy had securing onsite inspections of Soviet missiles in Cuba. Why, Mechem asked, would the U.S. "...place 100% of our security in an international organization (United Nations) which lacks the traditions of representative government...?"[297]

Young Republican National Federation Chairman Leonard J. Nadasdy was back in New Mexico and also addressed the convention. His speech, described in the press as rollicking, denounced the "credit card government" in Washington.[298] He critiqued the Kennedy administration for its tough measures with the steel industry and the detention of a government whistleblower. He called on the GOP to be a vocal loyal opposition.

The convention that year brought a new element to New Mexico YRs, a Miss Young Republican contest. Earle Bursum had led in organizing the competition. The contest was not of the typical bathing beauty type, she stated.[299] It celebrated other qualities and gave young women the opportunity to be recognized for political accomplishments and public speaking abilities on topics of party history or trends. How a contestant presented herself on the stage was important, but the emphasis was on knowledge, character, and accomplishment. Barbara McKim of Albuquerque was the first to earn the New Mexico title.

During the business of the convention, the Young Republicans elected their officers for the coming two years. Holm Bursum III won a second term as president, but it was not his unanimous-vote victory of 1961. He had an opponent, something he was not aware of until just before the convention. Questioned about his chances, Bursum said simply, "You don't run unless you think you can win." Then he added, "We are encouraging as many people as we can to run for all the offices."[300] Despite the surprise opposition, Bursum won 142 votes out of the 176 cast. His election had come about in a rousing show of support from his peers. His victory is reminiscent of the first Holm O. Bursum, standing before the Republican Party Convention in 1906, also a young man, also winning reelection as a party leader.

The thirty-four votes lost to Holm Bursum had gone to his competitor, Richard Ullrich, a Farmington geologist. As a "friendly opponent," Ullrich explained that he had no quarrel with Bursum's leadership.[301] He had tried for the vice presidency too, he said, just to add a bit of interest to the races. He and Bursum had been seen greeting each other warmly before the contest. Afterward, Ullrich and Julio Garcia of Santa Fe accepted appointments as special assistants to Bursum. Burt Sanborn became the associations' vice president; Colin McMillan, the executive secretary, and Patricia Trujillo, the recording secretary. Patricia Springer and John P. Mitchell, Jr. were reelected corresponding secretary and treasurer respectively, and

Richard Cheney and Rowena Greene became YR National Committee members. The new leaders came from all over New Mexico: Farmington, Albuquerque, Santa Fe, Las Vegas, Clovis, Roswell, and Las Cruces. They had built a truly statewide organization.

The delegates passed resolutions. In one, they endorsed Barry Goldwater for the presidency even though the Republican National Convention was a year away from nominating a candidate. "We loved Goldwater," Bursum said. "He spoke our language."

The most consequential resolution of the convention concerned the disliked 1963 pre-primary election law. The plan, initiated by the Young Republican Club in Dona Ana County, was to repeal it. The method was by referendum on the 1964 election ballot. It would be only the second time the referendum mechanism was used in New Mexico,[302] and it involved the same matter, to restore the direct primary to the people. The Young Republicans already had petitions in half of New Mexico's counties and would have all counties covered within weeks. Five hundred petitions were circulating in Bernalillo County, with the number soon to double.[303]

Next, the YRs elected delegates to the Young Republican National Federation convention in San Francisco. Bursum had declined to run for leadership of the YRNF, but he had another role. He planned to promote Albuquerque as a future convention site and to honor a local club leader. He could not have known it then, but the convention he was about to attend was to be one of the most contentious in Young Republican history. F. Clifton White, political organizer par excellence, was going to have much to do with what happened.

Previewing the Tensions of the Young Republican National Federation Convention

Toward the end of June 1963, the Republican Party was at a choice point as two leading candidates for the presidential nomination emerged: New York Governor Nelson Rockefeller, a liberal-leaning moderate, and Arizona Senator Barry Goldwater, a conservative. Although the Young Republican National Federation had a policy of not endorsing a presidential candidate before the senior party nominated one, primary politics always animated the conventions. 1963 was no exception as pressure built over the election of a new YR chairman. Backers of Rockefeller were not going to be preeminent at the convention. The higher enthusiasm was for Goldwater, but more than one faction supported him. As before in YRNF elections, those factions were about to clash. The contest was more about control of the organization than about debating ideology. A rift in political philosophy was not the reason for what transpired.

One of the Young Republican factions, including Len Nadasdy and the New York delegation, was supporting Charles McDevitt, a thirty-one-year-old attorney and legislator from Idaho. Another faction had put their support behind Donald E. 'Buz' Lukens, thirty-two, an attorney and clerk for the Rules Committee in the U.S. House of Representatives. Both Lukens and McDevitt espoused a conservative philosophy and favored Barry Goldwater for president, but McDevitt remained publicly neutral, observing the YRNF's policy about endorsements. Buz Lukens, on the other hand, made his enthusiasm for Goldwater a clear part of his campaign.

One of the factors in the accumulating tensions was the national Draft Goldwater Movement. That movement was about to light up the YRNF convention in ways both beneficial and not. Once again, it involved F. Clifton White. By 1963, White had aged out of Young Republican membership. Nevertheless, he remained avidly interested in the YRNF as a way to influence the senior party's presidential nominations. He had moved away from the Dewey and Eisenhower wings of the GOP years before and had transformed himself into a booster of conservatism. For months, he had been pursuing Barry Goldwater in order to gift him with a cadre of superbly organized young supporters. By February 1963, still, with no clear word from Goldwater about running, White and his group had become frustrated. According to Theodore White, they decided that they would draft the Arizonan whether he liked it or not, but Goldwater had become concerned about the publicity that the movement was generating for him.[304] He was not sure it was what he wanted. That summer, Clif White organized two demonstrations that caught Goldwater's attention in a new way.

Demonstrating at the 1963 YRNF Convention

White was about to launch a Draft Goldwater rally in the nation's capital in the summer of 1963. Set for July 4th, it was on the agenda of thousands, who were arranging trips to Washington, DC by chartered bus. First, however, White would do a test run in San Francisco. In late June, at the Young Republican National Federation convention, he would practice his staging of a large-scale national demonstration for a conservative candidate.

While White finalized his plans, Holm and Earle Bursum and the New Mexico delegation arrived in San Francisco. At the elegant Sheraton-Palace Hotel, with its vaulted ceilings and gilded embellishments, they set up a hospitality suite in their bid to bring the next convention to Albuquerque. They named the suite Cocina de Carlos after restaurateur Carlos Montoya, who sponsored it, and they supplied it with the spice and color of New Mexico's food, décor, and dress.[305] They modeled the silver and turquoise jewelry of the Southwest, and among the women, there would be the flair of cotton fiesta dresses and the swirl of broomstick skirts.

As the delegations were arriving in San Francisco, Clif White mobilized his people. He meant for his surrogates to have a high profile at the convention and display the young wing's passion for Goldwater. Outgoing YRNF chairman, Len Nadasdy, remembered the situation:

> Clif White was ensconced in an upper suite in the hotel with communication lines to key delegations on the convention floor. The two candidates [for YRNF chairman] were Chuck McDevitt, a young lawyer from Idaho with six children and Donald 'Buz' Lukens, a political activist from DC. In an attempt to obtain a pledge of neutrality on the Presidential race, I met privately with Senator Barry Goldwater who was scheduled to speak at the convention. I explained that the YR national organization had a policy of not endorsing a candidate before the Republican National Convention. He seemed to agree with me and said that he would not endorse either McDevitt or Lukens. I also said that both of them privately were sympathetic to [his] candidacy....

Later, when Goldwater addressed the convention, he seemed to have gotten caught up in the crowd's excitement about him and to have abandoned his own neutrality, Nadasdy thought. When the moment came to elect a new chairman, tensions heightened. Nadasdy described the scene:

> Everyone knew that the delegate vote was very close to being even. We had set up a screen which showed each state's delegate vote followed by the vote for each candidate. Half way through the ballot, the screen went dark and had been disconnected so that no vote

totals were showing. We had been keeping a report of the votes at the podium. At the end of the balloting the convention secretary suddenly grabbed the mike and announced that Lukens had won by two votes. The convention went wild.... Our count showed McDevitt ahead by two votes. It was not possible to restore order and the police had to be called in....

As Nadasdy began to speak to the convention about the vote count, he heard shouts of "Go back to Russia," and a California delegate rushed him, attempting to take the gavel from his hand. In the confusion, Nadasdy recalled, Charles McDevitt told him to "let it go." He was withdrawing from the race, no longer interested in chairing such an organization, he said.

"It was one of the longest, bitterest, closest polling battles in the federation history," wrote Seymour Korman of the *Chicago Tribune*.[306] The journalist watched as the disagreements on the floor turned physical at times. Yet at the election's conclusion, Charles McDevitt was photographed giving Buz Lukens a generous congratulatory hug.[307] Senator Hugh Scott of Pennsylvania, in San Francisco to speak to the convention, counseled the young people "not to beat each other to bits and to stand ready to support the party's Presidential and Vice Presidential candidates, whoever they may be."[308]

As for the New Mexico delegation, the Young Republican National Federation did not accept their bid to host the 1965 convention in Albuquerque. That honor went to Miami, but the New Mexicans enjoyed another kind of recognition. It was a point of pride for them that their nominee, Hoyt Pattison of Curry County, was named runner up for Outstanding Young Republican Club Chairman of America."[309]

As the convention ended and delegations dispersed, Leonard Nadasdy spoke to the press.[310] He did not recognize some of the people at the gathering, he said. They were unfamiliar among the ranks of Young Republicans and perhaps were members of the John Birch Society and other extreme groups, he speculated. To him, they did not seem to be conservatives or any other type of Republican. Their favored candidate, Buz Lukens, certainly was not a Birch Society adherent, Nadasdy acknowledged, yet he had appeared to cater to those who were. The event left Nadasdy worried about the presidential campaign. He hoped that Barry Goldwater could distance himself from the kinds of people who had disrupted the convention and instead "surround himself with conservatives," he told his interviewer.

As for the two men who had run to lead the Young Republicans, both went on to high public office.[311] By 1993, Charles McDevitt had become chief justice of the Idaho Supreme Court. Donald 'Buz' Lukens, following the path of other YRNF chairmen, soon won a seat in Congress. His career would be marred, however, by court cases involving financial and personal improprieties. In 1990, he would be defeated in the Ohio Republican primary by John Boehner, the future speaker of the U.S. House of Representatives.

Holm Bursum III did not go on record about the turmoil of the Young Republican National Federation convention of 1963. He likely was in accord with Leonard Nadasdy as his friend tried to keep order among the delegates and proceed with a fair election of a chairman. What they discussed privately is not known. The difference that Bursum might have made as a candidate for the chairmanship can only be guessed at. Some elements are predictive, however. He was an experienced leader, a proponent of party unity, and a man of personal warmth. He might have had a fair chance of keeping the disparate elements of the YRNF together. Patricia Hutar must have thought that he could have led the rapidly transforming organization when she picked up the telephone to call him earlier that year.

Gearing Up for Goldwater Again

In 1963, as the Young Republican National Federation's power struggles progressed, a trend was coming into focus. Many people in the country were inspired by Barry Goldwater. Clifton White, his dress rehearsal in San Francisco finished, staged a National Draft Goldwater rally in Washington, DC. He brought in his busloads of avid supporters from around the country—seven thousand people in all—to gather at the National Guard Armory. Theodore White noted that only three other events at the armory had drawn more people, two of them being Eisenhower's and Kennedy's inaugurations."[312]

Clifton White's strategy was having its effect. Barry Goldwater began to look at running against the incumbent President John F. Kennedy. The president was his friend from their days together in the Senate, but Goldwater deplored what he saw as the accumulation of federal powers in the Kennedy administration. As the Arizona senator incubated the idea of his candidacy, he could not have been unmoved by what he saw happening around him. He had just witnessed the deluge of enthusiasm for him at the YRNF convention and then at the July 4th National Draft Goldwater rally. Two years earlier, according to Theodore White, Goldwater had visited Kennedy in the Oval Office. Kennedy had asked him bluntly about his desire for "this job."[313] At the time, Goldwater had replied that he was not interested. How things had changed.

Len Nadasdy thought Goldwater would be nominated but was not optimistic about his candidacy. "In my mind, Barry Goldwater stood and spoke for an America unfettered by over-regulation.... [H]e was committed to re-establishment of the constitutional principles of government," he said. But many voters, he thought, had become accustomed to federally-funded benefit programs. He doubted that Goldwater's message would speak to them.

Back home in New Mexico, Holm Bursum was out of the whirl of national politics by his own choice. With summer coming to a close, he got to work on a big Bernalillo County Republican event that would bring all parts of the party together, from senior members to the Teen Age Republicans. It was the kind of intergenerational political work that he liked. In a play on the Republicans' acronym for the Grand Old Party, he and the planners called the event GO-Picnic.[314] It was expected to draw up to three thousand people.

Confronting Partisanship in the Nonpartisan City Commission Elections

In September, a controversy arose in Albuquerque's municipal election. A move appeared to have been made to give Democrats a majority on the city commission. Since the city's charter mandated nonpartisan elections, the situation did not look good. For a decade, a group called the Citizens Committee had worked to restore good governance in city hall by endorsing candidates who ran on a nonpartisan basis. Care was taken that two Republicans, two Democrats, and an Independent served on the commission so that no party dominated. In 1963, however, with two seats vacant, the committee chose two Democrats to run. Both had relatively high profiles in their party: Ralph S. Trigg and Emanuel Schifani.[315] Given the makeup of the rest of the commission, a Trigg and Schifani win would tip the balance to the Democrats.

Holm Bursum III made a statement. The executive board of the

Citizens Committee has become "...completely one-sided with Democrats now," and its nonpartisan nature lost, he said.³¹⁶ Previously, he reminded people, the Republican Party had supported the committee and appreciated its reform work. The press speculated that Bursum himself might run. He had been seen at the city clerk's office picking up filing papers.³¹⁷ Instead, he helped form the Committee for Non-Partisan Government. "We don't want to take over the commission...," Bursum stated. "[W]e just want to balance it."³¹⁸ The new group endorsed William A. Gardner, a past Young Republican club president. Gardner pointed out that too many commissioners of the same party could adversely affect personnel and contracting decisions at city hall.³¹⁹ It was a point not lost on people who remembered the days of one-party state rule in New Mexico.

On Election Day in October, in a race of eight candidates, Schifani and Trigg won the two commission seats with over 7,000 votes each. Gardner, who had entered the campaign late, won an impressive 5,001 votes.³²⁰ The balance on the City Commission had tipped to one party, but it had not gone unnoticed and unchallenged. The new Committee for Non-Partisan City Government had taken a stand and made a strong electoral point.

Bringing One-Person One-Vote to Legislative Representation in New Mexico

While Holm Bursum III was doing his part to revitalize the two-party system, something else was transpiring that would help change the political balance in New Mexico. David Cargo had been observing the way New Mexicans were represented in the state legislature, and what he saw displeased him. The people elected their representatives by county, not by population-based districts. Each county, no matter how sparsely settled, had at least one representative. The system was imbalanced, giving the rural counties disproportionate power over urban ones. Simply put, rural people were over-represented in the legislature at the expense of those in larger population areas like Albuquerque.

Cargo saw another problem. Candidates for the New Mexico House ran at large in their counties. Instead of appealing to constituents in specific geographic areas, they had to run county-wide. The system tended to disadvantage candidates of political or ethnic minorities. Cargo filed a suit to reapportion and district New Mexico for the election of its state legislators. His was a one-person-one-vote initiative, and it was on trend with national developments. There was, however, resistance to face in New Mexico. Cargo described his reform adventure in his memoir *Lonesome Dave*.

As he was preparing his case, Cargo had been watching *Baker vs. Carr*, which was before the U.S. Supreme Court.[321] In 1962, the Court, upholding the one-person-one-vote principle, decided that state legislative districts must be apportioned on the basis of population. Cargo moved on his case. *Cargo vs. Campbell* was assigned to State District Court Judge Caswell Neal of Carlsbad, an individual whom Cargo respected as a legal scholar.

The State of New Mexico, Cargo said, asked for the dismissal of the case.[322] State attorneys contended that legislative apportionment as it existed was neither unconstitutional nor discriminatory. As for Cargo's concern about underrepresented Bernalillo County, its rapid population growth was not stable, the state argued. In the post-World War II period, Albuquerque had grown due to an influx of federal military and contract personnel. Given the changeable nature of the federal presence in New Mexico, the new people could be considered transitory residents, the state attorneys asserted. Therefore, making an accurate population count in such a community was difficult, they said. Cargo pushed back.[323] In the courtroom on August 26, he called to the witness stand Dr. James Edwards, a labor market analyst. Edwards stated that Albuquerque's labor force was more stable than the state assumed. Political scientist Dr. Frederick C. Irion also testified—with great feeling, Cargo said—concluding that New Mexico's current apportionment was an offense to democracy.

Judge Caswell Neal considered the facts and compelled Governor Jack Campbell to call the legislature into special session. Neal specified outcomes.[324] Given New Mexico's population, each legislative district should have 14,409 constituents regardless of where the county boundaries lay. It meant that, of the state's thirty-two counties, twenty would lose some of their House representation. Neal set a deadline for reapportionment: November 1.

With consternation and after hard work and an extended deadline, the legislators passed apportionment and districting bills. One bill set up weighted roll-call voting. It was creative and meant to ensure that no county lost its seat to reapportionment. David Cargo described the plan as the legislature presented it.[325] Under the weighted formula, the representative from the sparsely-populated Catron County, for example, would have his or her vote counted at .20. The representative of the more populous Socorro County would have his or her vote counted at .70. Still larger counties would be entitled to full votes and, in some cases, would have more than one representative. Cargo found the solution exasperating.

After the legislature's work in the special session, Governor Jack Campbell signed the apportionment and redistricting bills. Judge Caswell Neal studied them and responded. On December 22, the banner headline of *The Santa Fe New Mexican* announced the decision: "Reapportionment Illegal."[326] Both laws violated the state constitution, the judge said. The legislature had to try again. Meanwhile, New Mexico faced a problem. The 1964 election was approaching, and candidates would have to file for their primaries in a few months. With the one-person-one-vote matter unresolved, it was not clear how the state would proceed with its legislative races. Judge Neal believed in the U.S. doctrine of the separation of powers. Reapportionment was the duty of the legislature, he stated, not of the courts; however, in the case at hand, the legislature had failed. The judge did not want to act from the bench, but the problem was looming. He devised a temporary solution for the upcoming election.

With the legislative situation in flux, journalist Will Harrison had a wry take on it. Reapportionment had come up as New Mexico was building the Roundhouse, its new state capitol. "Nobody knows how big to make the house and senate chambers, whether for fifty members or two hundred,"[327] he wrote facetiously. Reapportionment and districting would not be completed until later, but ultimately, the reform which David Cargo launched would benefit the two-party system in New Mexico.

Speaking Out: A YR Position on the International Wheat Deal

Young Republican clubs were places to study the issues of the day and take positions on them. In 1963 they had kept up with national, state, and local concerns, and toward the end of the year, they also considered an international one. Holm Bursum III urged the Bernalillo County YR club to review the Kennedy administration's support for a controversial wheat deal with the Soviet Union.

Although particular to its time, the wheat deal raised absorbing questions about presidential authority which are relevant today. Could the president approve commercial dealings with an unfriendly country without significant congressional involvement? Was it legal to extend credit to an adversarial government? The Johnson Act of 1934 barred U.S. citizens from extending any kind of loan to a country that had defaulted on obligations to the U.S.,[328] and another piece of legislation banned selling publicly-subsidized commodities to countries under communist control.[329] The president's brother, Attorney General Robert Kennedy, ruled that extending credit in the wheat sale to Russia was not the same as a loan, thus not prohibited.[330] Congress held hearings, attempting to determine if the Soviet Union was stockpiling wheat for geopolitical advantage. Administrative officials who testified were not sure. Questions also surfaced about the Democratic Party's connections to the private negotiators of the deal.[331]

The American Farm Bureau and the National Grange opposed the wheat sale, as did Richard Nixon and Barry Goldwater.[332] The Bernalillo County Young Republicans asked their congressional delegation to oppose the sale and published their position in the paper.[333] By the end of the year, master legislator Lyndon B. Johnson, by then in the Oval Office, brought presidential power and Congress together to make the deal happen. Regardless of the outcome, the YRs had used the routes available to citizens in a representative government and had entered the public discourse. Len Nadasdy, who called for more rigor, education, and action at the club level, would have been pleased. Patricia Hutar, who urged young people to stay engaged in the years between elections, would have been pleased.

It had been a momentous year for Young Republicans in presidential politics. Even with issues over factional control, their national federation had registered enthusiasm in the clearest terms for Barry Goldwater over his competitors. Columnist John Gizzi reflected on the significance of their 1963 convention, quoting *The Indianapolis News* editor M. Stanton Evans. Evans believed that for conservatives to have been able "...to nominate Goldwater in '64, they had to win the YR convention in '63. That convention was a decisive moment, and it presaged everything."[334]

In New Mexico, the Young Republicans had done their own bold work. They continued to organize for the party, and they had other objectives: to restore the state's direct primary and to keep Albuquerque's city elections nonpartisan. Their former president, David Cargo, had his special project: to make representation in the state legislature more equitable. Then, there was the next election. In less than a year, New Mexicans would be going to the polls again to vote in a presidential race. Up and down the ballot, the election would test the young people's work thus far. Then, just as the country got ready to celebrate Thanksgiving, a shattering event took place. In Dallas, Texas, on November 22, 1963, the fourth presidential assassination in U.S. history occurred, an act that affected all Americans, unsettling them deeply and uniting them regardless of what else separated them.

10

1964: Traces of Progress in a Profound Defeat

I thought of something my old coach at Staunton had often said: 'We win some, we lose some, and some get rained out; but we always suit up.'

—Barry Goldwater, U.S. Senator and Republican Candidate for President of the United States[335]

The 1964 presidential campaign did not turn out to be the one that people had anticipated. The shock of John F. Kennedy's assassination on November 22, 1963 changed everything. Earlier that fall, President Kennedy had reached gridlock with Congress. His budget, tax cut, and civil rights legislation had bogged down.[336] On civil rights, Kennedy had taken a moderate stand.[337] He needed to maintain the southern Democrats' support for his other initiatives while also fulfilling campaign pledges to African Americans. It was a fine line to walk, and neither the South nor the North was completely pleased. When a backlash against the civil rights movement intensified in the spring and summer of 1963, Kennedy sent a bolder civil rights bill to Congress. That summer, a poll showed a dip in his approval rating.[338] Many thought he was moving too far too fast on civil rights, yet others wanted more resolute action. Kennedy took a risk with his bill, especially given that his reelection was on the line. Then in November, the stunning news came out of Dallas, and the country reeled. Barry Goldwater, distraught over Kennedy's assassination, could not think of running for the presidency. He was finished with his candidacy, he told his wife.[339]

When Lyndon B. Johnson stepped into the presidency on November 22, the election, less than a year away, became a very new game. With superb legislative skill, Johnson pushed Kennedy's stymied tax-cut, budget, and civil rights bills through Congress. He evoked the Kennedy name, pledging to fulfill the deceased president's program as a way to honor him.[340] It was an appeal that carried Johnson into the campaign of 1964. His policies also prompted Goldwater to reconsider a presidential run. In the very unusual circumstances of the times, the Republicans in New Mexico began to build their ticket. They suited up and set out to win some elections.

Training and Organizing: The YRs in Winter and Spring

In January, Holm and Earle Bursum helped launch the 1964 campaign in New Mexico. The month before, they had celebrated five years of marriage, and during those years, they had given a good part of their time for party revitalization. They had become a high-profile pair on the state political scene, not to be missed at any GOP gathering, a beautiful, engaging young couple with a great heart for their party.

In mid-January, in the snowy mountain town of Ruidoso, Holm headed up a leadership school to train attendees from twenty-one Young Republican and Teen Age Republican clubs. He scheduled a range of speakers. Merle Tucker, businessman and candidate for governor, was among them. So was New Mexico's AFL-CIO Executive Secretary Wayne Brunner, who came to speak about labor's perspective on politics.[341] It was an agenda that offered a healthy juxtaposition of ideas to engage young minds.

On January 29, the attention turned to fundraising for the 1964 presidential campaign. In Albuquerque, the New Mexico Republicans joined 25,000 counterparts in twenty other cities in a push to raise 2.5 million dollars.[342] At a banquet in the Civic Auditorium and through the technology of closed-circuit TV, they heard Dwight D. Eisenhower, Richard Nixon, and Nelson Rockefeller address the party. The event also cabled in several primary candidates: Senator Barry Goldwater of Arizona, Governor William Scranton of Pennsylvania, and Governor George Romney of Michigan. Former President Eisenhower endorsed them all with a light-hearted comment that he would run for the vice presidency with any of them. For New Mexico, with only a few Electoral College votes, to be chosen as one of twenty-one sites may have been a nod to the rising prominence of the Sun Belt states. The Bursums worked to make the banquet happen, Holm helping with arrangements and ticket sales and Earle serving as part of the decorating committee. She recruited youth from the fifty-five-member Teen Age Republican Club to lend a hand. It was a mutual benefit. She acquired a lively young workforce and they an invitation to be part of an exciting national event with a creative and fun supervisor.

In March, another fundraiser was on the Bursums' schedule. Robert Dole and John B. Anderson headlined a YR event,[343] giving young New Mexicans a close look at two U.S. congressmen who would run for the presidency in the years to come.

Speaking Goldwater's Language

Meanwhile, on the national scene, F. Clifton White continued to organize for Goldwater, and conservatives and other groups across the country rallied as the senator's run for the presidency progressed. Holm Bursum had commented that Goldwater spoke the language of young conservatives like himself in the 1960s. The lexicon of that language was on full display in Goldwater's *The Conscience of a Conservative*, a volume assembled by his speechwriter L. Brent Bozell, Jr. and first published in 1960. The book became a popular item on college campuses and among conservative young adults elsewhere. In the run-up to the 1964 election, it was reprinted twenty times.[344] The book was a Cold War argument against the totalitarianism that Goldwater saw in the Soviet Union. Moscow, he felt, threatened the American way of life. He called on the United States to avoid Soviet-style tyranny by keeping its own central government constitutionally sound and its military defenses strong.

In 1962, Senator Goldwater also wrote "The Case for Conservatism," again in the context of the Cold War with Russia. He composed it as a contrast to the ideas of liberal New York Republican Jacob Javits. The essays became part of *The Great Ideas Today*, published by Britannica. Goldwater's words were vibrant, his syntax compelling:

> We find ourselves pitted against the total regimented society. We find ourselves contesting with the all-powerful state. We find ourselves in the role of guardian and defender of a just social system and a decent civil order. We find ourselves cast as the world's foremost possessor of the blessings that flow naturally from a governmental system founded on freedom for the individual.[345]

Conservatives recognized the spiritual aspects of human beings, Goldwater asserted. He believed that socialists, on the other hand, focused on material needs and wants to the exclusion of spiritual well-being. It was perhaps a reference to the Soviet Union's official doctrine of atheism. To contrast U.S. views with Soviet ones, Goldwater often mentioned Judeo-Christian tenets and spoke of God-given, unchangeable natural law. Overarching religious principles were one matter, but in later years, Goldwater cautioned against using religion in public life in ways he considered improper. He disagreed with religious groups that imposed their interpretations of religious morality on the entire country through specific legislation. He especially disliked groups' use of coercive methods with elected officials like himself.

Goldwater was a practical man. He moved quickly from philosophical abstractions to concrete policies. He critiqued the high taxes of liberal governments, which, having spent public dollars, had not succeeded in speeding up economic growth or reducing unemployment. He deplored deficit spending and inflation. He commented on the very structure of government, saying, "Our federal government is republican in form, not directly democratic."[346] The higher degree of democracy flourished at the state and local levels, he believed. Thus, the national government must interfere as little as possible with those governments closer to the people. The rights of all were to be respected, he said. Racism was to be confronted through moral persuasion rather than through the passage of laws that over-extended the power of the federal government. By encouraging individual enterprise, the United States could develop its economy and improve the quality of life for all citizens, he claimed.

On the international front, Goldwater saw the United States' problems with Cuba, Berlin, Southeast Asia, and Korea as symptoms of a weak foreign policy, one that bordered on appeasement. He opposed admitting the People's Republic of China to the United Nations and called for intervention in Cuba in response to Fidel Castro and his Russian allies. In the world as it was, Goldwater had no interest in nuclear disarmament, preferring an ample weapons supply as a deterrent to war. Similarly, he had little faith in the United Nations as an instrument of peace and justice, seeing it in more limited terms as a forum for international debate.[347]

Goldwater enjoyed political ideas, and his were resonating with a segment of the electorate. His campaign needed F. Clifton White's technical skills and extraordinary volunteer organization, but for input on political ideology, the senator was more inclined to turn to a person like Denison Kitchel.[348] Kitchel was an Ivy League lawyer who practiced in Phoenix. As he began playing a role in a possible Goldwater candidacy, Kitchel had concerns about some of the people who were gravitating to the campaign. They were the ones whose extremist ideology did not reflect Goldwater's kind of conservatism.

Clif White, concerned as well, screened his organization and removed people with less savory behaviors and positions.[349] Later, however, he helped produce a documentary called *Choice*, an analysis of voters' fears. In 1964, there were many worries among the citizenry. They ranged from the potential misuse of nuclear weapons to violence in the nation's communities. The documentary accurately conveyed the concerns of many voters, in Theodore White's opinion, but the images in the film disturbed Goldwater. The candidate "...declared it to be an inflammation of racism, and he suppressed it completely," White wrote.[350]

Goldwater's stand on civil rights was complex. He did not support racial segregation, and during his years in Congress, he had voted in favor of civil rights bills. In the course of his presidential campaign, however, he opposed the legislation that became the Civil Rights Act of 1964. President Lyndon Johnson and his congressional allies had strengthened the civil rights bill beyond what John F. Kennedy had proposed in 1963. The reworked bill was a problem for Goldwater. In his view, it was an unacceptable expansion of federal power, especially when that power reached into the operations of privately-owned businesses. Even wholehearted supporters of the bill were not sure how to ground the federal authority, debating whether it should be in the Constitution's Commerce Clause or the Fourteenth Amendment's Equal Protection Clause.[351] During the months of deliberation, Goldwater reiterated his opposition to segregation, but in the end, he cast a nay vote on the civil rights bill. He was one of the twenty-seven senators to do so, and twenty-one of them were Democrats from the Deep South or the bordering states. Goldwater found himself in the minority among his fellow party members. Of the thirty-three Republicans in the Senate, twenty-seven of them voted in favor of the bill.[352]

In the national excitement over the bipartisan passage of the Civil Rights Act of 1964 and, in the middle of a fast-moving campaign, Goldwater's vote was challenging to explain. It served almost as a Rorschach test for the electorate. Segregationists found comfort in it; civil rights proponents objected to it. At the very least, his vote obscured his support for a racially inclusive society. In Harvard Professor Louis Menand's opinion, Goldwater "...was not a segregationist, nor was he any kind of racist."[353] He had supported civil rights initiatives as a city council member in Phoenix, helping to integrate local public schools and other entities.

As voters worked out how they felt about Barry Goldwater, tensions were building inside the national campaign. F. Clifton White was being nudged to the outer edges of Goldwater's inner circle,[354] as he had been nudged by the Eisenhower people a decade before.

Bringing a New Component to the New Mexico Republican Party

In New Mexico, the prospect of a Goldwater nomination animated much of the Republican Party. The GOP ticket already included star candidates like Edwin Mechem and Jack Redman. Soon the party was going to send delegates to the Republican National Convention at the Cow Palace in Daly City, California. There they would cast their votes to nominate a presidential candidate. It was a privilege to be elected to the state's delegation, but those party members who reasonably could expect to go to California were about to be surprised. What happened at the New Mexico convention would affect the entire state party, eventually including its young wing. A new figure had come into their midst. He introduced a different thread into New Mexico Republicans' prevailing conservatism, and he brought like-minded people with him. The new figure was Anderson Carter, and he was running the Goldwater campaign in New Mexico.

Republicans had presidential nomination choices ranging from Arizona Senator Barry Goldwater, right of center, to New York Governor Nelson Rockefeller, left of center. Many in New Mexico leaned toward Goldwater, but, even with a fair amount of agreement about a nominee, the state party was about to sink into disharmony. It all stemmed from the selection of delegates to the national convention. Over a thousand party members had come to the Johnson Gymnasium on the University of New Mexico campus for their convention on June 13, and many were surprised when the focus quickly turned to Anderson Carter. He appeared to be running not only the Goldwater campaign but the Republican state convention. What he and his people were about to accomplish there was "...a stunning power play by Goldwater workers...," according to an

Associated Press report.[355] *The Santa Fe New Mexican* called Carter's work a "blitzkrieg" that tore "gaping holes in New Mexico's Republican Party."[356]

Some Republicans must have wondered what Anderson Carter was doing in their party. A big man with a genial smile, he was not an unknown quantity in New Mexico politics. In fact, he had a very high profile—as a Democrat. He was from the east side of the state. In 1952, when he was twenty-five and living in Portales, he won a seat in the New Mexico Legislature. He was talented and ambitious and rose to chair the powerful House Appropriations and Finance Committee. He made the news often. Political columnist Will Harrison, with his penchant for characterization, termed Carter "the out-sized chairman of the…Finance Committee."[357]

As a Democrat, Anderson Carter had been willing to take on the leaders in his party. In 1957, he challenged Joseph M. Montoya for the nomination to run in a special election—the one by which Montoya succeeded Congressman Antonio Fernandez. Then in 1960, Carter made a bold move against Governor John Burroughs.[358] Burroughs, he charged, was spending the state into bankruptcy and, with colleagues such as H. E. "Fats" Leonard, was trying to build a political machine. Carter decided that Burroughs needed to be defeated in the primary and co-chaired the campaign of his Democratic challenger Joseph Bursey. Governor Burroughs prevailed over Bursey, but he lost the general election to Edwin Mechem.

Apparently, passions had run high over Anderson Carter's evolving role in the Democratic Party. In 1961, Will Harrison's sharp pen noted that Carter had gotten into a political tiff at a Tesuque nightclub with a fellow Democrat who had served as Governor Burroughs' state liquor director. The commotion prompted the club owner to intervene.[359] By the time of that altercation, Carter already had sold his farm near Portales and moved to Lea County to enter the oil business. The following year, he left the Democratic Party and became a Republican.

In 1964, in his new county and his new party, Anderson Carter became passionate about electing Barry Goldwater to the presidency. When asked by a reporter if he would leave New Mexico to join the Goldwater campaign at a higher level, Carter said no, but then added, "…[A]s deeply committed as I am, I guess I'd go to Siberia for him."[360] Carter went on to praise F. Clifton White, who by then was firmly in place in the national campaign. White was, Carter said, "…one of the most capable people I've known." To trace how White and Carter met would make an interesting story. Perhaps White recruited the New Mexican back in 1962 when he was launching his Draft Goldwater movement and creating nine districts in the U.S. from which to organize. Regardless of the route to their collaboration, Anderson Carter was about to take on a huge role in the New Mexico Republican Party, and it started with the June 13 convention. Will Harrison described the scene in the Johnson Gymnasium in his vivid way:

> The New Mexico Republican Party has changed hands. The Saturday convention marched and wheeled to the command of new leaders.... [T]hey are youngish, conservative, mostly from eastern New Mexico, resolutely tough, and also characterized by a desire for anonymity.... They let the opposition...nominate any they wished for the national convention delegation and then proceeded to elect their own slate with huge votes.[361]

Harrison listed those who did not receive enough votes to become delegates.[362] They included veteran Republican leaders Art Trujillo and Willie Ortiz. Also named were Aileen Thompson, the state GOP vice chairwoman, and Lillian Foreman, the mother of West Texas Congressman Ed Foreman, himself a conservative Republican. Having illustrious party credentials and excellent GOP connections no longer guaranteed inclusion under Anderson Carter's leadership. However, after some wrangling, a few of the long-time members were allowed into the delegation, on the condition they would support Goldwater.

Willie Ortiz, who served as both the chairman of the Santa Fe County party and vice chairman of the state GOP, spoke on the record.[363] Many people were displeased, he said, by how the delegate votes were taken—by voice vote. It was unfair, he thought, because some counties used fractional voting, giving their voice vote a volume others could not match. Ortiz also protested the move to have all delegates pledged to Goldwater. Some at the convention favored Nelson Rockefeller and Henry Cabot Lodge, he pointed out, but they had not felt included. In the fallout, Ortiz was planning to call a meeting of Republicans in the northern counties of Santa Fe, Rio Arriba, Los Alamos, Taos, San Miguel, Mora, and Colfax. Some Republicans running for local offices there were talking about ending their candidacies, but Ortiz hoped to persuade them to stay.

Sara Balcomb, chair of the party in Los Alamos County, conveyed her delegation's discontent.[364] She also spoke about problems for Republicans in the general election if rifts from the state convention were not bridged. She wished that a gentler approach had been used. The Goldwater people had the majority, she said, and would have won regardless.

Others predicted that the distress in the party had endangered Edwin Mechem's campaign to retain his U.S. Senate seat. Goldwater, the preferred candidate of many, was not the issue, another ventured.[365] Some Goldwater supporters at the convention were just as concerned as others about the moves that the new guard made. People in Carter's group, they speculated, were newcomers to the party—probably recently registered as Democrats or independents—yet they had wielded controlling power at the Republican state convention.

When Carter himself was queried, he expressed optimism about his impact on his new party. He acknowledged that some people were angry, but he found that commonplace after a convention. "After all, the Republican Party is bigger than me or any individual..., he said."[366] He was counting on people to put matters in perspective and come together for the sake of the campaign. The new strand that Carter was weaving into the conservative-leaning New Mexico GOP seemed ultraconservative to some, but it was bringing new people into the party. Carter, like Holm Bursum, saw the east side as a region where the GOP could grow. Several stalwarts feared, however, that Carter's approach would be at the expense of the party in the northern counties where a more moderate strand of Republicanism coexisted with conservative ones.

The approach to political organizing that Anderson Carter was taking differed from that of another young leader. Holm Bursum III seemed more committed to a unified party. He understood its history and respected the roles that its elders were playing. In 1965, Bursum's and Carter's paths would cross in the Young Republican organization, and there would be a contest. In 1964, however, both men had a common cause—the election of Barry Goldwater and the entire ticket. To that extent, Carter had been correct. The GOP was bigger than any individual, and the whole party could, and, for the most part, would come together for the campaign.

Campaigning in the Summer and Fall

David Cargo, running for his second term in the New Mexico House of Representatives, faced challenges from both parties. First, the Democrats, he felt, had set up an obstacle to his reelection. Cargo's 1963 reform had created population-based legislative districts, and suddenly Bernalillo County had double its number of House seats. The Democratic-controlled legislature had drawn the new district lines, giving Cargo a pro-labor territory that included the East Mountains with rural villages such as Chilili and Tijeras.[367] Perhaps the Democrats hoped that the Michigan-born, urban-based Republican Cargo was not a natural fit for the constituency, but accepting an outsider's role was not in the young man's nature. He relished his new district and campaigned on, undaunted.

Cargo also felt a challenge from some Republicans. The Anderson Carter movement in New Mexico's GOP seemed to promote adherence to a single political ideology. It was clear by then that Cargo did not wholly embrace the Goldwater message, and a woman at the Bernalillo County party convention warned him of the consequences. Cargo quoted her as saying, "...[U]nless you have Goldwater tattooed across your forehead, you are going to lose, and I mean it!"[368] Cargo kept running on his own terms, again not greatly concerned.

On the east side, Republicans kept at the business of building the party in the solidly Democratic counties. The GOP's profile was rising, and the Young Republicans were part of the reason. Through public appeals, they welcomed Democrats. In Clovis, for example, Young Republican Colin McMillan emceed a gathering open to young people interested in politics, regardless of party affiliation.[369] All over the state, YR clubs and their Teen Age Republican club protégés worked wholeheartedly to spread the party message and get out the vote.

Getting the Pre-Primary Convention Law on the Ballot.

In the middle of the campaign, Holm Bursum III and the New Mexico Young Republicans had a parallel project—a bipartisan one involving a referendum. It was the petition drive to put the new pre-primary convention law on the November ballot for possible repeal. Led by Tom Reader, the drive had started the year before with the Young Republican Club in Dona Ana County and had spread statewide. By summer, the leaders had moved into the last phase of their work. On June 18, Holm Bursum went on KNME TV's "Shirtsleeve Session" with host Tony Tiano to discuss the drive.[370] Bursum's fellow guests made up a bipartisan panel: Henry A. Kiker, Jr., the Democratic Party county chairman; Tom Garcia, treasurer of Republican Jack Redman's congressional campaign, and

Imogene Lindsay, a Democratic candidate for a legislative seat. All agreed that the pre-primary convention law needed to go.

In the hectic last days, the YRs pushed to ensure that New Mexicans could vote on whether or not to restore the direct primary. It had been a long and intricate process. To meet the state constitution's stipulations, the organizers had had to conduct research and do their math. The number of their petition signers had to equal ten percent of the vote in the gubernatorial race in the previous election. In 1964, that meant they needed a total of 24,713 valid signatures from at least twenty-four of New Mexico's thirty-two counties.[371] As the petition-filing deadline approached, the Young Republicans faced even more hurdles, including some unexpected ones. It was a suspenseful time as they confronted barrier after barrier, and more than once, the state's attorney general had to weigh in.

The petitions circulating in the counties had to be submitted to the secretary of state in Santa Fe for signature verification. July 3 was the deadline. Missing it would mean that the repeal question could not appear on the election ballot. To ensure they would not be derailed by the upcoming July Fourth holiday, Holm Bursum and his colleagues drove the petitions to Santa Fe on Thursday, July 2. He and Las Crucens Tom Reader and Oscar Syfert appeared in Secretary of State Alberta Miller's office.[372] In a cordial exchange, they handed Miller their bundle of petitions. There was just one problem; Eddy County's petitions were still out, and the next day, the long holiday weekend would start. In a considerable accommodation, Miller kept her office open late as the young men waited for the last sheaf of signatures to arrive from southeastern New Mexico by plane. Tom Reader, keenly aware of the time and all that was at stake, called his contacts in Eddy County for updates.

It helps to remember that the young people were working without the devices that make communication easy today. They had no cell phones, computers, scanners, printers, or even much access to photocopiers. Theirs were the days of landlines, typewriters, carbon copies, and tedious correction methods involving abrasive erasers or chalky tape. High-volume copying of documents meant running off specially prepared sheets on machines with inked drums, some of which had to be hand-cranked. For quick contact, organizers in the mid-1960s did not even have fax machines, only fixed-line telephones and telegraph offices. Furthermore, overnight delivery services across the great spaces of New Mexico were up to them to arrange—by private car or plane or by packages entrusted to Greyhound. There was no FedEx.

In the relatively low-tech scenario that summer, Bursum and his colleagues pressed on, but as July 2 wound down, Eddy County's petitions still had not arrived. Although Friday was the deadline, the state was closing offices for the long holiday weekend. Monday should be the new deadline, the YRs reasoned, but there was no assurance it would be. Too near their goal to take risks, Bursum and another colleague, Dr. E. W. Bundy, found another way to file. On Friday, with the last petitions finally in hand, they showed up on Alberta Miller's doorstep in Albuquerque to complete their delivery.[373] Bursum and Bundy considered the documents duly filed, but Miller, understandably cautious, was not sure.

On Monday morning in Santa Fe, Secretary Miller began to process the petitions.[374] The job started with the staff's alphabetizing the nearly 25,000 names of the petition signers. Miller also sought legal counsel, asking the attorney general to review the unusual conditions of the Friday filing. Assistant Attorney General Oliver Payne's opinion came quickly. It was favorable to the petitioners, affirming their assertion that the deadline rightfully fell on Friday.

Prospects for repeal began to look promising again, but a new challenge came later in July. The state was up against a tight deadline to verify and certify the petitions.[375] The task was enormous, requiring the secretary of state to work with over thirty county clerks. The clerks, in turn, had to verify that petition signers in their counties met legal requirements. One complication in the verifying process reflected the customs of the times. The year before, the state legislature had passed a law permitting women to register to vote using their first names rather than their husbands' names or initials. In 1964, a woman whose voter registration was still under her husband's name may have signed the referendum petition using her own name. The sorting out of proper identities took time. The attorney general granted Secretary Miller an extension of ten days to complete the checks.

Miller's staff randomly had sampled some counties' petitions and found discrepancies between the clerks' lists of disqualified names and their own. In Bernalillo County, for example, the clerk had found some signers to be ineligible because they were not registered voters when, in fact, the secretary's staff found that they were. However, when the process was completed, Miller, even with her more generous count, found that the number of petition signers who were properly registered as voters had fallen short. On July 23, she announced that the Pre-Primary Convention law would not appear on the November ballot and notified Holm Bursum and his colleagues.[376] More than a year of Young Republican work was about to go down the drain.

The leaders were daunted—momentarily. Quickly, new ideas occurred to them, ones that involved a tremendous amount of labor. They decided to recheck the petitions themselves and, if the results warranted it, they would consider a lawsuit to bring about the referendum. Then, Republican State Senator Lawrence H. Prentice stepped in.[377] A candidate for attorney general that year, Prentice acknowledged Secretary Miller's careful work. However, he disagreed with a premise she had used. The petition signers had to be qualified electors, he said, but not necessarily registered voters. Secretary Miller again turned to the attorney general's office for an opinion. Assistant Attorney General Oliver Payne essentially agreed with Prentice, and Attorney General Earl Hartley declared that the referendum to repeal the statute would appear on the ballot after all.[378]

The petition drive to hold a referendum on the Pre-Primary Convention law had succeeded, and it was news. Political reporter Fred Buckles called the victory "rousing" and gave credit to Reader, Bursum, and Bundy as the leaders.[379] Will Harrison admitted that he and others had not thought the Young Republicans could complete their drive. He had assumed that the YRs' name alone would have turned a great many people away from their cause, but he and the skeptics were "eating crow," he said.[380] New Mexicans' second-ever referendum was going forward, and it was on the same topic as before, the repeal of the pre-primary convention.

Aspiring Beyond Defeat: November 3, 1964

On Election Night, Republicans from party elders to teens gathered at their county headquarters across New Mexico to watch the returns come in. They were the ones who had organized the fundraising dinners, handed out campaign literature in store parking lots, and walked the neighborhoods talking with voters about their ticket. They had been part of an exciting exercise in the great U.S. tradition of government for the people. They, like their Democratic counterparts, started the evening of November 3 with high hopes for their candidates, but it turned out to be a disheartening stretch of hours for the GOP as the opposition swept the elections nationwide.

First, there was the crushing defeat at the top of the ticket, with Goldwater winning 52 electoral votes to Johnson's 486. The strong showing by President Johnson impacted down-ballot races across the United States. Democrats picked up seats in Congress, achieving two-thirds majorities in both the House and the Senate. For Joseph M. Montoya in New Mexico, it meant the realization of a long-desired goal. As he wished, he had glided through the Democratic primary in June with no opposition and had gone on to the general election to win a seat in the U.S. Senate. He defeated Edwin L. Mechem by 30,619 votes.[381] Democrats also kept the state's two seats in the House of Representatives. Democratic Governor Jack Campbell was re-elected, and both chambers of the state legislature retained Democratic majorities. In a final blow, the referendum to repeal the pre-primary convention law failed.

1964 would be the last time Edwin Mechem appeared on the Republican ticket in New Mexico, ending an era in electoral politics. In the bleak results, Holm Bursum looked for encouraging data. Mechem had been defeated, but he had polled ahead of the national ticket, winning 147,001 votes compared to Goldwater's 133,398 in New Mexico.[382] Jack Redman had taken on the futile challenge of running as a Republican in an at-large congressional race, but against the odds, he had garnered 154,231 votes,[383] the most of any Republican on the ticket.

The other uplifting news was in the legislative races. State representatives Hoyt Pattison and David Cargo, among others, retained their seats. Pattison's victory was a good sign. It showed that his win two years earlier in a Democratic stronghold had not been an anomaly. Likewise, Cargo's win must have pleased him mightily. He had prevailed despite the challenging district that the Democrats had created for him. He had prevailed despite his fellow Republican's warning about his tepid response to the Goldwater message. Cargo also could take satisfaction in other legislative victories. By going to court to bring about equitable representation in the state legislature, Cargo had produced a good effect for other Republicans in the 1964 election. Will Harrison said it well. He gave Cargo and Judge Caswell Neal credit for the districting "…which this year led to the election of eight Albuquerque Republican representatives who would surely have lost had they been candidates at large as in the past."[384]

Overall, the New Mexico GOP had grown in places where it had not been strong before, and the revitalized Young Republican clubs had drawn in people in their teens and early adult years. For the long term, the signs were there—sometimes literally—that the Republican Party was still a contender. One message scrawled on a party headquarters window in Alamogordo was prophetic. On Election Night, GOP volunteer Gigi King had attempted to cheer up the crowd. She paid special attention to the group from the local Teen Age (TAR) Republican Club.

Over the summer and fall, the TARs had brought the idealism, creativity, and fun of youth to the '64 campaign.[385] Although they could not yet vote, they jumped into electoral politics. They wrote letters about candidates to the local paper and composed and bought campaign spots on the radio. They even created a good-humored spectacle that made the news. Paul Mapes and his fellow club members borrowed a farmer's donkey to serve as the Democratic Party mascot and adorned it with a cardboard rendering of Barry Goldwater's black-rimmed glasses. The donkey's placard read, "If I could, I would vote Republican." With their playful prop, the teens distributed literature around town in the last days of the campaign.

Downcast over the Election Night results, the TARs got ready to leave party headquarters, but before they were out the door, Gigi King handed each one a small U.S. flag. Then, she wrote on the building's window: "Just you wait. We'll be back in '68." She had the spirit. The Republicans might have lost one, but they were going to suit up again. In just four years, those adolescents filing out the door would be young voters ready to go to the polls.

If New Mexico's Republicans could have looked ahead, they would have seen that 1968 was going to be an extraordinary year for them. Their electoral achievements were going to be staggering when compared to those earlier in the decade.

As for the Goldwater supporters around the country, their candidate had been defeated, but his movement was not done. Louis Menand cited political writer Rick Perlstein's assertion that Barry Goldwater had been a part of the youth rebellion of the 1960s—as much a reaction against the moderate/liberal East coast establishment as those on the left.[386] Commentators on the Sixties usually focus on the Kennedy brothers, the civil rights movement, and radical leftist college students, Menand continued, but another impulse drove part of the young resistance to the conservative end of the spectrum. Those young people had been inspired by a silver-haired standard-bearer from Arizona.

History has shown Barry Goldwater to be "...as much a man of the nineteen-sixties as Abbie Hoffman or Malcolm X, and, what's more, his shadow looms a good deal larger than theirs," Menand asserted, again drawing on Perlstein. From his perspective in 2001, Menand went on to say that "it's not only that more politicians today sound like Goldwater than like Tom Hayden. More politicians today sound like Goldwater than like Lyndon Johnson."[387] Holm Bursum, who spoke Goldwater's language, was one for whom the Arizonan's words carried into the twenty-first century.

11

1965: Transitions at Home and a Peace Mission Abroad

Inspire us with wisdom, all of us, of every color, race and creed, to use our wealth, our strength, to help our brother, instead of destroying him.
—Conrad Hilton, 1957[388]

1965 was the Bursums' last year in Albuquerque. Holm and Earle prepared to leave their stylish, modern house in New Mexico's largest city for a charming vintage home in a town whose population had not yet reached six thousand. Holm was about to act on his long-deferred plan to join his father in banking in Socorro. "I'd intended to work at the bank in Albuquerque for two years, but I stayed seven," Bursum said, with a touch of retrospective wonder at how long his tenure had been. He had built up his professional credentials, of course, but his political organizing also had kept him in Albuquerque. Working to restore a two-party system in New Mexico had taken time. The results at the ballot box had been modest thus far, and in the mid-1960s, both the state and nation were on political tracks different from Bursum's own. Nonetheless, he had done the work he set out to do. He had helped find those enduring seeds of political life beneath the hard-crusted, one-party landscape, and the flourishing would come.

In 1965, tensions in the world grew. Conflict in Southeast Asia escalated, bringing the U.S. into combat against Soviet-supported North Vietnam. War, so prevalent in the first half of the 20th century, had prompted Bursum's relative Conrad Hilton to speak out for more depth of understanding and goodwill in the global community. Bursum himself would take part in an international effort in 1965. He would confer with young European leaders, some of them from countries that had been at war with his own during his lifetime. Meanwhile, six months of intense political work in New Mexico lay ahead of him.

Monitoring the Pre-Primary Convention Law

In 1965, Bursum continued to monitor the direct primary matter. Although the referendum to end the pre-primary convention had not passed in 1964, the ballot-box results were encouraging. Of the 114,000 people who voted on the referendum, 85,000 favored repeal.[389] The vote was three-to-one for the abolition of "the odious pre-primary convention," the *Albuquerque Journal* editorialized.[390] The referendum failed only because the votes on it, as a percentage of all votes cast in the election, did not meet the constitutional standard. Simply put, not enough voters had marked their ballot one way or the other on the pre-primary question. Thus, they created a void in which the votes of those who did respond could not be considered. The legislature should step up to repeal the law, the *Journal* said. When the next session opened in Santa Fe in January of 1965, the lawmakers were ready to do just that.

Many Democrats were on board with ending the pre-primary convention and had been for over a year. In 1964, at their party convention, discontent over the nominating process had erupted, and it had "...people screaming from one end of the state to the other," as Will Harrison described it.[391] Convention-goers had two observations on the topic. First, the pre-primary law seemed to have been passed to benefit the senatorial campaign of Joseph M. Montoya. Second, Clinton P. Anderson, still a driving force in the party, had dominated the candidate selection.[392] Many legislators walked out of the convention hall on Saturday, February 22, and into the state capitol on Monday, February 24, ready to vote the pre-primary convention law off the books. In the special legislative session, State Senator George Amaya, Democrat from McKinley County, drafted the repeal legislation. A number of his prominent partisans signed it, including the powerful Tibo Chavez of Valencia County,[393] a former lieutenant governor. The bill did not make it through the legislature in 1964, however.

The Young Republicans assessed the situation. The legislative repeal effort of 1964 had failed. The referendum on the 1964 election ballot had failed, but the bipartisan support that Holm Bursum III predicted had held fast. In the 1965 session, the New Mexico House passed a bill, sixty-to-thirteen, to repeal the pre-primary convention law.[394] The bill moved to the Senate, where a drama was about to be staged. Clinton P. Anderson, watching developments from his office in Washington, saw where the repeal effort was headed. He promptly booked a flight to New Mexico.

Anderson had considerable heft in the United States Senate despite his being from a sparsely populated western state. He held important positions, chairing the Committee on Aeronautical and Space Sciences and the Joint Committee on Atomic Energy. He had succeeded in many endeavors—journalism, private business, government administration, and international humanitarian service—but legislative work seemed to be his particular niche. From the 1950s into the '60s, he helped pass landmark bills that changed the nation, advancing civil rights and establishing Medicare.[395] Clinton Anderson wielded power in Washington because he first wielded power in New Mexico.

Arriving in Santa Fe on a winter day in 1965, Anderson got to work caucusing with the Democratic state senators to save New Mexico's pre-primary convention law from repeal. In the view of the *Albuquerque Journal*, he was interfering in a strictly state legislative matter.[396] Anderson was a prominent individual, the paper noted, who was using his prestige in an unseemly manner. Undeterred, Anderson moved ahead. His party held twenty-eight of the thirty-two seats in the New Mexico Senate, giving him much to work with. He pressed his points with the Democratic caucus, but he did not convince everyone. When the repeal vote was taken, it was sixteen to sixteen. Clearly, many had broken with their party leader on the issue. With the vote evenly split, attention turned to the Senate's presiding officer, Democratic Lieutenant Governor Mack Easley. In that tense moment, Easley broke the tie against repeal, leaving the pre-primary convention on the books.[397] Clinton Anderson had his victory.

Holm Bursum III and the Young Republicans responded. "The franchise has been taken away from all the people and given to the political bosses," they stated. They began to look into other methods of reform.[398] They had brought the issue into broad public awareness, and it was going to stay there awhile. Bursum called for Republicans, Democrats, and independents to come together to restore the direct primary.[399] They would not have to wait long.

Two years later, the Democratic-majority legislature would pass a bill to repeal the pre-primary law, and the new governor, a Republican, would sign it. For those who had worked so long for it, the repeal was a great success, but it would not last even a decade. By 1976, New Mexico had returned to the old convention system of selecting candidates to run in primaries. As before, one man's name would be associated with the change. With the pre-primary system back in place, Joseph M. Montoya would be re-nominated easily that year, but it would be his last political win. He would lose the general election to the GOP's Harrison Schmitt, a young Apollo 17 astronaut. Although his career ended in defeat, Montoya had had many victories. His great desire, the pre-primary convention system, was one of them, and it persists into the twenty-first century.

Presiding over the Biggest YR Convention Yet

Holm Bursum III wrapped up his leadership of the New Mexico Young Republican Association in May of 1965, and he did it with style. The young man who had walked into the historic Alvarado Hotel to start his political organizing in 1961 stood at the podium in Albuquerque's new Holiday Inn and called his last convention to order. In his four years of leadership, he had become a respected figure in the young wing of the Republican Party at both the state and national levels, and he had not yet turned thirty-one.

The YRs were planning an exciting, star-studded event to run from May 13 to 15. "It will be the biggest convention we've had.... It will be our fifth one. Each has been bigger than the last, and this will top all the others," Bursum told the press.[400]

The growth in the Young Republican Association over four years indeed was striking. David Cargo had reported eight convention attendees in 1959, but in 1965 two hundred fifty delegates and a hundred alternates showed up.[401] Bursum brought in public affairs consultant F. Clifton White as a featured speaker. Just forty-seven in 1965, White was the man who had brought young power to presidential politics from Eisenhower's campaign in 1952 to Goldwater's in 1964. On the program with White were YR leaders from Colorado and members of Congress from Kansas and North Carolina. Candidates running for president of the Young Republican National Federation came to campaign for New Mexico's support at their upcoming convention. The state's prominent Republicans were at the YR gathering—from Ed Mechem, Frances Lee, Jack Redman, and Tom Bolack to David Cargo and Anderson Carter. Carter led a delegate-seating challenge from a Lea County group that the Young Republican Association had not yet chartered, and the little dust-up made the news.

Looking forward to 1968, the convention focused on the coming presidential election. Kansas State Senator Scott Van Sickle addressed the group, pointing out that by '68, half the people in the U.S. would be under twenty-five years old. The demographics had great implications for a rejuvenated electorate, giving the Young Republicans an opportunity. Van Sickle charged the association with bringing in new young voters. Train regional leaders, he urged the YRs, and give them delegated authority; train campaign managers. Make voter registration drives year-round affairs. Put in the work, he encouraged the group. "[T]he biggest organization builder is work," he said, leaning on the idea that there is no substitute for door-to-door, house-to-house campaigning.[402]

Another contest for young women was on the agenda, and Marianne Waddell of Otero County had entered. Just graduating from high school, she had been on an award-winning debate team and was a political organizer. She had started a vibrant Teen Age Republican (TARs) club in her county and served as its first president. She had recruited her fellow teens, attended campaign rallies, raised funds, and gone door to door in her town to campaign for the GOP ticket. She had done the work and moved directly from the TARs into a Young Republican club. With poise, a political resume, and public speaking skills, Marianne Waddell became the young woman to represent New Mexico at the YR national convention in Miami.[403]

Before the convention ended, Holm Bursum and Nancy Burke won their elections as New Mexico's committee members in the Young Republican National Federation. Tom Nord of Roswell took Bursum's place as president. Nord was another example of an individual who transitioned quickly from YR leadership into government service. After serving as a Young Republican chairman in Carlsbad and moving to Roswell, Nord was elected as Chaves County's sheriff. He became a well-regarded leader in law enforcement, taking on the presidency of the new Sheriffs' Association of New Mexico.[404]

It had been a spectacular weekend, a fitting finale to Holm Bursum's state Young Republican leadership. On Monday morning, he was back at the bank, back at his day job, and ready for the next round of political challenges. One was coming up in June.

Covering a Cliffhanger Election: The Bernalillo County Young Republican Club President

Bursum, New Mexico's new YR national committeeman, stayed active in the Bernalillo County Young Republican Club. The club had been his home base throughout his time in Albuquerque, and, as its robust press coverage indicated, it had become a newsworthy political organization. One person looking at the Bernalillo County YRs with great interest was Anderson Carter, three hundred miles away in southeastern New Mexico.

The Bernalillo club prepared to elect new officers at its June meeting. Two groups had slated candidates, one associated with Bursum and the other with Carter. Carter's interest in backing a slate so far from home may have been strategic, intended to enhance his power in the whole party. The Bernalillo County club played a big part in state YR conventions, and Carter, fresh from his takeover of the senior GOP assembly the year before, knew the value of conventions. At thirty-eight, he was close to aging out of the Young Republicans, but he still had time. He was going to maximize his presence in both wings of the party.

Bursum, who had witnessed Carter's actions at the senior party's convention in 1964, was attentive to his interest in the Young Republicans in 1965. Although he rarely issued public statements about intraparty differences, Bursum made an exception. Carter's influence in the young wing of the party concerned him, he told *The Albuquerque Tribune* editorial writer A. C. DeCola.[405] Carter had established his power in the senior party and should maintain boundaries of control between it and the young wing, in Bursum's opinion. His unusual candor about an internal party matter might be explained by a technique the editor used. "Tony DeCola had a habit of calling people around five in the morning," Bursum recalled in amusement, "before anyone is really awake." Overall, he maintained his discretion. As he told his associate Cindy Lam years later, it was good to remember his father's words during tense moments. "If you're in an argument and you think it would feel really good to say something," the elder Bursum had counseled, "you probably shouldn't say it. You can't take back a spoken word."

Although Holm Bursum III preferred being circumspect, the Young Republican matter was about to become an ongoing news story. The Albuquerque press saw a tough fight shaping up and understood its implications.[406] The spotlight was on the two candidates running for the presidency, both students at the University of New Mexico. Dennis Howe, the incumbent, was backed by Carter while Brad Zeikus, the club's vice president, had Bursum's support. As tensions escalated, Eddie Mahe's name also came up. He was an officer in the state Young Republican Association and seemed to some like a good compromise candidate. Zeikus stated that he would consider supporting Mahe if his opponent would do likewise, but Howe rejected the idea. Mahe himself shut down further talk of his candidacy by declaring for Howe.

In the lead-up to the election, Albuquerque reporters talked with faction leaders, many of whom were two thousand miles away at the Young Republican National Federation convention in Miami. Holm Bursum, as a national committeeman, had expected to be with the delegation in Florida, but his bank duties kept him home. An alternate took his place. Anderson Carter, on the other hand, was at the convention, in the thick of the action. Reached by phone, he confirmed to a reporter that he was not a participant in the Bernalillo County club but stated his firm support for Dennis Howe. Howe had increased club membership, Carter stated and added, "I would like to claim the credit that is due me."[407] Perhaps Carter was alluding to his influence in the club. With his pronouncement, the lines were drawn. Brad Zeikus decided to stay in the race. "It is an all or nothing affair now," Zeikus said.[408]

On Saturday afternoon, June 19, *The Albuquerque Tribune* declared, "Young Republicans of this county, embroiled in one of the liveliest organization rows in years, will elect a president tonight...."[409] The paper speculated that a hundred members would show up. The *Albuquerque Journal* predicted a full house.[410] As it turned out, at eight p.m. on that June night, more than three hundred young people crowded into a meeting room at the First National Bank.[411] Some had just arrived, fresh from Miami. They had left the national Young Republican convention early to take part in the club election.

In the packed room, through two hours of adrenaline and suspense, leaders sorted out credentials challenges and seated the members eligible to vote. At ten p.m., the meeting finally got underway. It lasted until after midnight. In a very close election, Dennis Howe defeated Brad Zeikus. The vote was 110 to 108, and it was breaking news.[412] Although the results had come about in the wee hours of the morning, the *Albuquerque Journal* managed to print a small election bulletin on the Sunday paper's front page. A page-one article detailing the evening's events followed on Monday.

Carter's candidate had won over Bursum's. Carter himself was getting ready to run for a high public office, and he appreciated the power of Young Republicans to boost a campaign. In 1966, he would win the GOP nomination to run for the U.S. Senate. He would oppose Clinton P. Anderson, the leader of his erstwhile party, and he would lose. No one beat Senator Anderson. Carter, however, would extract one plum from his campaign against the renowned Democrat. He would win Anderson's home county of Bernalillo, a significant achievement.[413]

From Albuquerque to Socorro by Way of Western Europe: Travels for Peace Channeling Conrad Hilton

Holm Bursum stayed with the Bernalillo County Young Republican Club well into Dennis Howe's new term, but his time in Albuquerque was nearly over. As he was preparing for his move back to Socorro, he took an international detour. Days after the YR club's elections, Bursum was on a flight to London. He joined a delegation to help bridge rifts in the post-war North Atlantic community by building relationships with young political leaders in Europe.

In the first half of Holm Bursum's life, conflicts abroad had drawn the country into war at close intervals. From World War II to combat in Korea and Vietnam, soldiers and their families on both sides suffered, and U.S. resources were diverted from more constructive pursuits. The end to war seemed an elusive goal, but people hoped for it.

One of the eloquent voices for peace in mid-century America belonged to someone Bursum knew well, Conrad Hilton, his grandfather's cousin. Bursum had grown up in the Hilton family's hometown. He played where the Hilton children had played, and he knew their stories. He had even seen the penciled marks on a wall in the old Hilton home that tracked the growth spurts of the younger set of children, the one called Boy and others. By the 1950s, Conrad, the most famous of the family, had become an international entrepreneur. He lived a glamorous life with homes in California and New York, and, for a time, he had been the husband of Zsa Zsa Gabor and the father-in-law of Elizabeth Taylor.

With his New Mexico roots and his aura of celebrity, Conrad Hilton often made the local news.[414] In 1960, he came to kick off the Socorro fiesta and golf tournament named for him. There to welcome him home were Mayor Holm Bursum, Jr., his first cousin once removed, and his longtime friend, attorney William Keleher of Albuquerque. Two years later, on the golden anniversary of statehood, New Mexico honored Hilton with a plaque. At twenty-four, he had been the youngest member of the state's first legislature in 1912.

Holm Bursum III spent time with Hilton when he came to Socorro and remembered, in particular, a long conversation with his famous relative at a kitchen table after a family funeral.[415] It made a great impression on the younger man. What Hilton thought mattered to Bursum, and Hilton had thought a great deal about war and peace.

Conrad Hilton knew armed conflict from a personal perspective. He had left Socorro as a young man in 1918 to fight in the First World War in Europe, and later, he saw two of his sons off to serve in the Second World War. In the post-war '50s, Hilton pondered the state of the world as armed combat transitioned into the Cold War between the Soviet Union and the United States and their respective blocs. "Our sons had fought the war," he wrote. "Our part would be to fight for the peace."[416] Hilton was well into his career as a hotelier then--an entrepreneur who was buying some of the county's grand hotels, including the Palmer House in Chicago, the Mayflower in Washington, DC, and the Plaza and the Waldorf-Astoria in New York. He also went abroad to establish Hilton Inns in places as diverse as Mexico City, Madrid, Istanbul, and Bangkok. He found himself enchanted by the cultures of them all.

Dialog and diplomatic alternatives to global war were the trends in the 1950s, and Hilton, who had a great love for the world in all its variety, wanted nothing less than peace rooted in regard for humankind. He had been raised by his mother to practice prayer, and he often had stepped through the doors of Socorro's San Miguel Catholic Church for that purpose. He had ideas about achieving global harmony. One concerned sending an entreaty heavenward. He composed a prayer for peace that circulated widely in the U.S. in the 1950s.[417] He also directed a message to his fellow citizens and, by extension, the Western world. Addressing the National Conference of Christians and Jews in El Paso in 1957, he spoke bold and prescient words:

> The world does not belong to the Christians and Jews in the fashion we once thought. Certainly since the 16th Century the Western nations have dominated the economic life of the world. We have walked over it, often in roughshod arrogance, bad manners

and tactlessness. Then the arrogance turned on us and became two fratricidal world wars—when the West fought itself. Out of these wars came the demand for one world.[418]

A third of humans, Hilton said, lived outside the Western and Soviet blocs. He reminded his audience that Asia had prevailed up until the rise of the West. History, as taught in our culture, he continued, did not fully recognize the brilliance of Asia and Africa. Instead, we seemed to regard people of other continents as bystanders to Western achievements, failing to acknowledge the great contributions other peoples have made to human progress. Hilton also addressed the West's almost exclusive focus on Christian and Jewish faiths, his eloquence preserved in an *El Paso Times* article.[419] "...[W]e have too long ignored Buddha, Confucius, and the tribal beliefs of Africa," he said. He urged "...that we try to understand and value each other's histories and fonts of history—not just the Judeo-Christian but world history: to understand and value the past of the uncommitted third of the world." That part of the world is composed of people of color, he pointed out, and they are asking for their rightful place in global affairs. Citing historian Arnold Toynbee, Hilton continued, "...the West will have its just place, but no more than its just place in the world." The Judeo-Christian community could help achieve global unity, he said, "...embracing all the spiritual riches of the world, all the cultures of the world, all the peoples of the world—including the uncommitted third."

Hilton's young cousin, Holm Bursum III, was about to join a dialog for understanding and peaceful relations. In Bursum's case, he and his political peers abroad would be searching for common ground after one of the fratricidal Western wars that Hilton had lamented.

Attending the North Atlantic Conference of Young Political Leaders

Given that European conflicts had spread into global wars twice in the first half of the twentieth century, the West was looking for a new strategy. One was the mutual defense pact called the North Atlantic Treaty signed by several European and North American countries. The treaty's implementing organization became known as NATO, and NATO's mission generated other groups that supported it. One day Holm Bursum received an extraordinary opportunity from one such group.

When Bursum was invited to attend the North Atlantic Conference of Young Political Leaders in the summer of 1965, Europe was about midway between the end of World War II and the establishment of the European Union. It was an exciting time to be meeting the future leaders of a new international order. Bursum and the Young Republicans in New Mexico had been following developments in Europe and had stated their opposition to Soviet actions, notably the building of the Berlin Wall and the U.S.S.R.'s entry into a controversial wheat deal with U.S. suppliers. Now Bursum could exchange perspectives with European counterparts on the same side of the Cold War divide. The United States was sending twenty-five delegates to the North Atlantic Conference, thirteen Young Democrats and twelve Young Republicans. One of the YRs was Bursum's friend Leonard Nadasdy.

Holm Bursum's traveling companion to Europe was Earle. The month-long trip marked their second time abroad as a couple. In 1963, as private citizens, they had toured countries on the Mediterranean coasts of Europe, Asia, and Africa. Since Holm had a public role in 1965, their trip entailed a stop in Washington, DC for briefings. The delegates gathered in the capital for meetings with State Department and Atlantic Council officials. Vice President Hubert Humphrey also met with the group, discussing Europe's efforts to work together peacefully in the Common Market. There were, however, problems, he said, between the Inner Six members of the Market (France, Italy, the Low Countries, and West Germany) and the Outer Seven (the United Kingdom, the Scandinavian countries, Switzerland, Austria, and Portugal). With help from the Atlantic community, Humphrey thought, the problems could be solved.[420] The delegates were learning the challenges of defining the common good, not only among those who had been enemies but also among those who had been allies. None of it was easy.

After the Washington briefing, the delegation flew to England. For the first week, the North Atlantic conferees settled in at the University of Oxford fifty miles from London. The school, dating from the 12th Century, presented a splendid silhouette of domes, towers, and spires. Its architecture told its history, with styles ranging from Saxon, Gothic and Baroque to Neoclassical and 1960s Functionalist.[421] In the great halls, the young politicos of the North Atlantic world listened to a series of leaders: Prime Minister Harold Wilson of the United Kingdom; Lord Chalfont Alun Arthur Gwynne Jones, minister for Foreign and Commonwealth Affairs, and Pierre Mahias, General Secretary of the Atlantic Treaty Association.[422]

Later, Bursum and the others traveled to Brussels and Paris for briefings at the North Atlantic Treaty Organization (NATO) and Supreme Headquarters Allied Powers Europe (SHAPE). It was "the most interesting thing I've ever done," Bursum said in a report back to the *Albuquerque Journal*.[423] His time in Britain and on the continent had given him insights into evolving international relations. He saw the young Europeans' desire for what he described as a super-government, a United States of Europe. They knew the structures for such a union would not come quickly, but the first steps had been taken through closer trade agreements. More cooperation in the North Atlantic region also was on their agenda. The French conferees candidly wished for new leadership in their country to forge better binational and international relations. They appreciated President Charles de Gaulle and his wartime service to France, but they found his challenging posture toward the U.S. unhelpful. They knew he was popular at the polls and impossible to defeat. They would wait out his time of political power, Bursum said. The reunification of Germany also entered the discussions. Already, the Germans pointed out, the east and west sectors of their country were negotiating trade agreements.

When the formal sessions ended, the North Americans and Europeans paired up for more individual relationship building. The Bursums traveled on to Germany with their conference partner and now host Peter Corterier of Karlsruhe. They saw the post-war conditions in his country and noted the people's productivity and determination. Only twenty years had passed since the end of combat, but the destruction of World War II no longer could be seen, Bursum reported.[424]

In 1990, when Germany reunified and in 1992, when the European Union emerged from the Treaty of Maastricht, Holm and Earle Bursum could appreciate more than most Americans just how long the changes had been in process. Their friendship with Peter Corterier lasted a lifetime. They hosted him in New Mexico in the 1970s, showing him the Socorro area's intriguing convergence of an ancient past and a high-tech future and taking him to their ranch so near the Trinity site with its World War II implications.

Throughout their lives, both Corterier and Bursum would engage in public service. In the late 1960s, Corterier took a seat in the German parliament. Under Chancellor Helmut Schmidt in the early 1980s, he became deputy foreign minister and later served as secretary-general of the North Atlantic Assembly of NATO.[425]

Although Bursum pursued a career in private business, he served publicly in many capacities as well.⁴²⁶ In 1967, Governor David Cargo appointed him to the New Mexico Civil Defense Council, which he chaired. He and the legislators, military advisors, and educators on the council took up the charge of state preparedness in cases of military strikes and other disruptions to infrastructure and public health. In 1970, he received a White House appointment to the National Public Advisory Commission on Economic Development. That year, he and ex-Governor Tom Bolack became part of the National Advisory Board for the U.S. Small Business Administration. In the matter of elective offices, Bursum remained local. He served on the Socorro City Council from 1974 to 1978 and chaired the Socorro County Commission from 1981 to 1983. In 1995, he began his best public service work, chairing the New Mexico State Highway Commission for eight years.

In 1965, the many public roles of Peter Corterier and Holm Bursum III still lay ahead of them. When they said their goodbyes in Germany that summer, they were two young political actors, one twenty-nine, the other thirty, who had shown promise as leaders and a willingness to foster rapport within the post-war North Atlantic community.

Moving Home

Back from Europe, Holm and Earle finished up their time in Albuquerque. That fall, one of New Mexico's most famous political writers suddenly was gone. Will Harrison, fifty-eight, died of a heart attack in November.⁴²⁷ Although the columnist could ruffle feathers, Holm Bursum thought he was fair. He was willing to say he had misread a situation, as he had when he complimented the Young Republicans for getting the direct-primary referendum on the 1964 ballot and admitted he had thought they would fail. He would be missed for his incisive and highly readable commentary on the colorful politics and governance of New Mexico.

In their last month in Albuquerque, the Bursums still were making the news, but this time the focus was on Holm IV, five, and Elizabeth, four. A *Journal* photographer captured a storybook scene of the children intent on wrapping a gift for an upcoming Christmas gathering. Thirty Bursum and Powell family members were due in Albuquerque, and Elizabeth, in her classic smocked dress, and Holm IV, in his formal jacket, were getting ready. They were among the Albuquerque children caught up in the "mystery and secrecy" of the season, as the *Journal* phrased it.⁴²⁸ In the new year, the Bursum siblings' lives would change as they left a city of more than 200,000 to grow up in their father's hometown of 5,500.

In earlier days, Conrad Hilton had written that Socorro could stir a person. It still could. The old rivalry between it and Albuquerque to be New Mexico's predominant city was long over. Albuquerque had won, but the smaller city had more than its share of treasures with a highly-rated university and fine historic buildings. Not far away were the Alamo Navajo Reservation and vestiges of pre-contact Pueblo communities. The deserts, river lands, and mountains of the region offered places for economic development but also for national forests and wildlife preserves. Socorro looked in two directions: in one case, to a fascinating past of diverse Indigenous societies and European migration, and in the other, to an intriguing future of research into atmospheric physics and cosmic listening. Holm and Earle Bursum were going to spend the rest of their lives honoring both directions.

12

1966–1968: A Party Set to Celebrate

[T]he trend was toward a rule of 'one man one vote.'
—David Cargo[429]

Holm Bursum III and David Cargo had differed about the operation of the Young Republican Association for a short time in the early Sixties, but they had a common interest in the well-being of their party and state. Before long, their work would converge. In 1966, as Bursum settled into life in Socorro and became a vice president at First State Bank, Cargo was savoring an election victory and getting ready to move into the governor's mansion in Santa Fe. He was only the second Republican to win the gubernatorial office since 1928. In his new role, Cargo got ready to make his next contribution to the two-party system. Again, it would entail legislative reapportionment and districting, this time at the congressional level.

Holm Bursum: Settling in at Home

It probably was not lost on Holm Bursum that he might have been the one to go to Santa Fe at some point after having led New Mexico's Young Republican Association. A colleague, he recalled, was going to put his name in for the GOP's gubernatorial nomination, but Bursum had discouraged it. He would have been an excellent candidate. He knew politics and government, and he knew New Mexico in all the richness that his grandfather had outlined for President Taft in the statehood quest nearly sixty years before. The young Bursum also had name recognition throughout the state. He had visited every corner of it. As his national YR colleagues had known for some time, Bursum had a considered political philosophy and the interpersonal skills that would have made him an attractive presence in any electoral pursuit. When he was in his eighties, Bursum reflected on the governor's race that had not materialized. "I didn't have an organization, and I didn't have the money," he said. Then, his eyes twinkling, he added, "I think my father would have fired me. I had just started at the bank."

As Bursum stepped away from statewide political leadership, turned down high-level candidacies, and got ready to move home, he felt the change. He acknowledged that, as he and Earle were preparing to leave Albuquerque, they wondered how it would be to live in Socorro. "But about twenty minutes after we got here," he said, looking out at his town many years later, "we knew it was going to be fine." The couple would have two more children, Julia and Michael, and the third and fourth generations of Bursums would take their places in the life of the community.

The Bursums and Socorro soon were to lose one of their brightest lights, however. Betty Bursum died in 1969. She was sixty, a woman of great warmth and generosity, gone too soon. The mention of her name, to the present day, brings smiles and fond memories of her gracious presence. She had been in public service, but it was her personal touch that made her a legend. From acquiring wheelchairs for those who needed them to baking a cake for a family she knew was expecting visitors, Betty Bursum and her kindnesses still are part of people's stories.

A few years after his mother's death, Holm Bursum III began running for local offices, as his parents and grandfather had done. Combining his City Council and County Commission terms, he served for six years. He supported New Mexico Tech through foundation work, and like his grandmother and father, he accepted gubernatorial appointments to public boards. The young politico, who had organized all over New Mexico, returned home to apply his skills to new kinds of public work.

David Cargo: Making Changes in New Mexico's Congressional Elections

For his part, David Cargo got to work on the next one-person-one-vote campaign to bring better representation to the people. After he had helped secure state legislative districting, he began to focus on districts for New Mexico's two seats in the U.S. House of Representatives. Once again, the work was not going to be easy. Cargo was about to face the weighty opposition of the four men who made up the state's congressional delegation at the time.

  Cargo first raised the notion of congressional districting in 1965 while he still was a state legislator. He was no fan of the at-large system of electing New Mexico's representatives to the U.S. House. In other states, congressional candidates had to appeal only to people in their geographic districts, but in New Mexico, they had to appeal to the whole state. Naturally, the at-large system made it more difficult for a candidate from Cargo's minority party to win. The last Republican elected to the House from New Mexico was Albert G. Simms in 1928. Simms lost his reelection bid to Dennis Chavez in 1930 and returned home to Albuquerque to farm.[430] He soon was to marry his fellow member of Congress, Ruth Hanna McCormick of Illinois. She, the daughter of Ohio's Mark Hanna, had lost her reelection campaign also. As the Democratic Party rose to great power throughout the country, Albert and Ruth Simms built up their farm at Los Poblanos along the Rio Grande and patronized the arts. Simms died in 1964, having seen only Democrats fill his old New Mexico congressional seat all those years.

  Republicans were not the only candidates disadvantaged by New Mexico's at-large congressional elections. The absence of districts also weighed against candidates of Hispanic heritage regardless of party, Cargo thought. After Dennis Chavez moved on from the U.S. House to the Senate in 1935, no other members of his ethnic group won his old seat for over thirty years. The situation improved when New Mexico got a second congressional seat in 1942, and Antonio M. Fernandez and Joseph M. Montoya won elections to fill it. However, with New Mexico's changing post-war demographics, some worried that statewide congressional elections might go mainly to Anglos. In 1965, when Cargo introduced a congressional districting bill in the New Mexico House of Representatives, his coalition of backers included Hispanic legislators. "…[T]hey knew that it was extremely difficult for a Hispanic to get elected to Congress in at-large elections," Cargo said.[431] The coalition appreciated that districting would offer more opportunity for election success, he added.

  As Cargo prepared his bill, Congress was working on one to specify how states districted for House seats. New Mexico and Hawaii stood out as the only states still electing their members at large. Representative Emanuel Celler, a Democrat of New York, offered to exempt New Mexico in the bill, according to Congressman Tom Morris.[432] As it turned out, Morris might have benefited from the exemption. The congressman had been running successfully in at-large elections in New Mexico since 1958, but geographic districts could change his odds.

Back in Santa Fe, Cargo's districting bill ran into problems. Democratic Governor Jack Campbell did not favor it, nor did Speaker of the House Bruce King and other legislative leaders. However, a coalition of sixteen Republicans and twenty-six Democrats managed to pass it. Then the ax fell. Cargo recalled the situation vividly in *Lonesome Dave*.[433] After the passage of the bill, New Mexico's senators and representatives in Washington boarded flights and headed home, arriving in Santa Fe to talk with the legislators of their party. Promptly Cargo's bill was brought back to the floor. As the state representatives assembled in their chamber, they must have been quite aware of who was present in the gallery behind them. If they had turned to look, they would have seen a formidable foursome. U.S. Senators Clinton P. Anderson and Joseph M. Montoya and U.S. Representatives Tom Morris and E. S. Johnny Walker all took front row seats, watching as the New Mexico House voted again, Cargo remembered. The bill went down to defeat: fifty-seven to eighteen.[434] Most of the Democrats from the first vote evidently had come home.

Cargo, dismayed by the Democratic leaders' power play, was not finished. In 1967, he returned to the capitol as the newly-elected governor and reintroduced legislation to create two congressional districts. Eventually, the bill passed both houses of the legislature, and he signed it.[435]

New Mexico's powerful congressional delegation had resisted Cargo's reform. Nevertheless, two House districts had become a reality, and the Democratic leaders had big decisions to make. Senators Anderson and Montoya and others looked at the geography and considered the incumbents: Tom Morris and E. S. Johnny Walker. The two men had succeeded in at-large elections, but now the puzzle was how to assign each one to the district where he had the best chance to win. Morris, they agreed, would run in the northern district. Walker would run in the south.[436] Their strategy did not work. Morris, whose roots were in eastern New Mexico, was not able to run well enough in the northern counties of the state. He may have needed the southern counties to balance the vote, but they no longer were part of his constituency. Walker, despite having once lived in Silver City, did not win in the south.

Fabian Chavez, Jr., the well-regarded public servant of long standing, attributed his party's loss of both congressional seats in 1968 to serious miscalculations. Some went back several years, and it was no surprise that the problems involved the pre-primary convention. "The Democratic Party had set itself up for failure," Chavez claimed.[437] It might have been better to let congressional candidates arise out of a direct primary election instead of from conventions controlled by party leaders. The bosses, as it turned out, were not infallible.

Fabian Chavez offered biographer David Roybal a back story to explain 1968. In 1964 he, the majority leader of the New Mexico Senate, had entered the Democratic primary to run for Congress. He wanted to try for the seat that Representative Joseph M. Montoya would be vacating to run against Senator Ed Mechem, but Chavez had neither Anderson's nor Montoya's support. At the Democratic pre-primary convention, E. S. Johnny Walker, not Fabian Chavez, was the top vote getter. Chavez did get on the primary ballot by petitioning, but with the top leaders pulling for Walker, he did not prevail. Chavez believed that he would have won the at-large congressional seat if he had been supported to run in 1964. He also believed that he would have retained the districted seat against a Republican contender four years later, given his strength in the northern counties. Chavez was not alone in that assessment. Prominent Democrat James 'Bud' Mulcock stated that, if properly assigned to districts in 1968, Tom Morris and Fabian Chavez would have won and held their seats into the twenty-first century.[438]

Instead, in the 1968 election, the Democrats watched in great surprise as Manuel Lujan, Jr. won the northern congressional race and Ed Foreman the southern one. For the first time in forty years, Republican representatives from New Mexico were headed to the U.S. House. As David Cargo expected, the House races made an important point. The drawing of geographic districts apportioned by population could be good for congressional candidates of various ethnicities and for the two-party system.

Checking in on the Revitalization of the Republican Party

1968 was an excellent year to take stock of what had come of the Young Republicans' partnership with the senior party over the past seven years. In the general election, the following happened:

Presidential candidate Richard Nixon, who lost New Mexico in

1960, won it in 1968.
New Mexicans elected Republican David Cargo to his second term as governor.
Republicans Manuel Lujan, Jr. and Ed Foreman won the state's two congressional seats.
Republicans in New Mexico House races won 37% of the seats, up from 9% in 1959.[439]
Republicans in the New Mexico Senate held 40% of the seats, up from 13% in 1961.[440]

Just four years later, Republican Pete V. Domenici of Albuquerque made history in a statewide election. He had started his public service career back in 1966 as a member of the Albuquerque City Commission. Among his local causes was one that did not succeed—saving the iconic Alvarado Hotel from the wrecking ball in 1970. The magnificent building, the site of so many auspicious political events, had fallen, but new venues for history-making had opened up. It was a time when both major parties were on the move, and in 1972, Domenici became the first Republican in New Mexico elected to the U.S. Senate in thirty-eight years. He took the seat long held by Clinton P. Anderson, the lion of the Democratic Party. Anderson's health finally had forced his retirement. In Washington, DC, Domenici, like his predecessor, became a powerful figure. He chaired the Budget Committee and the Committee on Energy and Natural Resources and built a reputation for bipartisanship in pursuit of a balanced budget.[441] Domenici served for thirty-six years, leaving office as Anderson had—in retirement, not in defeat.

Reviewing New Mexico's Congressional Districts[442]

With districting in place, New Mexico's U.S. House races became less predictable and more exciting than they had been in a long time. After Republicans won both seats in 1968, Manuel Lujan, Jr. held his in District 1 for twenty years, but Ed Foreman in District 2 served only one term. In 1970, Foreman lost to Democrat Harold L. 'Mud' Runnels. Runnels, who worked in the petroleum industry, did well in the great southern expanse of mountains and deserts, farmlands and oil fields. He was from one of the region's richest corners—Lea County in the Permian Basin. As a conservative Democrat, he became undefeatable.

The evolution of District 2.

In August 1980, in the middle of a reelection campaign in which Runnels was unopposed, he died. Both parties scrambled to find candidates, but the GOP was out of luck. The state's attorney general, a federal judge, and an appeals court all agreed on that point. Since the Republicans had not nominated anyone in their primary to run against Runnels, they could not have a candidate on the ballot in November. It was then that Joe Skeen, the veteran GOP leader, attempted a stunning feat. The rugged fifty-three-year-old Hondo Valley rancher announced his campaign as a write-in candidate. It was a brilliant move. Skeen was a gregarious and skilled politician who had come within one to two points of winning the governorship in 1974 and 1978. He knew he was a viable candidate, but he had not entered the congressional race earlier in 1980 because, he implied, he had not felt the need. Harold Runnels "was [as] good a Republican as you can be and still be a Democrat,"[443] he explained in his amiable way. Through his write-in campaign, Skeen defeated both the Democratic Party's official nominee and Runnels' widow Dorothy, who, like him, was running as a write-in.

For the next thirty-eight years—from 1981 to 2019—Joe Skeen and his GOP successor, Steve Pearce, represented District 2 in all terms except one. That one term came about in 2008 when Pearce sought another office, opening the way for conservative Democrat Harry Teague to win the seat. Teague, a Hobbs oil-industry businessman, served only until his predecessor ran again. Steve Pearce reclaimed the seat by defeating Teague in 2010 and kept winning until he retired from Congress in 2019.

With Pearce not running in the 2018 election, Democrat Xochitl Torres Small performed a feat as impressive as Joe Skeen's nearly forty years before. The personable young woman with a dynamic campaign approach upset a pattern. She became the first woman and first person of Hispanic heritage to represent District 2. In other ways, she diverged from the standard that had been set. Previous representatives had had their origins on the east side of the state and had been in oil or ranching businesses. She, on the other hand, was a water rights attorney who had grown up in

Dona Ana County. Her more moderate political stands placed her to the left of her predecessors. In 2020, however, Torres Small lost her reelection bid to an ex-state legislator, one whose promise as a GOP candidate Holm Bursum had foreseen. The winner, Yvette Herrell, had honed a conservative message that resonated with the majority of voters. A realtor in Otero County and a member of the Cherokee Nation, Herrell has brought her own engaging approach and set of firsts to the representation of District 2.

The evolution of District 1.

District 1, which Manuel Lujan, Jr. first represented beginning in 1969, has had a very different history from its companion district in the south. The northern district was reconfigured in 1982 after New Mexico grew large enough to have a third representative in Congress. The new District 1 was no longer the expansive upper half of the state. It became geographically small but densely populated, consisting largely of Albuquerque. Lujan, transitioning to a mostly urban constituency, kept winning the seat. Over the years, the district has become competitive for both parties, but it was a showcase for GOP revitalization for a very long time. Lujan and his fellow Republicans Steve Schiff and Heather Wilson held the seat consecutively from 1969 to 2009.

The ethnic diversity among successful candidates for the District 1 seat also has been impressive. It began with Manuel Lujan, Jr.'s long tenure. His distant relative Michelle Lujan Grisham, a Democrat, also served District 1. Then in 2018, Deb Haaland won the seat, becoming one of the first women of Indigenous heritage to be elected to the U.S. Congress. Haaland had just been reelected in 2020 when President-elect Joe Biden nominated her to be secretary of the U.S. Department of the Interior. Her path from Congress to a presidential cabinet is one that at least four other New Mexicans have taken. Two of them, Albert Bacon Fall and Manuel Lujan, Jr., preceded Deb Haaland as head of the Interior Department.

The creation of District 3.

District 3, created in 1982, mirrors District 2 in that it leans heavily to one political orientation. The newest district, however, is inclined toward the Democratic Party. Only one time did voters send a Republican to the U.S. House. Covering northern New Mexico, District 3 includes part of the Navajo Nation and most of the Pueblos, as well as Santa Fe, Espanola, Taos, and the High Plains agricultural lands. Throughout the years, candidates of Hispanic heritage, such as Bill Richardson and Ben Ray Lujan, have done well in the district. In 2020, Teresa Leger Fernandez, an attorney with experience in tribal sovereignty and civil rights law, became the first woman to represent the district.

Overall, the creation of districts changed an old dynamic in New Mexico. From 1930 through 1966, the winners of U.S. House seats had been determined essentially by the Democratic Party. Furthermore, those perpetually victorious Democratic candidates often had been pre-selected at the party's pre-primary conventions where top leaders influenced who became House candidates. Since the leaders resisted geographic districting in favor of at-large elections, the old ways resulted in the power becoming concentrated in one region. In the fifty-six years between statehood and congressional districting, three-quarters of New Mexico's members of the U.S. House were men from the northern half of the state. When the 1968 reform created districts, the winning candidates' political, cultural, and geographic diversity increased immediately. And the unexpected kept happening. More women ran and won. Ultimately, the voters benefitted. When they could elect their representatives by district, people in various regions could express their political will more precisely. For that, David Cargo, one of New Mexico's prominent Young Republicans of the 1960s, could take his bow. He helped moved his adopted state toward more democratic representation.

By the late 1960s, New Mexico was en route back to a two-party system. Hoyt Pattison, an early success in that decade, reflected on the Young Republican (YR) movement.[444] The clubs gave young people opportunities to develop as leaders. As a YR chairman himself, Pattison practiced skills that prepared him for the state legislature. In his club, he dealt with some dissidents, he said, thereby learning how to further a group's goals despite an active few who tried to obstruct them. Several of his YR peers joined him in the legislature, including George Bannister, Frank Bond, Bob Johnson, and Ralph Pruitt. Their success was due in part to Holm Bursum III, Pattison stated, "...to his getting us organized."[445] The rebuilding of the young wing had helped the entire party, Pattison thought. As bonds grew stronger between the YRs and the senior party, the veteran politicians became great supporters of emerging young leaders. Edwin L. Mechem, in fact, was the key to Pattison's becoming chair of the Curry County Republican Party. "How do you say no to Ed Mechem?" he asked with a smile.[446]

The Young Republicans had set up clubs in most of New Mexico's counties and had taken on some of the senior party's legwork, as Holm Bursum had planned. Together, the party's two wings had done the critical work of finding candidates, raising funds, and encouraging voters. In the process, they had restored a political party, making it a solid intergenerational one where young people felt welcomed and encouraged to participate. When David Cargo's districting work created new opportunities in legislative and congressional races, both wings of the Republican Party were ready to make the most of them.

13

And Then: Seven Young Republicans in Middle Age and Beyond

Politics is just like flypaper. Once you get involved, you are stuck.
—Patricia Hutar, 1976[447]

As the Young Republicans in our story entered middle age, they continued their public work. They came out of the 1960s politically skilled, understanding the interplay of principle, power, and strategy in policymaking and resource distribution. Many branched out from partisan work to other kinds of civic engagement. All served in their own ways, some through elective or appointive positions or in partnership with those who held office. One moved into presidential campaigning and another into international electoral consulting. In the work of their later years, they produced some outstanding results. We follow seven of them with brief looks at their accomplishments: Patricia Hutar, Anderson Carter, David Cargo, Hoyt and Joy Pattison, and Holm and Earle Bursum.

Patricia Hutar

Holm Bursum's Young Republican colleague, Patricia Hutar, moved from national to international work in her forties.[448] It started with an appointment. In 1974, she was President Richard Nixon's choice to represent the U.S. on the United Nations Commission on the Status of Women. Nationally, she already had built her credentials as a women's rights advocate. Since 1969, she had served on the White House Task Force on Women's Rights, and, when the long-awaited Equal Rights Amendment (ERA) entered the ratification process, she supported it.

In the late 1970s, Hutar took her talents and perspectives on women's rights across the Atlantic to Geneva. She headed a bipartisan

U.S. delegation to draft the Convention on the Elimination of All Forms of Discrimination against Women (CEDAW). Governments ratifying CEDAW agree to establish and protect women's rights in civic and political areas. According to one researcher, Hutar was "a skilled negotiator," able to bring communist-bloc countries to an agreement on provisions.[449]

A decade later, Patricia Hutar teamed up with her partner from the Goldwater campaign, F. Clifton White, who had just created the International Foundation for Electoral Systems (IFES).[450] Through IFES, they worked with both emerging and older democracies in places like West and North Africa, the Middle East, and Eurasia. Hutar became vice president of the foundation board. The nonprofit still flourishes with bipartisan and international leadership and personnel. IFES consults globally to help make electoral systems more functional, ethical, and inclusive of those who have been marginalized, including women. It was a fitting affiliation for Patricia Hutar. From her days as a very young precinct captain in Chicago, she had worked for full citizen participation in the political process. Part of her legacy is an award in her name, which recognizes a public servant who has supported good democratic practices.

David Cargo and Anderson Carter

Back in New Mexico, "Big Anderson Carter roared into town like an East Side tornado," declared the *Alamogordo Daily News* in 1966.[451] Carter invited such analogies in his bold run against Senator Clinton P. Anderson that year. Although he won Anderson's home county, Carter lost the election. Buoyed up nonetheless, he decided to run for Senator Joseph M. Montoya's seat four years later. First, he had to win the primary, and there he faced David Cargo. Republicans, so rattled by Carter in 1964, had a clear ideological choice in 1970: left-of-center Cargo or quite-to-the-right Carter. The latter beat the former nearly two to one,[452] but in the general election, Carter lost to the liberal Senator Montoya. Montoya, who had taken New Mexico politics by storm himself as a young man, still was running strong in 1970.

Between and beyond his Senate races, Anderson Carter took up the cause of putting Ronald Reagan in the White House.[453] In 1968, he organized New Mexico for Reagan but could not deliver the party's full delegation to him as he had done for Goldwater. Carter had come up against the power of Edwin Mechem, who was heading the Nixon presidential campaign in the state. In 1976, when Reagan ran again, Carter was a regional director in his national campaign. On Reagan's third try in 1980, Carter rose to deputy chair of field operations. Leaving the campaign early, he returned to it only to head New Mexico's delegation to the Republican National Convention. When Reagan won the nomination on the first ballot, Carter went home. After more than sixteen years of zealous work with the GOP, he stepped off the political stage.

Anderson Carter was a considerable organizer in his new party, but for sheer success in getting elected as a Republican, David Cargo outperformed him. In 1966, Cargo transitioned smoothly from his second term as a state representative to the governor's office. He was a rarity in the state, a liberal-leaning Republican in high office. In 1968, to Cargo's surprise, his future opponent, the very conservative Anderson Carter, worked for his reelection in a contested gubernatorial primary race.[454]

Cargo's gubernatorial style was similar to the one that he had debuted as the Young Republican president. He was known as a colorful, unpredictable official who announced policy initiatives through the media and kept his staff off-guard in the process.[455] Despite an unorthodox style, Cargo achieved. He established libraries and state parks and built roads in rural areas. He helped revive the film industry in the state, and in good humor, took a bit part in a movie or two. He ran for office several more times in the 1970s into the 1990s, but his governorship was his last elected public service. His greatest legacy may be his work to see that New Mexicans had better legislative and congressional representation through districting and apportionment.

Hoyt and Joy Pattison[456]

Hoyt Pattison was one of the Young Republicans of the 1960s that Holm Bursum III often mentioned from his political organization years. Pattison, for him, was a model of a YR who succeeded in elective office and became a principled leader. From the Democratic eastside, Pattison brought his gift for bipartisan coalition-building to the two-party system. When he took a seat in the New Mexico House of Representatives in 1962, he learned how to operate in the extreme minority. Except for a fleeting, one-member majority in the early 1950s, Republicans had been the minority in the House since 1931. Not until the late 1970s, with Pattison's help, did the party achieve something close to sustained majority power.

In the spirit of strategic bipartisanship, Republicans in the House coalesced with right-leaning Democrats like John Mershon and George Fettinger of Otero County. The majority caucus then did not belong to the Democratic Party but to the Conservative Coalition. The Republicans held a greater number of seats in the coalition. Consequently, Pattison, as minority leader, had more influence in guiding legislation and influencing committee assignments than his position normally would have entailed.[457] The Conservative Coalition held through three sessions.

Hoyt Pattison spoke of those people who made his twenty-two years in legislative office productive and positive. Foremost was his wife. Gracious and graceful, Joy Pattison has had leadership roles in GOP groups since the 1960s. She served as an officer in her Young Republican Club, presided over her county Republican women's organization, and held office in the state Republican Women's Federation. For two decades, January was the month that she organized her family for the move to the state capital. Packing for a multi-week stay over two hundred miles away was one matter. Another was meeting with her four children's teachers to prepare for the young Pattisons' education during the sessions. The annual move became tiring, but the rewards were there. She befriended legislative spouses of both parties. They gathered regularly to enjoy the cultural offerings of Santa Fe, and their children formed new friendships. The Pattisons looked for the best in public life and were spared the worst. Families of elected officials sometimes say how painful life can be because of politically-motivated attacks on their loved ones. In their case, Joy Pattison said, it was not a problem. Her husband, known for his integrity, was not often a target of incivility.

The partnership of Joy Pattison in Hoyt Pattison's legislative career formed its solid foundation. The collegiality of other legislators also was important. Pattison remembered that Otero County's Vincent M. Lee, son of rancher Oliver Lee, helped orient him to his new world of lawmaking. Senator Lee, his face pleasantly weathered, his rancher's hat a part of his formal dress, took an interest in the freshman representative from Curry County. He noticed Pattison's early frustration with the drawn-out processes of lawmaking and advised the young man that patience and the passage of time could bring the results he was seeking. Other memorable colleagues included talented policy analysts Frank Bond, a Santa Fe attorney and rancher; George Buffett, a businessman and cousin of Warren Buffett, and Max Coll, a Young Republican from Roswell who became minority whip. Coll's service took a twist, however, as he changed location and parties. For most of his thirty-two years in the legislature, Max Coll was a Democrat from Santa Fe.

Throughout his political campaigning, Pattison lost two elections, his first and last. In 1960, when he initially ran, the state's east side did not have a strong base of Republican voters. In 1984, he lost his thirteenth race due to reapportionment. He had kept his seat through one reapportionment, but in a subsequent one, he did not. The changes had taken many of his old precincts out of his electoral reach.[458] His new district ranged from mid-Curry County to up to Union, taking in much of Quay in between. It pitted Pattison against Cliff Moreland, a Quay County Democrat who had served in the Conservative Coalition with him.

Pattison took the defeat well. He could look back on what he had done for the state and his High Plains region. He spoke especially about the financing of rural public education. He had a good relationship with the National Education Association of New Mexico. He helped schools in places such as Melrose, Grady, Elida, Floyd, Lovington, Clayton, Roy, San Jon, Logan, and Tucumcari.

After nearly a quarter of a century of public service, the Pattisons returned home to revitalize their farming business. It had suffered financially. In a conversation about the sacrifice that public service can be for an elected official, Hoyt Pattison added without a pause: "If you're honest." He rebuilt, but occasionally he has wondered how big his farming operation might have become if he had devoted full time to it—if he had limited his legislative work to just a few terms. At their pretty country home amid the lush green croplands of eastern New Mexico, Hoyt and Joy Pattison spoke about their long years as a family in public life. Although it cost them, they knew the value of the service they had taken on.

Holm Bursum III and Earle Bursum

A traveler on Interstate 25 between Socorro and Truth or Consequences will see a magnificent sculpture of steel and glass to the east, rising more than thirty feet above the desert floor. The sculpture and the complex beyond it are meant to evoke a journey along the ancient trail known as the Camino Real, the royal road that linked Mexico City with Santa Fe in Spanish colonial times. The trail was not new, even in the sixteenth century. It had been a trade route for Indigenous societies before the Europeans came to the western hemisphere. In the twenty-first century, Earle Bursum, serving on the Museum of New Mexico Board, helped illuminate the Camino Real story.

Continuing north on I-25 as it parallels the Camino Real, the traveler will come to a junction with a more modern road: Interstate 40 in Albuquerque. The interchange, known as the Big I, had become one of the nation's major bottlenecks in the 1990s. It was a hazard that affected both cross-country and inner-city traffic, and it needed a solution. Again, a Bursum played a role in a New Mexico road matter. Holm O. Bursum III, chair of the State Highway Commission, helped work out a solution that relieved congestion on the Big I.

Combining their years of service, Holm and Earle Bursum spent two decades in appointive positions—in one case to preserve New Mexico's history and cultures and in the other to support its economic development through a better highway system.

Improving Roads: Holm Bursum III, Chair of the State Highway Commission

His years with the New Mexico State Highway Commission were among his most satisfying, Holm Bursum was quick to say. His commitment to the commission stemmed from his interest in economic development, but possibly another element factored in. Highway projects may have tied into his love of work done under the big skies of New Mexico. Bursum was a banker who looked entirely at home behind his desk, but it is not hard to imagine him as the rancher that he had planned to be. All his life, he had the suntanned look of an outdoorsman, and his hands, well-manicured, still were the hands of one who knew how to work with them. As his biographer Ron Hamm said, Holm Bursum was a contractor at heart. He enjoyed operating earth-moving equipment and working on construction projects.

When Governor Gary Johnson appointed him to the New Mexico State Highway Commission in 1995, Bursum found his new passion. He formed a solid partnership with Pete Rahn, the secretary of the Department of Highways and Transportation. What they achieved in miles of road improvements is notable, especially because the communities' economies improved along with the pavement. The highway program's success is among the memorable stories in Ron Hamm's *The Bursums of New Mexico*, data-based and enlivened by the first-person accounts of Secretary Rahn, Chairman Bursum, and Governor Johnson.[459]

Bursum and Rahn understood the parochialism that could creep into state highway work. It meant that road improvements at times became political rewards. The two new officials preferred a more analytical systems approach. They looked for long-range economic development, and to that end, they invited bipartisan community input and buy-in through meetings held around New Mexico. They built innovative funding mechanisms and worked with contractors who had new ideas about road construction.

Among Bursum's and Rahn's better-known highway improvements were the big ones—the four-laning of U.S. Route 550 from Bernalillo to the Four Corners region, for example, and the reconstruction of the Big I in Albuquerque. There were other projects as well, ones that served communities away from the more urbanized areas of the state and that helped them develop economically. One such project, on U.S. Route 54, caught the attention of Economic Development Research (EDR) Group, a Boston-based company that examines development in the context of investment decisions, programming, and policy.

Reconstructing U.S. Route 54

Every road has its story. Those U.S. highways and interstates in New Mexico generally originate far away, passing through lands of great beauty and history and promise. U.S. Route 54 is one of the several long roads connecting the state with distant parts of the country. From western Illinois, Route 54 crosses the Mississippi and heads south and west. Nearly twelve hundred miles later, it ends in El Paso, Texas.[460] In New Mexico, the State Highway Commission decided to improve the stretch in Otero County from Alamogordo south to the Texas border.

For people in Otero County, U.S. Route 54 was vital. For over half a century, it had served both commercial and military purposes. It had been taking residents to El Paso's urban offerings, to large medical facilities, specialized shopping, and a busy airport. People also drove 54 en route to the international border, crossing at Ciudad Juarez to enjoy Mexico's markets, restaurants, and cultural events. In turn, the road brought people north to Otero County's attractions, to the glittering dunes of White Sands and to the evergreen forests of the Sacramento Mountains, where hiking, horse racing, and skiing drew people out of the desert.

U.S. 54 was as important to the military as it was to civilians. During World War II, the U.S. Army established an airfield in Otero County, which later became Holloman Air Force Base. A site for guided-missile development and tactical-combat training, Holloman brought in military personnel, scientists, and engineers from far beyond New Mexico. The nearby town of Alamogordo boomed. In ten years, its population more than tripled, from 6,783 in 1950 to 21,723 in 1960.[461] The local economy had become tied to what was happening at Holloman, and Holloman worked with Fort Bliss Army Post in El Paso. U.S. 54 linked the two facilities.

For all the purposes that it served, the rough road between Alamogordo and El Paso presented drivers with a narrow pavement and less than adequate shoulders. By the 1990s, it had become dangerous for the high volume of traffic that it carried daily. People who commuted from El Paso to work at Holloman felt the hardship, and the federal government considered transferring some of the Air Force programs to El Paso, Holm Bursum stated.[462]

In 1999, the State highway program under Bursum and Rahn got to work to reconstruct U.S. Route 54. In an environmentally-conscious move, the contractors used 1.5 million pounds of recycled tires as part of the asphalt mix. It was a first for New Mexico highway construction. In 2002, at a Highway Commission meeting in Ruidoso, Ford Motor Company gave the state a $200,000 check to cover the cost of the recycled rubber.[463] By 2001, a faster and safer four-lane highway replaced the old road, and a relief route reduced the traffic through Alamogordo.

In 2007, the EDR Group completed its assessment of New Mexico's investment in U.S. 54.[464] The American Association of State Highway and Transportation Officials (AASHTO) published the assessment as a case study. Not much time had passed between the project's completion and the study, but the economic indicators were encouraging. Using pre and post-project data, the researchers reported the following about Otero County:

The number of jobs increased by 6.67%.
Business sales increased by 10.47%.
Personal income per capita increased by $5,527 or 23%.
Property values as determined by median house value increased by 4.14%.

Some of the most noticeable benefits came from the new relief route.[465] Named for Charlie T. Lee of the Oliver Lee family, the route reduced congestion. As big trucks and other through-traffic vehicles were diverted from Alamogordo's White Sands Boulevard, the businesses there enjoyed safer access for their customers. The relief route did more than untangle traffic in town; it also stimulated new growth. PreCheck, Inc., a Houston-based company providing health-care worker background checks, established a branch along the route. As a result, 150 new jobs came to town. The very location played into the company's decision to set up shop in Alamogordo since new land along the route had been designated for development. State and local governments offered incentives as well. As recently as 2018, PreCheck was expanding the number of jobs in Alamogordo, and other businesses have located on or near the Charlie T. Lee Memorial Route.

Overall, economic distress in the county decreased during the study period, according to the ERD Group (now EBP). Some of that decrease could be attributed to highway improvements. Even before the study was published, the region had felt the impact of the work. The Otero County Commission and the Alamogordo Chamber of Commerce recognized the extent to which the New Mexico State Highway Commission had made U.S. 54 a route of safe travel and economic development. The county declared September 19, 2002 to be Holm Bursum III Day in appreciation of his leadership in highway improvement.[466]

Celebrating New Mexico's Past: Earle Bursum, Museum Regent

While the U.S. 54 improvements were underway, Earle Bursum was in the process of highlighting another road in New Mexico, a very old one. Her work, like her husband's, stemmed from an appointment. Governor Garrey Carruthers chose Earle Bursum to serve as a regent on the New

Mexico State Museum Board, and Governor Gary Johnson reappointed her. For twelve years, she helped oversee some of the state's treasures, including the Palace of the Governors on Santa Fe's plaza, the Museum of Fine Arts, and the Museum of Indian Arts and Culture.

The new regent, a student of history, was good at honoring the past. With her husband, she celebrated the heritage of their county, and they began by restoring an adobe house in Socorro. They turned the nineteenth-century structure into their beautiful family home, caring for the great old trees around it, making the courtyards into lush and shady retreats. They preserved other vintage buildings in town and commissioned murals. They helped publish books on New Mexico history and established a gallery of historic photographs at First State Bank. The gallery became a community project, with Socorroans offering their prized photos for copying and inclusion. The images show stunning scenes: a long-ago procession to the Church of San Miguel, as beautiful as an Ansel Adams; Geronimo at the rail station, quietly waiting, and the flooding of the Rio Grande in 1929, with San Marcial standing in a watery nightmare, soon to be a ghost town.

On property that they owned out of town, Earle and Holm welcomed an archaeological excavation. Headed by Dr. Michael Bletzer, the project uncovered ruins of perhaps the old Piro town of Teipana. The Bursums and the owners of adjacent lands, Charles and Jessie Headen and Barbara Remington, helped support the dig. As Paul Harden notes, Teipana may have been the very community that aided Juan de Onate and his advance guard of colonists in 1598—in essence, the first Socorro.[467] As artifacts emerged from the excavation, the Bursums agreed to serve as their custodians and shared them in public venues.

New Mexico architecture, art, literature, history, and archaeology all were part of Earle Bursum's life, and she brought her appreciation and hands-on experience to the regent's position. For a portion of her tenure, she served as the secretary-treasurer. She saw the New Mexico Museum through several gubernatorial administrations, a change of directors, and board differences over the very structure of the museum system.[468]

In 1998, the New Mexico Museum launched a project, one especially compelling for Bursum with her central New Mexico perspective. She and her colleagues worked with the legislative and executive branches to establish a state monument south of Socorro. It would celebrate an old trade route, the one known as El Camino Real de Tierra Adentro, the Royal Road of the Interior Land. The work of the Museum community and their associates brought spectacular results.

Some years before the monument's construction started, New Mexican scholars and government officials had approached their counterparts in Mexico to explore a common past. In 1994, they agreed to study the Camino Real together, and it launched a collaboration between the New Mexico Museum and El Museo Historico de Ciudad Juarez.[469] The work also led to shared archives in Zacatecas, student exchanges, joint archaeological digs, and more.

The imagined El Camino Real International Heritage Center began to materialize, and its position near the Camino Real became part of the message. Instead of being in Santa Fe or Albuquerque, it was to stand on a spot above the old road itself, the part called the Jornada del Muerto south of Socorro. The planners chose a soaring steel structure to announce the Heritage Center and the Jornada trail. In colors of rust and sky, with an opening like a gateway, the sculpture catches the eye from a distance and anticipates the trek along the Camino Real. The artist Greg Reiche, who grew up in Socorro, called his creation Camino de Suenos, Road of Dreams.[470]

Inside the Heritage Center, the design was meant to invite the public on a journey, one symbolizing the travels of European colonists coming from Mexico. The visitors first would enter a replica of the grand plaza of Zacatecas. It marked the point where the first colonizer, Don Juan de Onate, started his expedition under the authority of the Spanish Crown. From the Mexican plaza, in its terra cotta colonial richness, the visitors would begin their walk. Their destination would be a representation of Santa Fe's plaza at the end of the hall—a thousand miles in a few steps.

Museum curators began to assemble the goods of the bygone people of the Camino Real. The possessions of the colonists would be displayed: simple wooden furniture, dishes, trunks, books, santos, and retablos. From the Bursum, Headen, and Remington properties, Teipana's products would rest in glass cases: red and black pottery, metates, flutes, tools, and jewelry. The exhibits would tell stories—of the European people who boldly left the lands they knew for unknown ones and of the Indigenous people who had lived on those lands for a very long time. The products of Teipana indicate that the Piro people had done well in their Rio Grande region. They had been constructing homes, growing crops, transacting business, making music, governing, worshipping, and raising their children along a major trade route well before their contact with the Spanish colonists. When the beleaguered colonists did arrive, Teipana's residents had sufficient food and the graciousness to offer help.

Outside the Heritage Center, an observation deck would go up and an artist's vision of a ship's mast, a reference to the colonists' comparing the desert to an ocean. Beyond the deck, the famed Camino Real itself would be visible. Although traces of it are faint in the Jornada del Muerto, the Camino Real's story there has been coming to light, thanks to researchers and public servants like Earle Bursum. They helped show us that, before the Europeans came, Indigenous people had made a trail in the Jornada, away from the Rio Grande. It was a ninety-mile shortcut running parallel to the mountains but a risky one unless travelers knew the secrets for surviving it. The key was finding obscure water sources along the way.[471]

The Camino Real is among the oldest roads in North America, once extending from the southern Rockies to the Valley of Mexico and rich with intersecting routes. Carroll L. Riley evokes the extent of the many trails and their lively traffic in pre-contact times.[472] From his writings, we can imagine the arterial tracks that branched out in various directions from the main road. One, starting near Teipana and Pilabo, could take travelers west from the Rio Grande all the way through Arizona to Sonora's Pacific waters. En route, they would come to Zuni, a robust center of commerce, itself several days' walk from the Piro river towns. Along the complex of roads, Indigenous porters carried salt, ceramics, turquoise, garnets, and peridot from the Pueblo north and seashells, parrots, macaws, and copper bells from the Mexican south. Travelers also transmitted the ideologies and innovations of one society to another, creating a lively exchange network. The long trail and the arterial tracks had known many footsteps by the time the Spanish colonists arrived and claimed them as royal roads.

Once the Camino Real and other roads in the Americas became part of European empires, new people and products began to spread quickly between the two hemispheres. Along the Rio Grande, the Piro lands became involved in the global exchange. From the sixteenth century onward, the roads first established by Indigenous people "...placed New Mexico within the broad orbit of international trade," writes Gabrielle Palmer.[473]

On November 19, 2005, El Camino Real International Heritage Center opened its doors to share what had been learned about the old road. Throughout the day, nearly three thousand people showed up. Indigenous and Hispanic performers offered music and dance. Others demonstrated Navajo weaving, Pueblo arts, and colonial retablo painting. A matanza, the roasting of a pig in the centuries' old way, provided a feast for the occasion.[474]

For several years after that day, Earle Bursum served the center she had helped bring to life. Beyond her terms as a regent, she stayed active with El Camino Real International Heritage Center foundation. As part of her work, she selected books on the region's history and culture for the gift shop.

For twelve years, the public enjoyed taking that symbolic trip along the Camino Real from the plaza of Zacatecas to Santa Fe. Then in 2017, the State of New Mexico closed El Camino Real International Heritage Center as a cost-saving measure, but it still can be toured virtually. Thanks to the work of the Friends of El Camino Real Historic Trail, the center exists as text and image to present the ancient road to the visitor.[475] Even in cyberspace, it is an elegant, evocative, and educational complex, a part of Earle Bursum's legacy.

Working to Restore the San Miguel Mission and the Loma Theater

By 2003, both Holm and Earle Bursum had ended their formal service to the State of New Mexico. In 2014, Earle's death would conclude the coffee-only date that had brought the striking college senior together with her dashing Air Force captain. In their remaining years as a couple, they spent time with their beloved family, which came to include ten grandchildren. They enjoyed sports and other activities with their friends, to whom they offered great hospitality. Socorro's well-being always was high on their agenda. Holm continued as president and CEO of First State Bank and served on the New Mexico Tech Foundation Board. Earle stayed engaged with her Camino Real work.

San Miguel Mission and School

In 2013, the time came for the Bursums to join the community in restoring the San Miguel Catholic Church on El Camino Real Street. The old mission had stood on that spot for almost four hundred years, its beauty showing in the soft lines and warm colors of Pueblo-influenced design. Flanked by domed towers, it had opened its doors to many generations of Catholics in Socorro. In 2010, however, it closed due to structural problems. With help from the New Mexico Institute of Mining and Technology and other sources, planners applied to the Conrad N. Hilton Foundation for a grant to restore the church and associated buildings.

Holm Bursum was part of the project. As Cindy Lam, his executive assistant, remembered, "He spent numerous hours attending meetings, contacting individuals requesting funding, crunching numbers and putting together proposals, meeting with contractors and church officials, etc...."[476] He made a generous personal donation, and his work contributed to the project's completion in a timely and professional way. A Presbyterian, he was pleased to help with the restoration of a Catholic church, she said. The need was there, and he had resources. It was a good match. "And," she added, "he never wanted recognition for his good deeds. That's just how he rolled."

The Reverend Andrew J. Pavlak saw the appreciation that Holm Bursum had for Socorro's iconic old mission. Serving at San Miguel at the time, the clergyman knew Bursum as a bright, personable man, a helpful community partner in the church's restoration. He was like a pastoral figure in a secular context, Father Pavlak said, adding that he offered "great support and interest, and understanding." He recalled a statement that Bursum often made: "Whatever you need, let us know."[477]

The Hilton Foundation, a California-based humanitarian organization, granted $1.1 million to the Archdiocese of Santa Fe. In gratitude, the archdiocese recognized Holm Bursum III and his son Holm IV as having provided a connection to their cousin Steven M. Hilton, chairman of the foundation.[478] Steven Hilton had a particular interest—a grandfather from Socorro, a certain individual who in his young years often had gone to the San Miguel Catholic Church to pray.

The Loma Theater

In the secular sphere, Holm Bursum had his eye on another institution to revitalize, the Loma Theater. It had closed in 2014, and he wanted the people of Socorro to be able to enjoy evenings out at the movies again. The town had had a theater for films since 1912 or 1913, Paul Harden tells us.[479] First called the Guild and then the Gem, it had been about to occupy a new venue on the city plaza when the flu pandemic of 1918 hit. By order of the state, the theater remained closed for months. Its building was renovated in the '30s and renamed the Loma Theater. It thrived until it went up in flames in 1956—at the very moment that *The Day the World Ended* was on the screen. Fortunately, Harden writes, the audience evacuated without casualties. The fire prompted the theater's relocation in 1958 to the old

Price-Lowenstein Mercantile Building on Manzanares Street. The building once had been a store owned successively by two families. Then, the State of New Mexico used it for the National Guard Armory, and eventually, it housed the Loma Theater through a lease.

In 1972, the Bursums bought the Price-Lowenstein building. They entered into relationships with a succession of theater owners through nearly half a century of showing films to the people of Socorro. Over the years, as movie-going evolved, film rental companies and television were offering new options, and the audiences in theaters became smaller. The Bursums helped the Loma owners maintain a downtown facility by lowering the rent more than once, Harden states. In 1982, the Loma was remodeled to accommodate the scaled-down audiences and make more room for First State Bank next door. In 2008, the theater doors closed, but three years later, a new company bought the business. First State Bank remodeled the space again, adding new stadium seats, Holm (Cuatro) Bursum IV, said.[480] In 2014, however, the Loma shut down again. By then, it was a matter of technology; the management company did not have the equipment at the Loma to show digitalized first-run movies.

The Bursums explored ways to bring the Loma Theater back to the community. It led to a private/public partnership with the New Mexico Institute of Mining and Technology. With a lease of ten dollars a year from First State Bank, the school invested in upgraded equipment and found a new managing company. Tech students and all of Socorro once again had a movie theater. Michelle Lujan Grisham, a U.S. representative at the time, commended Tech President Stephen G. Wells for bringing the facility—now state-of-the-art—back to Socorro.[481]

On the evening of November 3, 2017, the Loma reopened with a street party hosted by New Mexico Tech, the City of Socorro, and First State Bank. The people came; food was plentiful; the hosts spoke. One of them was Cuatro Bursum, First State's chief operating officer. He shared the story of the theater and its restoration. The partners in its restoration, he said, had brought "...a little piece of Socorro history back to life." Then came his invitation: "Ladies and gentlemen, let's go to the movies."[482] The feature film *Thor: Ragnarok*, starring Christopher Hemsworth and Natalie Portman, was about to begin.

It was a perfect gift: a modern theater in a lovingly preserved building of the nineteenth century. Not far from the town's charming old plaza, near colorful restaurants and bars, the Loma was an ideal centerpiece for an evening out. A very pleased Holm Bursum III remarked that Socorro had gotten its magic back.[483] It was not a casual statement. There was something extraordinary about a town in a rugged desert land that—through raids and conquests, droughts and floods, revolts and displacements, economic booms and busts—has kept its communal heart beating for more than half a millennium.

As Patricia Hutar once said, "Politics is just like flypaper."[484] It is a compelling aspect of human society, and once individuals have involved themselves in political life, they are likely to be present for the long term. That was true of Holm Bursum III and many of his young colleagues of the 1960s. Although Bursum moved on to decades of less partisan public work and much nonpartisan community development, he was a mainstay of the Republican Party all his life. He figured prominently in the state campaigns of presidential candidates from Richard Nixon to George W. Bush.[485] He supported state and local candidates, mentoring some.

As part of his family legacy, he also inherited a seat at an extraordinary gathering of politicians in Albuquerque. He joined the OBs, a lunch group of Republicans who had been meeting since the mid-twentieth century. They had run for public office and lost their elections in the days of one-party governance. Long-time member Edwin L. Mechem, who had seen a few defeats, qualified for the OBs, as did Holm Bursum, Jr., who also had lost a share of races. As the years passed, Mechem became a highly regarded federal district judge and Bursum, Jr., a beloved retired mayor. The OBs granted Holm III a place at the table during the years he drove his father to Albuquerque to lunch with them. After the older Bursum died in 1989, Holm III came to occupy his seat as a full member. He still was attending the OB gatherings in 2018.

It was an elegant positioning of Holm O. Bursum III as a young political leader in New Mexico's fifth decade. He was the grandson of a man who worked to create the state government in 1910 and the protégé of another who had helped restore its integrity in the 1950s. It gave the young Bursum a unique perspective but not a driving desire for high office himself. He was similar to his mentor Edwin Mechem in that way. Mechem ran only under sustained pressure, and Bursum turned down all but local races. Two political men, a generation apart, preferred supporting candidates to being candidates. They seemed to enjoy what it took to rebuild the GOP from the ground up. They canvassed the state they loved, going to the farmlands and ranchlands and to the small towns and urban centers in search of voters, volunteers, and contestants for a sustainable two-party system. Vibrant political engagement meant better government in their view, and in their words and deeds, they were good for New Mexico.

Epilogue

...I love this land of sunshine, its rocks and rills, its plains and hills, its peoples and their traditions.
—The first Holm O. Bursum, in a speech on New Mexico statehood in 1906[486]

On the chilly morning of December 11, 2018, the Garcia Opera House on Abeyta Street in Socorro opened its doors to a subdued gathering. The building itself symbolized the delight that the Bursum family had long taken in New Mexico and its cultures. More than a hundred years before, the first Holm Bursum bought the Opera House.[487] It was a long and rather grand structure of thick adobe walls, twenty-foot ceilings, wooden floors, fluted columns, and murals personifying music and drama. The building had materialized in the 1880s, the vision of businesswoman Francisca Garcia, who dreamed of bringing traveling opera companies to Socorro. After her ownership, it passed to another and then to the Bursums. For years, it served as a community center for gatherings as varied as GOP conventions, college basketball games, high school graduations, and wedding balls. Eventually, a feed store and a skating rink came to occupy it. Then, in the late 1950s, it turned into a storage space for the community.

In 1983, Bursum's son, Holm, Jr., wanted to restore the old building. He applied to the New Mexico Historical Society for a grant and matched it. As the renovation proceeded, he spared no expense to make the opera house the best it could be. The process captivated him. "You get excited," he said. "All the workers became historians and restoration experts. It's been a lot of fun."[488] The Garcia Opera House came alive again for Socorro. It was a grand venue once more, the place for plays, concerts, banquets, and weddings—and in 1989 for the funeral of Holm Bursum, Jr. himself.

Twenty-nine years later, the funeral of his son Holm Bursum III was about to begin, and people from all parts of New Mexico filed into the Opera House. Among them were a future congresswoman, federal district judges, state legislators, business associates, and friends—all to join the family and people of Socorro in contemplating their loss. Soon every seat was taken, and people lined the walls of the old hall. Eulogies came from Bursum's children and from colleagues—tributes to a warm and loving father, an upright and affable community partner, and a generous benefactor. One memory from Lieutenant-Governor John Sanchez reflected Holm Bursum's sustained stature in political life. Early in his electoral pursuits, Sanchez, a young Albuquerque businessman, was advised that there was "a man in Socorro" he needed to meet.[489] It was a charming anecdote, one that more than a few young candidates could tell. Holm Bursum had become the kind of party elder he had appreciated when he was their age.

He was a man with "plans, projects, interests," Michael Bursum said of his father, acknowledging that the family had had little time to prepare for his passing. Many of his projects involved the common good. He had taught his children, his son said, "...that life is not about hoarding wealth but sharing your time, talents and resources."[490] Not even two months before, Holm Bursum, at age eighty-four, had been operating a backhoe on a construction project. He had started the work with his son Cuatro Bursum, with jobs for Socorro in mind. He prized his town—always and in all its expressions, from Pilabo to the community of his own time. He had his family's love of the land and people, voiced by his grandfather Bursum in his 1906 take on Samuel Francis Smith's "My Country, 'Tis of Thee."

Only weeks before he died, Holm Bursum III had been making his daily trip from home to First State Bank. He was a community banker with the caring concern for local development and philanthropy that the label implies.[491] Beyond the label was character. Cindy Lam spoke of him in his professional life.[492] He had classic notions of honesty and circumspection. Generosity was another lived value. People came to know of his work on big community projects, Cindy Lam said, but his small acts of kindness, which others did not see, were the most impressive to her. "I was fortunate enough to sit next to him and witness the little things that he did for so many," she said. He would never imply that they were of lesser status "... because they were in need. He would look them in the eye, shake their hand and wish them well," even in cases where he knew they "had no way of repaying him," she remembered. He was kind to everyone regardless of their backgrounds or political beliefs, and his example affected her life:

> Watching how he treated others literally made me change the way I think and behave toward others. He taught me that you can disagree with someone and still respect their point of view and if you listen long and hard enough, you might even learn something from them.... He genuinely lived what he believed and was the most humble man, other than my own father, that I have ever known.[493]

An image remains of one of Holm Bursum's walks through the bank lobby in his last year of life. An observer would notice the tall, robust man, his dark hair silvered, making his way through the spacious room. One by one, as customers and employees look up and see him, lights come on—in people's eyes and in their smiles. They offer him hellos, addressing him as "Mr. Bursum." He returns the greetings with equal warmth, by name, and frequently in Spanish. He has a natural dignity and an appealing modesty. In his unassuming way, he probably has not fully realized the impact of his life on the people and institutions to whom and to which he has given his best.

NOTES

Chapter 1. A Young Challenge to One-Party Politics

1. Ron Hamm, *The Bursums of New Mexico: Four Generations of Leadership and Service* (Socorro, New Mexico: Manzanares Street Publishing, 2012), 345.
2. Rosa Walston Latimer, *Harvey Houses of New Mexico: Historic Hospitality from Raton to Deming* (Charleston, SC: The History Press, 2015), 28.
3. Frederick C. Irion, "The 1962 Election in New Mexico," *The Western Political Quarterly*, 16, no. 2 (1963): 449, http://jstor.org DOI:10.2307/444959.

Chapter 2. The First Bursums in a New and Ancient Land

4. Hamm, *The Bursums of New Mexico*, dedication page.
5. J. Bart Campbell, "Senator Started Life as a Bottle Washer," I.N.S. [International News Service], *The Oregon Daily Journal*, November 27, 1921, newspapers.com.
6. Meskwaki Nation, "Meskwaki: A Brief History," accessed June 14, 2020, https://meskwaki.org/about-us/history/.
7. Campbell, "Senator Started Life as a Bottle Washer;" Holm Bursum, Jr., interviewed by Martina Franklin, transcript, Socorro County Historical Society, Oral History Tapes, 1, accessed August 3, 2018, http://socorro-history.org/ARCHIVES/h_bursum_jr01.pdf.
8. Holm Bursum, Jr., interview.
9. Ibid.

10. Ibid.
11. Campbell, "Senator Started Life as a Bottle Washer."
12. Ibid.
13. "The Death of Mrs. C. L. Wolfinger at Los Angeles," *Alamogordo News*, May 19, 1932, newspapers.com.
14. Campbell, "Senator Started Life as a Bottle Washer."
15. Paul Harden, "Apache Warriors—Part 1," accessed June 4, 2019, http://socorro-history.org/HISTORY/PH_History/200903_apache01.pdf. Published by *El Defensor Chieftain*, March 7, 2009.
16. Paul Harden, "Teipana Pueblo—The First Socorro, Part 1," accessed May 15, 2019, http://socorro-history.org/HISTORY/PH_History/201207_teipana_1.pdf. Published by *El Defensor Chieftain*, July 14, 2012; "Teipana Pueblo—The First Socorro, Part 2," accessed May 15, 2019, http://socorro-history.org/HISTORY/PH_History/201208_teipana_2.pdf. Published by *El Defensor Chieftain*, August 4, 2012.
17. Paul Harden, "Mission Churches—Part I: The Mission Churches in Socorro County," accessed June 21, 2019, http://socorro history.org/HISTORY/PH_History/200708_missions1.pdf. Published by *El Defensor Chieftain*, August 4, 2007.
18. Ibid.
19. Conrad N. Hilton, *Be My Guest* (New York: Simon and Schuster, 1957), 26.
20. Hamm, *The Bursums of New Mexico*, 11-12.
21. Holm Bursum, Jr., interviewed by Martina Franklin.
22. Ibid.
23. David L. Caffey, *Chasing the Santa Fe Ring: Power and Privilege in Territorial New Mexico* (Albuquerque: University of New Mexico Press, 2014), 190.
24. Robert W. Larson, *New Mexico's Quest for Statehood: 1846-1912* (Albuquerque: University of New Mexico Press, 1968), 196.
25. Donald R. Moorman, "A Political Biography of Holm O. Bursum: 1899-1924" (PhD diss., University of New Mexico, 1962), 23-24, 27-28, accessed July 6, 2020, https://digitalrepository.unm.edu/cgi/viewcontent.cgi?article=1245&context=hist_etds.
26. Caffey, *Chasing the Santa Fe Ring*, 191.
27. U.S. House of Representatives, "Overview of New Mexico Politics, 1848-1898," New Mexican Politics, History, Art & Archives, accessed May 30, 2019, https://history.house.gov/Exhibitions-and-Publications/

HAIC/Historical-Essays/Continental-Expansion/New-Mexican-Politics/.

28. David V. Holtby, *Forty-Seventh Star: New Mexico's Struggle for Statehood*, (Norman: The University of Oklahoma Press, 2012), 246-247.

29. Language Policy Web Site, "Language Rights and New Mexico Statehood," U.S. Commission on Civil Rights, accessed June 11, 2019, www.languagepolicy.net/archives/nm-con.htm.

30. Ibid.

31. "Andrews Named for Delegate," *Albuquerque Journal*, September 30, 1906, newspapers.com.

32. Ibid.

33. Richard Melzer, "Life in the Luna Mansion: Valencia County's 'Downton Abbey,'" accessed October 8, 2018, http://www.news-bulletin.com/news/features/life-in-the-luna-mansion-valencia-county-s-downton-abbey/article_248f7f64-ccbb-11e8-a1b6-0319292ca21f.html.

34. "Andrews Named for Delegate."

35. "Andrews on First Ballot," *Albuquerque Journal*, September 29, 1906, newspapers.com.

36. "Andrews Named for Delegate.

37. "Hon. W. H. Andrews Renominated for Delegate to Congress;" "Continued as Chairman," *Albuquerque Citizen*, October 1, 1906, newspapers.com.

38. Hamm, *The Bursums of New Mexico*, 83-84.

39. "What Statehood Advocates Claim," *Arizona Daily Star*, August 29, 1905, newspapers.com.

40. Ibid.

41. Ibid.

42. Larson, *New Mexico's Quest for Statehood*, 250.

43. Donald R. Moorman, "A Political Biography of Holm O. Bursum: 1899-1924," 108-109.

44. Hamm, *The Bursums of New Mexico*, 86-87.

45. "Odessan's Father in 'Western Hall of Fame,'" *The Odessa American*, August 2, 1965, newspapers.com.

46. Hamm, *The Bursums of New Mexico*, 86-87.

47. Ibid., 87.

48. Larson, *New Mexico's Quest*, 261-262.

49. Ibid.

50. "Good Will Taft's Word to Indians," *The Indianapolis Star*, October 16, 1909, newspapers.com.

51. "Good Will Taft's Word to Indians."
52. William A. Keleher, *The Fabulous Frontier: Twelve New Mexico Items* New Edition. Santa Fe, New Mexico: Sunstone Press, 2008, 220.
53. Ibid., 220-221.
54. "Taft at Banquet Reaffirms and Emphasizes His Statehood Promise," *The Santa Fe New Mexican*, October 16, 1909, newspapers.com.
55. Ibid.
56. Ibid.
57. Melzer, "Life in the Luna Mansion."
58. "Taft at Banquet Reaffirms."
59. Gordon R. Owen, *The Two Alberts: Fountain and Fall* (Las Cruces, New Mexico: Yucca Tree Press, 1996), 365.
60. C. L. Sonnichsen, *Tularosa: Last of the Frontier West* (Albuquerque: University of New Mexico Press, 1960), 69.
61. Keleher, *The Fabulous Frontier*, 217.
62. Ibid., 221-222.
63. Ibid., 222.
64. Ibid.
65. Ibid., 224.
66. Owen, *The Two Alberts*, 364.
67. Charles H. Harris III and Louis R. Sadler, *The Secret War in El Paso: Mexican Revolutionary Intrigue, 1906-1920* (Albuquerque: University of New Mexico Press, 2009), 1.
68. Donald Moorman, "A Political Biography of Holm O. Bursum," 97.
69. "Ready for Presidents," *El Paso Times*, October 10, 1909, newspapers.com.
70. "Fear of Plot on Taft's Life," *Indianapolis Star*, October 16, 1909, newspapers.com; "Taft and Diaz to Be Killed?," *The Brownsfield Herald*, October 15, 1909, newspapers.com.
71. "Ready for Presidents;" "Fluttering of Flags, Gathering of Soldiers Precede the Presidents," *El Paso Times*, October 12, 1909; "Throngs Already Begin to Arrive for the Event," October 13, 1909, *El Paso Times*; "Mr. Taft's Visit at El Paso," *The Deming Headlight*, October 15, 1909; "Taft and Diaz Make History for Two Great Nations," *El Paso Morning Times*, October 17, 1909. From newspapers.com.
72. "Ready for Presidents;" "Taft and Diaz Make History;" "Presidents Taft and Diaz Meet in El Paso," *The Roswell Daily Record*, October 16, 1909, newspapers.com.

73. Hamm, *The Bursums of New Mexico*, 93.
74. Owen, *The Two Alberts*, 368.
75. Richard Melzer, "'Safe and Sane' for Statehood: Making the New Mexico State Constitution of 1910," *Sunshine and Shadows in New Mexico's Past: Volume III, The Statehood Period*, R. Melzer, Ed. (Los Ranchos, New Mexico: Rio Grande Books, 2012), 26; F. Chris Garcia, Paul L. Hain, Gilbert St. Clair, and Kim Seckler (eds.), *Governing New Mexico* (Albuquerque: University of New Mexico Press, 2006), 27.
76. Melzer, "'Safe and Sane' for Statehood," 23.
77. Larson, *New Mexico's Quest for Statehood*, 281.
78. Ibid.
79. Ibid.
80. Joseph P. Sanchez, Robert L. Spude, and Art Gomez, *New Mexico: A History* (Norman: University of Oklahoma Press, 2013), 195.
81. Melzer, "'Safe and Sane' for Statehood," 35.
82. Hilton, *Be My Guest*, 65-66.
83. Ibid., 71-72.
84. Ibid., 73.
85. Hamm, *The Bursums of New Mexico*, 110-117.
86. Charlotte T. Whaley, *Nina Otero-Warren of Santa Fe* (Santa Fe, NM: Sunstone Press, 2007), 95-98.
87. Guthrie Smith, "Enthusiasm Runs High as Heads of Republican Ticket Tour Mora County," *The Columbus Courier*, September 22, 1916, newspapers.com.
88. Guthrie Smith, "Northeastern Part of the State Promises Majorities for the Republican Ticket," *The Columbus Weekly Courier*, October 27, 1916, newspapers.com.
89. "Bursum's Campaign for Governor Now Becoming Like a Triumphal March," *The Deming Headlight*, November 3, 1916, newpapers.com; "Mexico—New Mexico—and Wilson," *Western Liberal* (Lordsburg), November 3, 1916, newspapers.com.
90. Hamm, *The Bursums of New Mexico*, 120.
91. Owen, *The Two Alberts*, 404.
92. Hamm, *The Bursums of New Mexico*, 158-159.
93. "Mrs. Lowden Wins Hearts of New Mexico Women with Her Gracious Personality at State Reception," *Albuquerque Journal*, February 12, 1928, newspapers.com.
94. Ibid.

95. "Republican Women Finish Organization of State Council," *Albuquerque Journal*, April 26, 1931; "State Council of Republican Women Plans to Conduct Political School in Fall," *Albuquerque Journal*, July 12, 1931, newspapers.com.
96. Simon Kropp, *That All May Learn: New Mexico State University, 1888-1964* (Las Cruces: New Mexico State University, 1972), 229-261.
97. Linda Fresquez, "Book about Former NMSU Leader Hugh Milton to Debut at Homecoming," NMSU News Center, October 15, 2015, accessed August 3, 2019, https://newscenter.nmsu.edu/Articles/view/11455/book-about-former-nmsu-leader-hugh-milton-to-debut-at-homecoming.
98. Kropp, *That All May Learn*, 253-254; "Degree of Law Doctor for Murphy," *Las Cruces Sun-News*, May 21, 1939, newspapers.com.
99. "State College Investigation Order: Governor Says Will Look into Matter," *The Gallup Independent*, May 25, 1939, newspapers.com.
100. Kropp, *That All May Learn*, 260.
101. "State College Control Listed as Weakness," *Albuquerque Journal*, April 10, 1940, newspapers.com.
102. "Mrs. Bursum Says She'll Not Resign," *Albuquerque Journal*, April 12, 1940, newspapers.com.
103. "New College Regents Get NCAC Report," *El Paso Herald-Post*, April 16, 1940, newspapers.com.
104. Ibid.; "Mrs. Bursum Quits Board," *Albuquerque Journal*, April 19, 1940, newspapers.com.
105. Kropp, *That All May Learn*, 260-261; "New College Regents Get NCAC Report;" "Aggie Regent, Mrs. Bursum, Resigns Post," *El Paso Times*, April 20, 1940, newspapers.com.
106. Michael Bursum, email correspondence to author, July 21, 2019.
107. "GOP Executive Group Named," *Albuquerque Journal*, July 11, 1941, newspapers.com.
108. "Late New Mexico Rancher Named to Hall of Fame," *Albuquerque Journal*, June 28, 1965, newspapers.com; National Cowboy and Western Heritage Museum, "Hall of Great Westerners," accessed March 25, 2020, https://nationalcowboymuseum.org/hall-of-great-westerners/.

CHAPTER 3. DEMOCRATIC DOMINANCE: ONE-PARTY RULE IN THE 1930S AND 1940S

109. Frederick C. Irion, "The 1962 Election in New Mexico," *The Western Political Quarterly,* 16, no. 2 (1963): 449, http://jstor.org. DOI:10.2307/444959.
110. William A. Keleher, *Memoirs: 1892–1969, A New Mexico Item.* New Edition. Santa Fe, New Mexico: Sunstone Press, 2008, 135-136.
111. David Roybal, *Taking on Giants: Fabian Chavez Jr. and New Mexico Politics* (Albuquerque: University of New Mexico Press, 2008), 159-160.
112. New Mexico Legislature, "Political Composition—Legislative Sessions," accessed April 24, 2018, political_composition_since_statehood.pdf (nmlegis.gov). Office of the Secretary of State, Dianna Duran and Project Coordinators Patricia Winter and Karen Turri, *New Mexico Blue Book,* July 2015, Santa Fe, NM, accessed April 25, 2018, https://www.sos.state.nm.us/about-new-mexico/publications/blue-book/#. (Data on governors, secretaries of state, and attorneys general from the *Blue Book*, pages 179-180, 186, and 191, were compiled by Dan D. Chavez.)
113. Roybal, *Taking on Giants*, 75.
114. Keleher, *Memoirs*, 136, 139.
115. Ibid., 139-140.
116. Ibid., 140.
117. New Mexico Public Broadcasting Service, "Colores: The Tingleys," Michael Kamins, Producer, May 31, 1995, accessed June 13, 2019, https://www.newmexicopbs.org/productions/colores/clyde-carrie-tingley-of-new-mexico/.
118. Keleher, *Memoirs*, 140-141, 144-145.
119. "A Fateful Week," *Albuquerque Journal,* September 26, 1938, newspapers.com.
120. "Bursum Declares for Referendum on Primary," *Clovis News-Journal,* August 12, 1938, newspapers.com.
121. Suzanne Stamatov, "There Was a Time and It Was Tingley's," January 11, 2013, accessed May 19, 2019, https://newmexicohistory.org/?s=Clyde+Tingley. [Stamatov attributes the title to D. Ullrich Johnson from an article published in 1983.]
122. Roybal, *Taking on Giants*, 114-115, 95.
123. Keleher, *Memoirs*, 141-147.
124. Ibid., 148.
125. "Tingley Urges Platforms," *The Santa Fe New Mexican*, July 31, 1940; "Tingley Will Throw Hat in Ring for Governorship," *Clovis News-*

Journal, July 21, 1940. From newspapers.com.

126. "Six State Officials Indicted by Jurymen," *The Gallup Independent*, September 5, 1942, newspapers.com.

127. "Jurors Thanked by Judge Chavez," *Albuquerque Journal*, September 5, 1942, newspapers.com.

128. "State Press Comment: Liquor Dealers Intimidated?," *Albuquerque Journal*, May 9, 1950, newspapers.com; "Only 500 Dealers Got Vote Letters, Montoya Says," *Albuquerque Journal*, May 1, 1950, newspapers.com.

129. "State Press Comment: Buying Insurance from Politicians," *Albuquerque Journal*, July 30, 1950; Sanky Trimble, "State Machine to Back Miles for Governor," *The Santa Fe New Mexican*, February 2, 1950; R. L. Chambers, "Under the Capitol Dome," *Carlsbad Current-Argus*, March 5, 1950; Bob Brown, "Believes His Friends Helped Miles—Out," *The Santa Fe New Mexican*, November 12, 1950; Will Harrison, "No Bass Here, Just Us Suckers," *Las Vegas Daily Optic*, November 29, 1962; Joe Clark, "Capitol Slant," *Albuquerque Journal*, January 1, 1948. From newspapers.com.

130. Keleher, *Memoirs*, 149-152.

131. Paula Moore, *Cricket in the Web: The 1949 Unsolved Murder That Unraveled Politics in New Mexico* (Albuquerque: University of New Mexico Press, 2008).

Chapter 4. Republican Persistence: Cracks in the One-Party System

132. "GOP Leader Says Party Is Dead in New Mexico," *Albuquerque Journal*, November 14, 1948, newspapers.com.

133. "Young Republicans: The Lincoln Club of Roswell in Its New Quarters," *Albuquerque Citizen*, September 23, 1902; "Young Republicans Enjoy Pleasant Evening," *The Spanish American* (Roy, New Mexico, September 3, 1910; "Young Republican Voters Flock to Join County Clubs," *The Columbus Weekly Courier*, September 22, 1916; "Branch of the Young Republicans' League Formed at Santa Fe," *Albuquerque Journal*, January 16, 1920. From newspapers.com.

134. "Young Republicans Insist on 3 G.O.P. Women and Henry Sandoval as Price for Fusion," *Albuquerque Journal*, October 9, 1926, newspapers.com.

135. "Huge Republican Rally Here Closes Campaign; Victory Is Predicted," *Albuquerque Journal*, November 2, 1926, newspapers.com; "The County Result," *Albuquerque Journal*, November 4, 1926, newspapers.com.
136. "Chacon Head of Young Republicans," *The Santa Fe New Mexican*, August 21, 1944, newspapers.com.
137. "GOP Leader Says Party Is Dead in New Mexico," *Albuquerque Journal*, November 14, 1948, newspapers.com.
138. Ibid.
139. "Young Republican Club Forms Brigade," *The Deming Headlight*, March 10, 1950, newspapers.com.
140. Holm Bursum, Jr., interview.
141. "Young Bursum Leads 'Work and Sweat' Drive of Board to Rehabilitate Socorro County," *Albuquerque Journal*, August 24, 1941, newpapers.com.
142. Ibid.
143. Ibid.
144. "Brisk Fight Seen in Polls," *The Santa Fe New Mexican*, March 17, 1944; "GOP Takes Santa Fe, Las Cruces, and Raton," *The Santa Fe New Mexican*, April 5, 1944; "Santa Fe Grand Jury Indicts Six in Probe of Expense Accounts, Sharply Censures Miles," *Albuquerque Journal*, September 5, 1942. From newspapers.com.
145. "Gunderson Gives 'Hands Off' Pledge," *Albuquerque Journal*, May 12, 1944, newspapers.com.
146. Hamm, *The Bursums of New Mexico*, 196-198.
147. Morley Warren, "Democrats Fight It Out at Hobbs, Roswell; Republicans Take Socorro," *Las Cruces Sun-News*, April 7, 1948; "State Leaders Watch City Votes Update for Signs of a Trend," *Las Cruces Sun-News*, April 6, 1948; "Socorro Demos Lose in GOP Upset," *Albuquerque Journal*, April 7, 1948. From newspapers.com.
148. "Protecting the Public Purse," *Albuquerque Journal*, June 29, 1948, newspapers.com.
149. Roybal, *Taking on Giants*, 113-133.
150. "Pre-Primary Convention Gives Power Back to Parties," *Carlsbad Current-Argus*, March 15, 1949, newspapers.com; Art Morgan, "Long Fight against Suspension of Pre-Primary Convention Law Collapses, Attorneys Concede," *The Santa Fe New Mexican*, October 26, 1949, newspapers.com.

151. "State Police Escort Quip Stirs Retort," *Albuquerque Journal*, June 9, 1949, newspapers.com.

152. Ibid.

153. "State Press Comment: Using Good Sense," *Albuquerque Journal*, October 30, 1950, newspapers.com.

154. "Pickett Blasts Pre-Primary Law," *Albuquerque Journal*, April 28, 1949, newspapers.com.

155. Howard J. McMurray, "The 1954 Election in New Mexico," *The Western Political Quarterly, 12*, No. 4 (1954): 619, http://jstor.org DOI 10.2397/442814.

156. R. David Myers, "Making New Mexico Modern: Political Reforms of the 1960s," *Sunshine and Shadows in New Mexico's Past: Volume III, The Statehood Period*, R. Melzer, Ed. (Los Ranchos, New Mexico: Rio Grande Books, 2012), 100.

157. "Johnson Joins Chavez Camp at Rally Here," *Albuquerque Journal*, June 6, 1950, newspapers.com.

158. "Edwin Mechem, Jr. Wins Out in Dona Ana County," *Alamogordo News*, November 28, 1946, newspapers.com.

159. Edwin L. Mechem, interviewed by Emlen Hall and Maureen Sanders, unpublished transcript, May 28 (1997): A, 3-4; Judith L. Messal, "The Electoral Surprise of Mid-Century New Mexico: Edwin L. Mechem, Dennis Chavez, and the Gubernatorial Campaign of 1950," *Southern New Mexico Historical Review* XXIII, January 2016, 1-10.

160. Roybal, *Taking on Giants*, 123.

161. O. Hoyt Pattison, interviewed by the author, August 30, 2018.

162. Ibid.

163. "Mechem, Mason Hurl Charges at Miles Machine," *Las Cruces Sun-News*, November 3, 1950, newspapers.com.

164. Irene Fisher, "Chavez Said Miles Lost Over Coogler Murder," *Santa Fe New Mexican*, November 10, 1950, newspapers.com.

165. Irion, "The 1962 Election in New Mexico," 449.

Chapter 5. Holm O. Bursum III: Growing Up in the GOP

166. Hamm, *The Bursums of New Mexico*, 300.

167. Holm Bursum, Jr., interview.

168. Hamm, *The Bursums of New Mexico*, 277-278.

169. Ibid., 269.

170. Jon Hunner, *Inventing Los Alamos: The Growth of an Atomic Community* (Norman: University of Oklahoma Press, 2004), 71-72.
171. Hamm, *The Bursums of New Mexico*, 284-286.
172. Ibid., 285.
173. "U.S., School Yearbooks, 1880-2012"; New Mexico College of Agriculture and Mechanic Arts; Years: 1953, 1954, and 1956, Ancestry.com. *U.S., School Yearbooks, 1900-1999* [database on-line]. Provo, UT, USA: Ancestry.com Operations, Inc., 2010.
174. "Page Staff," *The Santa Fe New Mexican*, February 28, 1954, newspapers.com.
175. "Whatley May Make State Court Race," *Las Cruces Sun-News*, February 28, 1954, newspapers.com.
176. "Stockton Declared Official Winner by 1783 Margin," *Albuquerque Journal*, May 30, 1954, newspapers.com.
177. "Stockton Wins GOP Nomination to Oppose John Simms," *Clovis News-Journal*, May 5, 1954, newspapers.com.
178. "Mrs. Sporing, Carlsbad, President of GOP Women," *Albuquerque Journal*, October 17, 1961; "Mrs. Bursum Wins Socorro School Post," *Albuquerque Journal*, February 2, 1949; "Betty Bursum Dies After Illness, *Albuquerque Journal*, October 22, 1969. From newspapers.com.
179. Hamm, *The Bursums of New Mexico*, 288-290.
180. "In Sullins Review," *Albuquerque Journal*, February 26, 1952, newspapers.com; Michael Scanlon, "Radford's Most Famous Alumna Drops in for a Talk," *El Paso Times*, May 13, 1987, reprinted in "Tales from the Morgue," Trish Long, July 8, 2008, accessed July 10, 2020, https://www.elpasotimes.com/story/news/history/blogs/tales-from-the-morgue/2008/07/11/radfords-most-famous-alum/31477437/; "Colorful Pageantry Highlights Crowning of Sun Carnival Queen," *El Paso Times*, December 28, 1952, newspapers.com.
181. Elizabeth Spencer, conversation with the author March 14, 2019; Earle Bursum, interview by Ron Hamm, notes, September 28, 2010.
182. "Miss Earle Powell Named Engineer Queen," *Albuquerque Journal*, March 19, 1956, newspapers.com.
183. Hamm, *The Bursums of New Mexico*, 298.

CHAPTER 6. 1959-1960: EARLY YOUNG REPUBLICAN REVITALIZATION

184. Will Harrison, "Inside the Capitol," *The Gallup Independent*,

September 1, 1959, newspapers.com.
185. Theodore H. White, *The Making of the President 1960* (New York: Pocket Books, Inc., Cardinal Edition, 1961), 367.
186. Wayne S. Scott, "Mechem Urged, Not Endorsed by Young GOP," *Albuquerque Journal*, November 11, 1959, newspapers.com.
187. "State Republicans Gather Tonight," *Clovis News-Journal*, February 11, 1960, newspapers.com.
188. "Labor to Aid Pousma," *Albuquerque Journal*, January 14, 1960; "GOP Group Tosses Pousma into the Race," *The Gallup Independent*, November 9, 1959. From newspapers.com.
189. David Francis Cargo, *Lonesome Dave: The Story of New Mexico Governor David Francis Cargo* (Santa Fe, New Mexico: Sunstone Press, 2010), 51.
190. Will Harrison, September 1, 1959.
191. "State Republicans Gather Tonight."
192. Cargo, *Lonesome Dave*, 52.
193. Scott, "Mechem Urged, Not Endorsed."
194. "Finance Head for Young GOP Is Appointed," *Albuquerque Journal*, January 21, 1960; "Young GOP Meets Thursday," *Albuquerque Journal*, August 15, 1960, newspapers.com.
195. Roybal, *Taking on Giants*, 128-130.
196. Edwin L. Mechem, interview with Emlen Hall and Maureen Sanders, unpublished transcript, May 28 (1997): B 16-18.
197. Roybal, *Taking on Giants*, 130.
198. Maurice Trimmer, "Demo Collection Not All Inclusive," *Las Vegas Daily Optic*, May 8, 1959, newspapers.com; "Burroughs Ends Demo Collection," *Las Vegas Daily Optic*, May 12, 1959, newspapers.com.
199. "Democrats Register Statehouse Employees Plus Spouses," *The Santa Fe New Mexican*, February 23, 1959, newspapers.com; Tony Hillerman, "State Employees Sign Dem Pledge," *The Santa Fe New Mexican*, February 24, 1959, newspapers.com.
200. Richard Cheney, telephone interview by the author, August 2018 (day not recorded).
201. "GOP Unit Plans 'Truth Squad,'" *Albuquerque Journal*, September 4, 1960, newspapers.com.
202. Pattison, interview.
203. Ibid.
204. "Curry County Republicans Announce Full Slate of Candidates,"

Clovis News-Journal, May 8, 1960, newpapers.com.
205. Pattison, interview.
206. John A. Farrell, *Richard Nixon: The Life*, New York: Doubleday, 2017, 293.
207. Ibid., 294.
208. "Final Official Results Listed," *Albuquerque Journal*, November 29, 1960, newspapers.com.
209. Hoyt Pattison, interview.
210. "Final Official Results."
211. U S. House of Representatives, "Congress Profiles 86th Congress (1959-1961)," accessed August 11, 2019, https://history.house.gov/Congressional-Overview/Profiles/86th/; Congress Profiles: 87th Congress (1961-1963) https://history.house.gov/Congressional-Overview/Profiles/86th/.

CHAPTER 7. 1961: YOUNG REPUBLICAN LEADERS IN THE STATE AND NATION

212. Richard M. Nixon, *Six Crises*, Garden City, NY: Doubleday and Company, 1962, 416.
213. Ibid.
214. Farrell, *Richard Nixon*, 297-298.
215. Cargo, *Lonesome Dave*, 66.
216. "Mrs. Floyd Lee Attends Session in Washington," *The Santa Fe New Mexican*, July 10, 1957, newspapers.com.
217. Wayne S. Scott, "N. M. Young GOP Hit by Discord Over Convention, *Albuquerque Journal*, April 28, 1961, newspapers.com; "Young GOP Meet Will Apparently be Here May 6," *Albuquerque Journal*, April 30, 1961, newspapers.com.
218. "Charges Hit Young GOP Meeting Date," *Albuquerque Journal*, April 30, 1961, newspapers.com.
219. "Bursum Elected State President of Young GOP," *Albuquerque Journal*, May 7, 1961, newspapers.com.
220. Ibid.
221. Ibid.
222. "Young GOP Meet Under Way Here," *Albuquerque Journal*, May 6, 1961, newspapers.com.
223. "1962 Called GOP Key in '64 Race," *Press and Sun-Bulletin*

[Binghamton, New York], July 11, 1961, newspapers.com.
224. David Mazie, "New YR Chairman Started His Career with an FDR Emblem," *Star Tribune*, June 26, 1961, newspapers.com.
225. Theodore White, *The Making of the President 1964* (New York: Harper Perennial Political Classics Edition, 2010), 95.
226. White, *The Making of the President 1964*, 95.
227. White Bear Lake Yacht Club, "History," accessed June 29, 2019, https://www.wbyc.com/about-us/history.
228. "Young Republicans Elect Supporters of Nixon President," *The Tipton Daily Tribune* [Indiana], June 26, 1961, newspapers.com.
229. "Young Republicans Elect Supporters of Nixon."
230. "Sen. Goldwater Pledges Support," *Albuquerque Journal*, July 23, 1961, newspapers.com.
231. White, *The Making of the President 1964*, 92-94.
232. Ibid., 96.
233. "Young GOP Club to Get Charter," *Albuquerque Journal*, July 9, 1961; "Young GOP Head Wins Full Term," *Albuquerque Journal*, July 9, 1961; "Young GOP Club to Get Charter," *Albuquerque Journal*, August 4, 1961; "Santa Fe Unit of Young GOP to Get Charter," *Albuquerque Journal*, September 7, 1961; "Young Republicans to Meet at Clovis," *Lubbock Avalanche-Journal*, November 17, 1961; "Young GOP'ers Hear Skeen in Farmington," *Albuquerque Journal*, December 11, 1961. From newspspers.com.
234. "38 Appointments Are Announced by Governor Tingley," *Clovis News-Journal*, April 12, 1935, newspapers.com; "UNM Alumni Will Honor Frances Lee," *Albuquerque Journal*, June 15, 1978, newspapers.com.
235. "After White House Tea," *Albuquerque Journal*, April 15, 1960, newspapers.com
236. John Paul Mitchell, telephone interview with the author, August 23, 2018.
237. "Sen. Goldwater Pledges Support."
238. "'Re-Register' Drive Started by Young GOP," *Albuquerque Journal*, September 12, 1961, newspapers.com.
239. Joseph Alsop, "World Politics: Watchers of Mr. K in for Rugged Job; Zhukov and Others Attempted It," *The Santa Fe New Mexican*, September 20, 1959, newspapers.com.
240. "GOPers in Common Trap, says Democrat," *Albuquerque Journal*,

September 15, 1961, newspapers.com.

241. "Once It Was the Hotel of the Famous," *Albuquerque Journal*, August 25, 2980, newspapers.com.

242. "Young GOP Urged to Lead Youth in U.S.," *Albuquerque Journal*, November 10, 2961, newspapers.com.

243. Ibid.; "UNM Alumni Will Honor Frances Lee," *Albuquerque Journal*, June 15, 1978, newspapers.com; "Mrs. Floyd Lee Attends Session in Washington," *The Santa Fe New Mexican*, July 10, 1957, newspapers.com.

244. Rutgers Eagleton Institute of Politics, Center for Women in Politics, accessed July 8, 2020, https://cawp.rutgers.edu/history-women-us-congress.

245. "McManus Rules against Bid by Joe A. to Unseat Bolack," *The Santa Fe New Mexican*, November 8, 1961, newspapers.com; "Indian Voting Rights," *Albuquerque Journal*, November 9, 1961, newspapers.com.

CHAPTER 8. 1962: LOCAL ORGANIZING AND MIDTERM SURPRISES

246. Katherine Hatch, "Start at Precinct, Republicans Told," *The Daily Oklahoman*, December 9, 1961, newspapers.com.

247. Hamm, *The Bursums of New Mexico*, 300.

248. "GOP to Forego Statewide Fund Raising Dinner," *Albuquerque Journal*, January 5, *1962*, newspapers.com; "Young GOP Groups to Hear National Official," *Albuquerque Journal*, January 17, 1962, newspapers.com; "Charter Visitors," *Alamogordo Daily News*, January 21, 1962, newspapers.com.

249. "Young Republicans Confer," *Albuquerque Journal*, February 9, 1962, newspapers.com; "Talk Politics," *Albuquerque Tribune*, February 7, 1962, ancestry.com.

250. "GOP to Charter Two More Clubs," *Albuquerque Journal*, April 20, 1962, newspapers.com.

251. "Young Republicans Set Convention for Las Cruces," *Las Cruces Sun-News*, April 30, 1962, newspapers.com.

252. John P. Mitchell, telephone interview.

253. Dave Molina, "Cowboy Mayor Began with $90 in Pocket," *Clovis News-Journal*, October 28, 1962, newspapers.com.

254. Hoyt Pattison, interview with author, August 30, 2018.

255. "Mechem Explains Tax Increase in Election Year," *Albuquerque*

Journal, August 25, 1962, newspapers.com.

256. "State Financial Issue Hurled into the Campaign by Politicos," *The Santa Fe New Mexican*, September 24, 1962, newspapers.com.

257. Ibid.

258. "Small Donations Are Party Basis, Skeen Tells GOP," *Albuquerque Journal*, November 15, 1961, newspapers.com.

259. "Weekend Tour Set for Officials of Young GOP," *Albuquerque Journal*, August 3, 1962; "Republican Leaders Plan Deming Visit," *The Deming Headlight*, August 9, 1962; "Young Republicans Leaders on Tour," *Albuquerque Journal*, August 11, 1962. From newspapers.com.

260. "Young Republican Leaders on Tour."

261. Don Tripp, eulogy at the funeral of Holm O. Bursum III, Socorro, December 11, 2018.

262. "Young Republican Club of San Miguel Co.," *Las Vegas Daily Optic*, September 27, 1962, newspapers.com; "Over 200 Attend Republican Dinner," *Las Vegas Daily Optic*, October 2, 1962, newspapers.com.

263. "Action Overdue, Says Chairman of Young GOP," *Albuquerque Journal*, October 24, 1962, newspapers.com.

264. Rhodes Cook, "The Midterm Election of 1962: A Real 'October Surprise,'" Sabato's Crystal Ball, University Center for Politics, accessed September 20, 2019, http://centerforpolitics.org/crystalball/articles/frc2010093001/. See also Benjamin Schwarz, "The Real Cuban Missile Crisis," *The Atlantic*, February 2015, accessed July 19, 2020, https://www.theatlantic.com/magazine/archive/2013/01/the-real-cuban-missile-crisis/309190/.

265. Irion, "The 1962 Election," 450.

266. Bruce King with Charles Poling, *Cowboy in the Roundhouse: A Political Life* (Santa Fe, New Mexico: Sunstone Press, 1998) 69.

267. Pattison, telephone interview.

268. Mitchell, telephone interview.

269. "Canvassing Board Meeting Today, Can't Certify," *Las Vegas Daily Optic*, November 21, 1962, newspapers.com.

270. "Montoya, Joseph Manuel, 1915-1978," US House of Representatives: History, Arts & Archives, accessed June 24, 2018, http://history.house.gov/People/Detail/18432.

271. "White Defeated for Reelection by 26-7 Vote," *Albuquerque Journal*, January 10, 1939, newspapers.com.

272. "Montoya, Joseph Manuel."

273. Ibid.
274. "Here's Canvass Board's Primary Finals," *The Santa Fe New Mexican*, June 25, 1950, newspapers.com.
275. "Tom Montoya Succeeds Joe in New Mexico Senate," *Albuquerque Journal*, December 23, 1954, newspapers.com.
276. "Montoya, Joseph Manuel."
277. Will Harrison, "Inside the Capital: Most New Mexico Senators Appointed," *The Santa Fe New Mexican*, March 7, 1961, newspapers.com; Will Harrison, "Inside the Capital: Some Democrats Opposing the Election," *The Santa Fe New Mexican*, November 21, 1962, newspapers.com.
278. Roybal, *Taking on Giants*, 151; Roybal, 152; Will Harrison, "Fab and Alfonso in Bitter Clash," *Carlsbad Current-Argus*, March 13, 1961, newspapers.com.
279. Cargo, *Lonesome* Dave, 65.
280. "Mechem Looms as Top Prospect for Senate Post," *Albuquerque Journal*, November 20, 1962, newspapers.com; Will Harrison, "Inside the Capital: Not Much Dinero in the Senate Job," *The Santa Fe New Mexican*, November 23, 1962, newspapers.com.
281. Edwin L. Mechem interviewed by Emlen Hall and Maureen Saunders, unpublished transcript, June 18 (1997): B 18-19.
282. Will Harrison, "Inside the Capital: Nominates Bursum for the Senate," *Hobbs Daily News-Sun*, October 2, 1961, newspapers.com.
283. "Bolack Hails Court Ruling; Says He's Glad It's All Over," *Carlsbad Current-Argus*, June 6, 1962, newspapers.com.
284. "Teen Age Republican Party," *Albuquerque Journal*, November 28, 1962, newspapers.com.
285. "Bolack Meets with Young GOP Officers," *Las Vegas Daily Optic*, December 18, 1962, newspapers.com.
286. Hamm, *The Bursums of New Mexico*, 300.

Chapter 9. 1963: Tensions, Toil, and Tragedy

287. John Gizzi, "Modern Conservatism Marks 50 Years Since First Big Win," June 26, 2013, accessed September 28, 2018, https://www.newsmax.com/John-Gizzi/Young-Republicans-Goldwater-Reagan/2013/06/26/id/512047/.
288. Will Harrison, "Inside the Capital: Saps Don't Like Convention

Plan," *The Deming Headlight*, May 20, 1963, newspapers.com.
289. "Couple Directs 'Dimes' Campaign," *Albuquerque Journal*, January 25, 1963, newspapers.com.
290. Ibid.
291. Earle Bursum, interview by Ron Hamm.
292. "Couple Directs 'Dimes'" Campaign."
293. Marcia Kay Keegan, "Bright Splashes of Color Used Freely," *Albuquerque Journal*, March 1, 1964, newspapers.com.
294. Clarissa Start, "Busy Life with the Young Republicans," *St. Louis Post-Dispatch*, September 21, 1961; Richard Dudman, "Rightist Drive Started Four Years Ago," *Lincoln Journal Star*, December 28, 1964; "Patricia Hutar, 1926-2010," *Chicago Tribune*, May 14, 2010. From newspapers.com.
295. Start, "Busy Life."
296. "Big Ed Levels Blistering Attack at Democrats," *The Santa Fe New Mexican*, May 19, 1963, newspapers.com; "Mechem Says Washington in Hands of Arrogant Elite," *Albuquerque Journal*, May 19, 1963, newspapers.com.
297. "Big Ed Levels."
298. "Mechem Says Washington."
299. "Miss Young Republican Contest Set," *Albuquerque Journal*, May 8, 1963, newspapers.com.
300. "Bursum Faces Race in Young GOP Election," *Albuquerque Journal*, May 18, 1963, newspapers.com.
301. "State Young Republicans Back Goldwater," *Albuquerque Journal*, May 20, 1963, newspapers.com.
302. Garcia et al., *Governing New Mexico*, 59-60.
303. "GOP Stand Due on Pre-Primary Petitions May 18," *Albuquerque Journal*, May 3, 1963, newspapers.com.
304. White, *The Making of the President 1964*, 97.
305. "N.M. Young Republicans Seek National Convention," *Albuquerque Journal*, June 21, 1963, newspapers.com.
306. Seymour Korman, "Young GOP Elects Backer of Goldwater," *Chicago Tribune*, June 29, 1963, newspapers.com.
307. "Lukens Named National Chairman," *Carroll Daily Times Herald* (Carroll, Iowa), June 29, 1963, newspapers.com.
308. Korman, "Young GOP Elects."
309. "Young Republican at Clovis Honored," *Albuquerque Journal*,

August 30, 1963, newspapers.com.

310. "Disillusioned Young Republican Leader Makes Predictions," *The Algona Upper Des Moines* [from *Minneapolis Tribune*], August 22, 1963, newspapers.com.

311. "McDevitt Assumes Top Spot on Gem High Court," *The Times-News* (Twin Falls, Idaho), February 2, 1993, newspapers.com; Eric Bradley, "Donald 'Buz' Lukens, Disgraced Congressman," *The Cincinnati Enquirer*, May 24, 2010, newspapers.com.

312. White, *The Making of the President 1964*, 97.

313. Ibid., 98-99.

314. "3000 Expected for GOP Picnic Here," *Albuquerque Journal*, August 24, 1963, newspapers.com.

315. "McKim Accused of 'Partisanship' in City Election," *Albuquerque Journal*, September 18, 1963, newspapers.com.

316. "Robins Resigns GOP Party Post," *Albuquerque Journal*, September 19, 1963, newspapers.com.

317. "Nonpartisan Unit to Fight Citizens Committee Here Is Confirmed by Bursum," *Albuquerque Journal*, September 20, 1963, newspapers.com.

318. "Four More Candidates Enter Race," *Albuquerque Journal*, September 25, 1963, newspapers.com.

319. Ibid.

320. Dick McAlpin, "Schifani, Trigg Win City Commission Seats," *Albuquerque Journal*, October 9, 1963, newspapers.com.

321. Cargo, *Lonesome Dave*, 67.

322. Ibid., 79-80.

323. Ibid., 80-81.

324. Fred Buckles, "Session to Reapportion the Legislature Is Scheduled," *Albuquerque Journal*, September 5, 1963, newspapers.com.

325. Cargo, *Lonesome Dove*, 76.

326. "Reapportionment Illegal," *The Santa Fe New Mexican*, December 22, 1963, newspapers.com.

327. Will Harrison, "Inside the Capital: Task Too Much for Legislature," *Silver City Daily Press*, June 20, 1964, newspapers.com.

328. Robert S. Allen and Paul Scott, "The Allen-Scott Report: Credit to the Soviet Union Not Barred by '34 Johnson Act; Startling Ruling Reversal," *The Daily Herald*, October 8, 1963, newspapers.com.

329. "Editorial: Wheat Sale an Issue," *Austin American-Statesman*, October 30, 1963, newspapers.com.

330. Allen and Scott, "The Allen-Scott Report: Credit to the Soviet Union."
331. Ibid.
332. "Wheat Sale to Russia Opposed," *The News Journal* (Wilmington, DE), September 21, 1963, newspapers.com; Doris Fleeson, "Wheat Deal with Russia Is Helpful Principally to Republican Areas," *Quad-City Times* (Davenport, Iowa), October 15, 1963, newspapers.com.
333. "Reapportioning Action Termed 'Near Miracle,'" *Albuquerque Journal*, November 19, 1963, newspapers.com.
334. Gizzi, "Modern Conservatism Marks 50 Years."

CHAPTER 10. 1964: TRACES OF PROGRESS IN A PROFOUND DEFEAT

335. AZQuotes, "Barry Goldwater Quotes," accessed June 23, 2018, https://www.azquotes.com/author/5665-Barry_Goldwater.
336. Robert A. Caro, *The Years of Lyndon Johnson: The Passage of Power* (NY: Vintage Books, 2012), 345-346.
337. Clay Risen, *The Bill of the Century: The Epic Battle for the Civil Rights* (NY: Bloomsbury Press, 2014), 20.
338. Ibid, 101.
339. White, *The Making of the President 1964*, 100.
340. Caro, *The Years of Lyndon Johnson: Passage*, 430-433.
341. "Top Speakers Named for Young GOP 'School,'" *Albuquerque Journal*, January 8, 1964, newspapers.com; "Young GOP Unit Schedules Schools," *Albuquerque Journal*, January 18, 1964, newspapers.com.
342. Raymond Lahr, "Republicans Inspect Possible Candidates," *Las Vegas Daily Optic*, January 30, 1964; "GOP TV Dinner Here to Feature Contenders," *Albuquerque Journal*, January 5, 1964; "Dinner Decoration Unit Meets Today," *Albuquerque Journal*, January 10, 1964. From newspapers.com.
343. "GOP Speaker," *Albuquerque Journal*, March 30, 1964, newspapers.com.
344. Matthew Dallek, "The Conservative 1960s," *The Atlantic*, December 1995, accessed December 15, 2018, https://www.theatlantic.com/magazine/archive/1995/12/the-conservative-1960s/376506/.
345. Barry Goldwater, "The Case for Conservatism," *Britannica Online Encyclopedia*, 1, accessed January 18, 2019, https://www.britannica.com/topic/Barry-Goldwater-on-conservatism-1989999.

346. Ibid, 14.
347. Ibid, 16-17.
348. White, *The Making of the President 1964*, 99.
349. Ibid.
350. Ibid., 349-350.
351. Risen, *The Bill of the Century*, 47-48.
352. GovTrack.us, "H.R. 7152. Passage," accessed February 10, 2020, https://www.govtrack.us/congress/votes/88-1964/s409.
353. Louis Menand, "He Knew He Was Right," *The New Yorker*, March 26, 2001, accessed December 15, 2018, https://www.newyorker.com/magazine/2001/03/26/he-knew-he-was-right.
354. White, *The Making of the President 1964*, 363.
355. "Hill's Delegates Work to Upset Goldwater Coup," *The Santa Fe New Mexican*, June 14, 1964, newspapers.com.
356. Jim Colgrove, "Barry's Blitzkrieg Rips Gaping Holes in New Mexico's Republican Party," *Santa Fe New Mexican*, June 16, 1964, newspapers.com.
357. Will Harrison, "Inside the Capitol: Anderson Carter under Big Five," *The Deming Headlight*, February 3, 1958, newspapers.com.
358. "Bursey Names Rep. Carter as Campaign Co-Chairman," *Albuquerque Journal*, January 17, 1960, newspapers.com.
359. Will Harrison, "Inside the Capitol: Almost Violence over Burroughs," *Hobbs Daily News-Sun*, December 4, 1961, newspapers.com.
360. "Carter Is Content to Aid Goldwater in This State Only," *Albuquerque Journal*, July 17, 1964, newspapers.com.
361. Will Harrison, "Inside the Capitol: GOP Under New Management Now," *The Santa Fe New Mexican*, June 16, 1964, newspapers.com.
362. Ibid.
363. Colgrove, "Barry's Blitzkrieg;" Jim Colgrove, "Wounds Opened in GOP," *The Santa Fe New Mexican*, June 14, 1964; "Hill's Delegates Work to Upset." From newspapers.com.
364. Colgrove, "Barry's Blitzkrieg."
365. Ibid.
366. Ibid.
367. Cargo, *Lonesome Dave*, 84.
368. Ibid., 84-85.
369. "Curry Young GOP Group Sets Program," *Clovis News-Journal*, September 13, 1964, newspapers.com.

370. "Party Heads Agree on Repeal of Law," *Albuquerque Journal*, June 21, 1964, newspapers.com.
371. "Eddy County Pre-Primary Petitions Tardy," *Albuquerque Journal*, July 3, 1964, newspapers.com.
372. Ibid.
373. "Pre-Primary Petitions," *The Santa Fe New Mexican*, July 3, 1964, newspapers.com.
374. "Alberta Miller Asks Opinion on Deadline," *The Santa Fe New Mexican*," July 6, 1964, newspapers.com; "All Pre-Primary Petitions Filed within Deadline," *Albuquerque Journal*, July 7, 1964, newspapers.com.
375. "Deadline for Checking Pre-Primary Petitions Extended for 10 Days," *Albuquerque Journal*, July 19, 1964, newspapers.com.
376. "Pre-Primary Ballot Re-Check Shows Deficit," *Albuquerque Journal*, July 24, 1964, newspapers.com.
377. Fred Buckles, "Pre-Primary Fight Continues: Distinction between Voter, Qualified Elector Is Drawn," *Albuquerque Journal*, August 1, 1964, newspapers.com.
378. Fred Buckles, "Pre-Primary Convention Law to Be on Ballot, AG Decides," *Albuquerque Journal*, August 29, 1964, newspapers.com.
379. Ibid.
380. Will Harrison, "Nobody Questions Referendum Lists," *Las Vegas Daily Optic*, July 8, 1964, newspapers.com.
381. "Final Results in Top Races," *Albuquerque Journal*, November 6, 1964, newspapers.com.
382. Ibid.
383. Ibid.
384. Will Harrison, "Inside the Capital: David Cargo Is Legislator Called Most Contradictory," *Alamogordo Daily News*, November 20, 1964, newspapers.com.
385. Judith L. Messal, unpublished journal, 1964; "Prospecting for Votes," *Alamogordo Daily News*, November 2, 1964, newspapers.com.
386. Menand, "He Knew He Was Right."
387. Ibid.

CHAPTER 11. 1965: TRANSITIONS AT HOME AND A PEACE MISSION ABROAD

388. Hilton, *Be My Guest*, 272.

389. "Clint's Interference," *Albuquerque Journal*, February 14, 1965, newspapers.com.
390. "Up to the Legislature," *Albuquerque Journal*, November 12, 1964, newspapers.com.
391. Will Harrison, "Inside the Capital: Demo Convention Just as Planned," *Carlsbad Current-Argus*, February 26, 1964, newspapers.com.
392. "Abolish the Convention," *Albuquerque Journal*, February 25, 1964, newspapers.com.
393. "Pre-Primary Repeal Asked," *The Santa Fe New Mexican*, February 24, 1964, newspapers.com.
394. Will Harrison, "Inside the Capital: Wild Broncos Frequently Kick Over House Traces," *Alamogordo Daily News*, March 10, 1965, newspapers.com.
395. Clinton P. Anderson with Milton Viorst, *Outsider in the Senate: Senator Clinton Anderson's Memoir*, New York: The World Publishing Company, 1970, 262-297.
396. "Clint's Interference."
397. "Senate Kills Measure Calling for Return to Direct Primary," *Clovis News-Journal*, March 18, 1965, newspapers.com.
398. "New Pre-Primary Fight Planned by Young GOP," *Albuquerque Journal*, April 1, 1965, newspapers.com.
399. "Young GOP to Urge Pre-Primary Repeal," *Clovis News-Journal*, April 1, 1965, newspapers.com; "New Pre-Primary Battle Promised," *The Albuquerque Tribune*, April 1, 1965, ancestry.com.
400. "State Convention of Young GOP to Open Friday," *Albuquerque Journal*, May 9, 1965, newspapers.com.
401. Ibid; "Young Republicans Convention Sparked by Seating Question," *Albuquerque Journal*, May 15, 1965, newspapers.com; "Denver GOP Leaders Have Role in Session of Young Republicans," *Albuquerque Journal*, May 13, 1965, newspapers.com.
402. "Young GOP Given a Proposal on How to Captivate Friends," *The Albuquerque Tribune*, May 15, 1965, ancestry.com.
403. "Young GOP Darling," *Albuquerque Journal*, May 15, 1965, newspapers.com.
404. "Sheriffs Organize to Upgrade Image," *Albuquerque Journal*, September 8, 1968, newspapers.com.
405. A. C. DeCola, "Carter 'Influence' Over YR's Here May Spark Election Row," *The Albuquerque Tribune*, June 17, 1965, ancestry.com.

406. Ibid; Wayne S. Scott, "Battle Appears in Offing Here for Young GOP," *Albuquerque Journal*, June 17, 1965, newspapers.com.
407. "Carter Replies to GOP Critics," *Albuquerque Journal*, June 19, 1965, newspapers.com.
408. Wayne S. Scott, "Young GOP Rivals Trade Verbal Blasts," *Albuquerque Journal*, June 19, 1965, newspapers.com.
409. "YR Election Due Tonight," *The Albuquerque Tribune*, June 19, 1965, ancestry.com.
410. Scott, "Young GOP Rivals."
411. "Young GOP'ers Election is Won by Dennis Howe," *Albuquerque Journal*, June 21, 1965, newspapers.com.
412. "Bulletin," *Albuquerque Journal*, June 20, 1965, newspapers.com; "Young GOP'ers Election Is Won."
413. "U.S. Senator Contest," *Albuquerque Journal*, November 9, 1966, newspapers.com.
414. "Socorro Crowds Cheer Hilton in Fiesta Parade," *Albuquerque Journal*, May 29, 1960, newspapers.com; "Conrad Hilton Honored by N. M. Legislature," *Albuquerque Journal*, June 10, 1962, newspapers.com.
415. Hamm, *The Bursums of New Mexico*, 341.
416. Hilton, *Be My Guest*, 218.
417. Ibid., 271-274.
418. "Hotelman Discusses 'Uncommitted Third,'" *El Paso Times*, March 8, 1957, newspapers.com.
419. Ibid.
420. "Bursum Leaves for England, Politics Seminary," *Albuquerque Journal*, June 24, 1965, newspapers.com; "Vice President Briefs Young Political Heads," *The Albuquerque Tribune*, June 26, 1965, ancestry.com.
421. Oxford Royale Academy, "Types of Beautiful Architecture You Can See in Oxford," accessed July 19, 2019, https://www.oxford-royale.co.uk/articles/8-beautiful-architecture-oxford.html.
422. "Young Leader Named: Bursum Will Attend Atlantic Conference," *The Albuquerque Tribune*, June 23, 1965, ancestry.com.
423. "Holm Bursum III: European Conference Called Very Interesting," *Albuquerque Journal*, August 12, 1965, newspapers.com.
424. Ibid.
425. Alan Lee Williams, "In Memory of Doctor Peter Corterier," Mid Atlantic Clubs-Bonn, https://www.macbonn.de/en/events/notices/announcement-detail/news/detail/News/in-memory-of-doctor-peter-

corterier/.
426. "Other Boards Chosen: Albuquerquean Gets State Agency Post," *Albuquerque Journal*, May 4, 1967, newspapers.com; "Republicans Due Post," *Albuquerque Journal*, March 13, 1970, newspapers.com; "Two Appointed," *The Albuquerque Tribune*, March 13, 1970, ancestry.com; "Bursum to National SBA Advisors," *The Santa Fe New Mexican*, April 15, 1970, newspapers.com; Hamm, *The Bursums of New Mexico*, 268.
427. "Death Claims Will Harrison in Colorado," *Carlsbad Current-Argus*, November 19, 1965, newspapers.com.
428. "Mystery and Secrecy Abound as Christmas Approaches," *Albuquerque Journal*, December 19, 1965, newspapers.com.

CHAPTER 12. 1966-1968: A PARTY SET TO CELEBRATE

429. Cargo, *Lonesome Dave*, 69.
430. "Albert G. Simms, One of Top N.M. Developers Dies," *Albuquerque Journal*, December 30, 1964, newspapers.com.
431. Cargo, *Lonesome Dave*, 83.
432. Roybal, *Taking on Giants*, 156.
433. Cargo, *Lonesome Dave*, 82-83.
434. Ibid., 83.
435. Ibid.
436. Roybal, *Taking on Giants*, 210.
437. Ibid., 157.
438. Ibid., 210.
439. Office of the Secretary of State, Dan D. Chavez, "New Mexico Legislature," *New Mexico Blue Book*.
440. Ibid.
441. "State News in Brief: Alvarado Hotel Effort Fails Again," *The Santa Fe New Mexican*, February 17, 1970, newspapers.com; Keith Schneider, "Pete Domenici, Long a Powerful Voice on Fiscal Policy, Dies at 85," *New York Times*, September 13, 2017, accessed May 17, 2020, https://www.nytimes.com/2017/09/13/us/politics/pete-domenici-dead.html.
442. Office of the Secretary of State, Dan D. Chavez, "New Mexico U.S. Representatives (1912-Present)," *New Mexico Blue Book*, 170-171, accessed April 25, 2020. https://www.sos.state.nm.us/about-new-mexico/publications/blue-book/#; "Bingaman Denies Party Bias," *Albuquerque*

Journal, August 30, 1980, newspapers.com; "Court Turns Down Ballot Appeals by Skeen, Runnels" and "Voters are the Losers," *Albuquerque Journal*, October 9, 1980, newspapers.com.
443. Kate McGraw, "Big Joe Skeen…He Takes a Lickin' but Keeps on a Tickin,'" *Carlsbad Current-Argus*, September 16, 1980, newspapers.com.
444. Pattison, interview.
445. Ibid.
446. Ibid.

CHAPTER 13. AND THEN: SEVEN YOUNG REPUBLICANS IN MIDDLE AGE AND BEYOND

447. "ERA Still Trying," *Rushville Republican* (Rushville, Indiana), April 14, 1976, newspapers.com.
448. "People in the News: Gets UN Post," *Lancaster New Era* (Lancaster, Pennsylvania), January 1, 1974, newspapers.com.
449. Kelsey L. Campbell, "As the Indispensable Nation, the U.S. Must Lead in Eliminating Violence Against Women," *HuffPost*, November 25, 2014, updated January 25, 2015, accessed November 9, 2019, https://www.huffpost.com/entry/as-the-indispensable-nati_b_6218026.
450. Charles Stafford, "After 44 Years of Working in Politics, Now He's Worrying," *Tampa Bay Times*, October 9, 1988; "World Affairs Discussion," *St. Louis Post-Dispatch*, February 25, 1999; "Patricia Hutar 1926-2010: Active Leader in GOP Politics," *Chicago Tribune*, May 14, 2010. From newspapers.com. International Foundation for Electoral Systems, accessed March 14, 2020, https://www.ifes.org/who-we-are.
451. "Carter Keynotes Campaign Event," *Alamogordo Daily News*, June 5, 1966, newspapers.com.
452. Bill Feather, "Cargo Swamped in Senate Bid," *The Santa Fe New Mexican*, June 3, 1970, newspapers.com.
453. Fred Buckles, "Inside the Capital: State's GOP Delegation Split on Nixon, Reagan," *Alamogordo Daily News*, July 26, 1968; Robert B. [sic] Beier, "Carter to Drive for Reagan," *Albuquerque Journal*, October 19, 1975; Robert V. Beier, "New Mexicans Are Main Cogs in Three Presidential Campaigns," *Albuquerque Journal*, August 19, 1979; Richard Beer, "Work Pays Off for This State's Carter," *Albuquerque Journal*, July 13, 1980; Richard J. Cattani, "Reagan Cranking Up His Political Machine," *The Tampa Tribune*, July 14, 1980. From newspapers.com.

454. Cargo, *Lonesome Dave*, 316-317.
455. Roybal, *Taking on Giants*, 320.
456. Hoyt Pattison and Joy Pattison, interviews by the author, August 30, 2018, with follow-up phone conversations on November 16 and 17, 2018.
457. Dave Steinberg, "Anaya Targets House Speaker Battle," *Albuquerque Journal*, November 14, 1982, newspapers.com.
458. John Robertson and David Steinberg, "State Legislature Returns Strengthen GOP," *Albuquerque Journal*, November 7, 1984, newspapers.com.
459. Ron Hamm, interview by the author, March 7, 2019; Hamm, *The Bursums of New Mexico*, 309-316.
460. AASHTO, the American Association of State Highway Transportation Officials, "Project: U.S. 54 Widening & Relief Route (Alamogordo, New Mexico)," EconWorks, accessed June 4, 2018, https://planningtools.transportation.org/290/view-case-study.html?case_id=143.
461. Population.us, "Population of Alamogordo, New Mexico," accessed May 5, 2018, http://population.us/nm/alamogordo/.
462. Hamm, *The Bursums of New Mexico*, 312.
463. "New Mexico Highway Recycles Tires for Repaving," *The Santa Fe New Mexican*, July 16, 2002, newspapers.com.
464. "Project: U.S. 54 Widening."
465. Ibid.; PreCheck, "Healthcare Background Screening Firm PreCheck to Expand Presence and Create New Jobs in Alamogordo, New Mexico," February 12, 2018, accessed June 19, 2010, https://www.precheck.com/news/healthcare-background-screening-firm-precheck-expand-presence-and-create-new-jobs-alamogordo-nm.
466. Hamm, *The Bursums of New Mexico*, 312.
467. Harden, "Teipana Pueblo – the First Socorro, Part 2."
468. Anthony DellaFlora, "Opinions Divided Over Plan to Split Museum," *Albuquerque Journal*, June 12, 2000, newspapers.com.
469. Hollis Walker, "Mexico Finds Its Forgotten Trail;" "El Camino Real Inspires Projects Across Both Borders," *The Santa Fe New Mexican*, February 10, 1998, newspapers.com.
470. Keiko Ohnuma, "The Bigger the Project, the More Talents Needed," *The Sandoval Signpost*, June 2009, accessed April 9, 2020, http://www.sandovalsignpost.com/jun09/html/featured_artist.html.

471. Carroll L. Riley, "The Pre-Spanish Camino Real," in *El Camino Real de Tierra Adentro*, 13-19, Essays compiled by Gabrielle G. Palmer, Project Director, Cultural Resources Series, No. 11, 1993. June-el Piper and LouAnn Jacobson, Editors, Bureau of Land Management, New Mexico State Office, Internet Archives, accessed June 26, 2020, https://archive.org/stream/elcaminorealdeti2937palm/elcaminorealdeti2937palm_djvu.txt.

472. Ibid, 16.

473. Gabrielle Palmer, "El Camino Real de Tierra Adentro," *Southern New Mexico Historical Review*, VI, 1, January 1999, accessed July 27, 2020, http://www.donaanacountyhistsoc.org/HistoricalReview/1999/HistoricalReview1999.pdf

474. Polly Summar, "El Camino Real Center Tells Story of Royal Trade Route, Salutes Majestic Scenery," *Albuquerque Journal*, November 10, 2005, newspapers.com.

475. Friends of El Camino Real Historic Trail, accessed March 10, 2020, https://www.caminorealheritage.org/html/trail.html.

476. Cindy Lam, email message to author, July 14, 2020.

477. Rev. Andrew J. Pavlak, telephone interview by author, July 28, 2020.

478. Ashley M. Biggers, "A Town Called Help: The People Who Saved Socorro's San Miguel Mission," *New Mexico Magazine*, accessed April 4, 2020, https://www.newmexico.org/nmmagazine/articles/post/a-town-called-help-89583/

479. Paul Harden, "The Last Picture Show: History of the Loma Theater," accessed June 23, 2020, http://socorro-history.org/HISTORY/PH_History/200810_loma2.pdf. Published in *El Defensor Chieftain*, October 4, 2008.

480. Holm O. Bursum IV, "Loma Theater History," October 24, 2017, unpublished manuscript; The Loma Theater, accessed April 19, 2020, https://www.lomatheater.com/about.

481. Michelle Lujan Grisham, November 1, 2017, correspondence.

482. Bursum IV, "Loma Theater."

483. Scott Turner, "Socorro Celebrates Theater's Reopening," *El Defensor Chieftain*, November 9, 2017, accessed April 6, 2020, http://www.dchieftain.com/news/socorro-celebrates-theater-s-reopening/article_41165618-c4af-11e7-9c80-73e37807bea5.html.

484. "ERA Still Trying."

485. "Reelection Dinner Set at City Inn on Sept. 26," *Albuquerque Journal*, September 12, 1972; "Lujan, Domenici Assist Ford, *The Santa Fe New Mexican*, November 27, 1975; "2 County Aides for Bush Named," *Albuquerque Journal*, February 1, 1980. From newspapers.com.

Epilogue

486. "Hon. W. H. Andrews Renominated for Delegate to Congress: H. O. Bursum Re-elected Committee Chairman, His Ringing Address to the Convention," *Albuquerque Weekly Citizen*, October 6, 1906, newspapers.com.
487. U.S. Department of the Interior National Park Service. National Register of Historic Places Inventory – Nomination Form, August 13, 1974, accessed, March 10, 2020, https://npgallery.nps.gov/NRHP/GetAsset/NRHP/74001210_text; Sue Major Holmes, "Socorro Restores Historic Building to Old Grandeur," *El Paso Times*, March 11, 1985, newspapers.com.
488. Isabel Foreman, "Socorro's Garcia Opera House Reopens after Decades of Silence," *Albuquerque Journal*, January 24, 1985, newspapers.com.
489. John Sanchez, eulogy at the funeral of Holm O. Bursum III, Socorro, December 11, 2018.
490. Michael Bursum, conversation with the author, Socorro, December 11, 2018; eulogy at the funeral of Holm O. Bursum III, Socorro, December 11, 2018.
491. Kristine M. Newkirk, "Living History: New Mexico Banker Holm Bursum Helps Preserve His Hometown's Past," *Independent Banker*, August 1997, 65.
492. Cindy Lam, email message.
493. Ibid.

Bibliography

AASHTO, the American Association of State Highway Transportation Officials. "Project: U.S. 54 Widening & Relief Route (Alamogordo, New Mexico)." EconWorks. Accessed June 4, 2018. https://planningtools.transportation.org/290/view-case-study.html?case_id=143.

Anderson, Clinton P. with Milton Viorst. *Outsider in the Senate: Senator Clinton Anderson's Memoir*, New York: The World Publishing Company, 1970.

AZQuotes. "Barry Goldwater Quotes." Accessed June 23, 2018. https://www.azquotes.com/author/5665-Barry_Goldwater.

Biggers, Ashley M. "A Town Called Help: The People Who Saved Socorro's San Miguel Mission," *New Mexico Magazine*. Accessed April 4, 2020. https://www.newmexico.org/nmmagazine/articles/post/a-town-called-help-89583/.

Caffey, David L. *Chasing the Santa Fe Ring: Power and Privilege in Territorial New Mexico*. Albuquerque: University of New Mexico Press, 2014.

Campbell, Kelsey L. "As the Indispensable Nation, the U.S. Must Lead in Eliminating Violence Against Women." *HuffPost*. November 25, 2014, updated January 25, 2015. Accessed November 9, 2019. https://www.huffpost.com/entry/as-the-indispensable-nati_b_6218026.

Cargo, David. *Lonesome Dave: The Story of New Mexico Governor David Francis Cargo.* Santa Fe, New Mexico: Sunstone Press, 2010.

Caro, Robert A. *The Years of Lyndon Johnson: The Passage of P*ower. NY: Vintage Books, 2012.

Cook, Rhodes. "The Midterm Election of 1962: A Real 'October Surprise.'" Sabato's Crystal Ball. University of Virginia Center for Politics. Accessed September 20, 2019. http://centerforpolitics.org/crystalball/articles/frc2010093001/.

Dallek, Matthew. "The Conservative 1960s," *The Atlantic* (December 1995). Accessed December 15, 2018. https://www.theatlantic.com/magazine/archive/1995/12/the-conservative-1960s/376506.

Farrell, John A. *Richard Nixon: The Life*, New York: Doubleday, 2017, 293.

Fresquez, Linda. "Book about Former NMSU Leader Hugh Milton to Debut at Homecoming," NMSU News Center, October 15, 2015. Accessed August 3, 2019. https://newscenter.nmsu.edu/Articles/view/11455/book-about-former-nmsu-leader-hugh-milton-to-debut-at-homecoming.

Friends of El Camino Real Historic Trail. Accessed March 10, 2020, https://www.caminorealheritage.org/html/trail.html.

Garcia, F. Chris, Paul L. Hain, Gilbert St. Clair, and Kim Seckler (eds.), *Governing New Mexico.* Albuquerque: University of New Mexico Press, 2006.

Gizzi, John. "Modern Conservatism Marks 50 Years Since First Big Win," June 26, 2013. Accessed September 28, 2018. https://www.newsmax.com/John-Gizzi/Young-Republicans-Goldwater-Reagan/2013/06/26/id/512047/.

Goldwater, Barry. "The Case for Conservatism," *Britannica Online Encyclopedia*, 1. Accessed January 18, 2019. https://www.britannica.com/topic/Barry-Goldwater-on-conservatism-1989999.

GovTrack.us. "H.R. 7152. Passage." Accessed February 10, 2020. https://www.govtrack.us/congress/votes/88-1964/s409.

Hamm, Ron. *The Bursums of New Mexico: Four Generations of Leadership and Service*. Socorro, New Mexico: Manzanares Street Publishing, 2012.

Harden, Paul. "Apache Warriors—Part 1." Published in *El Defensor Chieftain*, March 7, 2009. Accessed June 4, 2019. http://socorro-history.org/HISTORY/PH_History/200903_apache01.pdf.

———. "Mission Churches—Part I: The Mission Churches in Socorro County." Published in *El Defensor Chieftain*, August 4, 2007. Accessed June 21, 2019. http://socorro-history.org/HISTORY/PH_History/200708_missions1.pdf.

———. "Teipana Pueblo—The First Socorro, Part 1." Published in *El Defensor Chieftain*, July 14, 2012. Accessed May 15, 2019. http://socorro-history.org/HISTORY/PH_History/201207_teipana_1.pdf.

———. "Teipana Pueblo—The First Socorro, Part 2." Published in *El Defensor Chieftain*, August 4, 2012. Accessed May 15, 2019. http://socorro-history.org/HISTORY/PH_History/201208_teipana_2.pdf.

———. "The Last Picture Show: History of the Loma Theater." Published in *El Defensor Chieftain*, October 8, 2008. Accessed June 23, 2020. http://socorro-history.org/HISTORY/PH_History/200810_loma2.pdf.

Harris III, Charles H. and Louis R. Sadler. *The Secret War in El Paso: Mexican Revolutionary Intrigue, 1906–1920*. Albuquerque: University of New Mexico Press, 2009.

Hilton, Conrad N. *Be My Guest*. New York: Simon and Schuster, 1957.

Holtby, David V. *Forty-Seventh Star: New Mexico's Struggle for Statehood*, Norman: University of Oklahoma Press, 2012.

Hunner, Jon. *Inventing Los Alamos: The Growth of an Atomic Community*. Norman: University of Oklahoma Press, 2004.

Irion, Frederick C. "The 1962 Election in New Mexico," *The Western Political Quarterly*, 16, no. 2 (1963): 449. http://jstor.org. DOI:10.2307/444959.

Keleher, William A. *The Fabulous Frontier: Twelve New Mexico Items*. New Edition. Santa Fe, New Mexico: Sunstone Press, 2008.

———. *Memoirs: 1892–1969, A New Mexico Item*. New Edition. Santa Fe, New Mexico: Sunstone Press, 2008.

King, Bruce with Charles Poling. *Cowboy in the Roundhouse: A Political Life*. Santa Fe, New Mexico: Sunstone Press, 1998.

Kropp, Simon. *That All May Learn: New Mexico State University, 1888–1964*. Las Cruces: New Mexico State University, 1972.

Language Policy Web Site, "Language Rights and New Mexico Statehood," U.S. Commission on Civil Rights. Accessed June 11, 2019. http://www.languagepolicy.net/archives/nm-con.htm.

Larson, Robert W. *New Mexico's Quest for Statehood: 1846–1912*. Albuquerque: University of New Mexico Press, 1968.

Latimer, Rosa Walston. *Harvey Houses of New Mexico: Historic Hospitality from Raton to Deming*. Charleston, SC: The History Press, 2015.

McMurray, Howard J. "The 1954 Election in New Mexico," *The Western Political Quarterly*, 12, No. 4 (1954): 619, http://jstor.org DOI 10.2397/442814.

Melzer, Richard. "'Safe and Sane' for Statehood: Making the New Mexico State Constitution of 1910," *Sunshine and Shadows in New Mexico's Past: Volume III, The Statehood Period*, R. Melzer, Ed. Los Ranchos, New Mexico: Rio Grande Books, 2012.

———. "Life in the Luna Mansion: Valencia County's 'Downton Abbey.'" Accessed October 8, 2018. http://www.news-bulletin.com/news/features/life-in-the-luna-mansion-valencia-county-s-downton-abbey/article_248f7f64-ccbb-11e8-a1b6-0319292ca21f.html.

Menand, Louis. "He Knew He Was Right," *The New Yorker*, March 26, 2001. Accessed December 15, 2018. https://www.newyorker.com/magazine/2001/03/26/he-knew-he-was-right.

Meskwaki Nation. "History." Accessed June 14, 2020. https://meskwaki.org/about-us/history/.

Messal, Judith L. "The Electoral Surprise of Mid-Century New Mexico: Edwin L. Mechem, Dennis Chavez, and the Gubernatorial Campaign of 1950," *Southern New Mexico Historical Review* XXIII, January 2016, 1-10.

Moore, Paula. *Cricket in the Web: The 1949 Unsolved Murder That Unraveled Politics in New Mexico*. Albuquerque: University of New Mexico Press, 2008.

Moorman, Donald R. "A Political Biography of Holm O. Bursum: 1899–1924" (Ph.D. diss., University of New Mexico, 1962), 23-24, 27-28. Accessed July 6, 2020. https://digitalrepository.unm.edu/cgi/viewcontent.cgi?article=1245&context=hist_etds.

Myers, R. David. "Making New Mexico Modern: Political Reforms of the 1960s," *Sunshine and Shadows in New Mexico's Past: Volume III, The Statehood Period*, R. Melzer, Ed. Los Ranchos, New Mexico: Rio Grande Books, 2012.

National Cowboy and Western Heritage Museum. "Hall of Great Westerners." Accessed March 25, 2020. https://nationalcowboymuseum.org/hall-of-great-westerners/.

Newkirk, Kristine M. "Living History: New Mexico Banker Holm Bursum Helps Preserve His Hometown's Past," *Independent Banker*, August 1997.

New Mexico Blue Book, Office of the Secretary of State, 2015–2016, Dianna Duran, Secretary of State, and Project Coordinators Patricia Winter and Karen Turri, July 15, 2015, Santa Fe, New Mexico. Accessed April 25, 2018. https://www.sos.state.nm.us/about-new-mexico/publications/bluebook/#

New Mexico Legislature, "Political Composition – Legislative Session." Accessed April 24, 2018. political_composition_since_statehood.pdf (nmlegis.gov).

New Mexico Public Broadcasting Service. "Colores: The Tingleys," Michael Kamins, Producer, May 31, 1995. Accessed June 13, 2019. https://www.newmexicopbs.org/productions/colores/clyde-carrie-tingley-of-new-mexico/.

Nixon, Richard M. *Six Crises*. Garden City, NY: Doubleday and Company, 1962.

Ohnuma, Keiko. "The Bigger the Project, the More Talents Needed." *The Sandoval Signpost*, June 2009. Accessed April 9, 2020. http://www.sandovalsignpost.com/jun09/html/featured_artist.html.

Owen, Gordon R. *The Two Alberts: Fountain and Fall*. Las Cruces, New Mexico: Yucca Tree Press, 1996.

Oxford Royale Academy. "Types of Beautiful Architecture You Can See in Oxford." Accessed July 19, 2019. https://www.oxford-royale.co.uk/articles/8-beautiful-architecture-oxford.html.

Palmer, Gabrielle. "El Camino Real de Tierra Adentro," *Southern New Mexico Historical Review*, VI, 1, January 1999. Accessed July 27, 2020. http://www.donaanacountyhistsoc.org/HistoricalReview/1999/HistoricalReview1999.pdf.

Population.us, "Population of Alamogordo, New Mexico." Accessed May 5, 2018. http://population.us/nm/alamogordo/.

PreCheck. "Healthcare Background Screening Firm PreCheck to Expand Presence and Create New Jobs in Alamogordo, New Mexico," February 12, 2018. Accessed June 19, 2010. https://www.precheck.com/news/healthcare-background-screening-firm-precheck-expand-presence-and-create-new-jobs-alamogordo-nm.

Riley, Carroll L. "The Pre-Spanish Camino Real," in *El Camino Real de Tierra Adentro*, 13-19, Essays compiled by Gabrielle G. Palmer, Project Director, Cultural Resources Series, No. 11, 1993. June-el Piper and LouAnn Jacobson, Editors, Bureau of Land Management, New Mexico State Office, Internet Archives. Accessed June 26, 2020. https://archive.org/stream/elcaminorealdeti2937palm/elcaminorealdeti2937palm_djvu.txt.

Risen, Clay. *The Bill of the Century: The Epic Battle for the Civil Rights*. NY: Bloomsberry Press, 2014.

Roybal, David. *Taking on Giants: Fabian Chavez Jr. and New Mexico Politics*. Albuquerque: University of New Mexico Press, 2008.

Rutgers Eagleton Institute of Politics. Center for Women in Politics. Accessed July 8, 2020. https://cawp.rutgers.edu/history-women-us-congress.

Sanchez, Joseph P., Robert L. Spude, and Art Gomez, *New Mexico: A History*. Norman: University of Oklahoma Press, 2013.

Schwarz, Benjamin. "The Real Cuban Missile Crisis," *The Atlantic*, February 2015. Accessed July 19, 2020. https://www.theatlantic.com/magazine/archive/2013/01/the-real-cuban-missile-crisis/309190/.

Sonnichsen, C. L. *Tularosa: Last of the Frontier West*. Albuquerque: University of New Mexico Press, 1960.

Stamatov, Suzanne. "There Was a Time and It Was Tingley's." January 11, 2013. Accessed May 19, 2019. https://newmexicohistory.org/?s=Clyde+Tingley.

U.S. Department of the Interior National Park Service. National Register of Historic Places Inventory – Nomination Form, August 13, 1974. Accessed, March 10, 2020. https://npgallery.nps.gov/NRHP/GetAsset/NRHP/74001210_text.

U.S. House of Representatives, "Overview of New Mexico Politics, 1848–

1898," New Mexican Politics, History, Art & Archives. Accessed May 30, 2019. https://history.house.gov/Exhibitions-and-Publications/HAIC/Historical-Essays/Continental-Expansion/New-Mexican-Politics/.

U. S. House of Representatives. "Congress Profiles 86th Congress (1959–1961)." Accessed August 11, 2019. https://history.house.gov/Congressional-Overview/Profiles/86th/; Congress Profiles: 87th Congress (1961-1963). https://history.house.gov/Congressional-Overview/Profiles/86th/.

"U.S., School Yearbooks, 1880–2012"; New Mexico College of Agriculture and Mechanic Arts; Years: 1953, 1954, and *1956*, Ancestry.com. *U.S., School Yearbooks, 1900–1999* [database on-line]. Provo, UT, USA: Ancestry.com Operations, Inc., 2010.

Whaley, Charlotte T., *Nina Otero-Warren of Santa Fe*. Santa Fe, New Mexico: Sunstone Press, 2007.

White Bear Lake Yacht Club. "History." Accessed June 29, 2019. https://www.wbyc.com/about-us/history.

White, Theodore H. *The Making of the President 1960*. New York: Pocket Books, Inc., Cardinal Edition, 1961.

Williams, Alan Lee. "In Memory of Doctor Peter Corterier," Mid Atlantic Clubs-Bonn. Accessed July 19, 2019. https://www.macbonn.de/en/events/notices/announcement-detail/news/detail/News/in-memory-of-doctor-peter-corterier/.

Index

A

Alamogordo Chamber of Commerce, 194
Albuquerque City Commission Election, 140-141
Amaya, George, 163
American Association of State Highway and Transportation Officials (AASHTO), 193-194
Anderson, Clinton P., 54, 65, 123, 164, 169, 179, 180-181
Anderson, John B., 148
Anderson, Robert O., 124
Apache Leaders, 23, 195
Archdiocese of Santa Fe, 199
Arnold, Julia Bursum, 12, 92-93, 177
Ashbrook, John, 103
Atlantic Council, 172

B

Baca, A. B., 63
Baca, Adolfo, 9
Baca, Elfego, 25
Baca, Rowena, 9
Baker vs. Carr, 142
Balcomb, Sara, 153-154
Bangerter, R. A., 63

Bannister, George, 185
Benavidez, G. L., 63
Biden, Joe, 183
Bishop, Ted, 97
Bletzer, Michael, 195
Bliss, Fanny, 9, 107-108
Boehner, John, 139
Bolack, Alice, 89
Bolack, Tom, 9, 86-87, 89, 108, 111-112, 114, 123, 126-127, 165, 174
Bond, Frank, 185, 190
Botts, Bob, 9
Bozell, Jr., Brent, 148
Brunner, Wayne, 147
Buckles, Fred, 158
Buffett, George, 190
Buffett, Warren, 190
Bulkley, John, 116
Bundy, E. W., 157-158
Burch, Dean, 131
Burke, Nancy, 166
Burroughs, John, 79, 83-84, 116, 152
Bursey, Joseph, 152
Bursum, Earle Powell, 9, 76, 82, 88, 92 129-130, 134,137, 147-148, 172-175,175, 191, 194-195, 197-198
Bursum, Elizabeth "Betty" (Puckett), 60, 73-75, 177
Bursum, Frank O., 20, 69
Bursum, Holm O., 11, 14-15, 19-25, 50-51, 56, 69, 87, 96, 203; organizing for statehood, 26-30; with President Taft, 31-36; writing the state constitution, 36-38; campaigns for governor, 38-41; in the U.S. Senate, 41; end of life, 45-46
Bursum, Jr., Holm O., 53, 56, 59-63, 66, 69-71,73-75, 124, 201
Bursum III, Holm O., 8-9, 10-11, 13, 62, 88, 91-93; birth to marriage, 69-77; political organizing, 14-18, 19-20, 29, 45-47, 51, 68, 81-82, 84, 87, 106-118, 126-127, 143-144, 147-148, 154, 185, 201-202; at Young Republican state conventions, 95-98, 132-135, 165-166; at Young Republican National Federation Conventions, 104-105, 128, 131-132, 135, 137, 139-140, 168; on Barry Goldwater, 105, 114, 135, 148,161; on Richard Nixon, 79, 125; Albuquerque city commission elections, 140-

141; pre-primary convention law repeal, 38, 65, 135, 155-159, 163-164; Bernalillo County YR election, 167-169; international peace conference, 162-163, 169-174; return to Socorro, 175-177; elective and appointive public service, 174; chairmanship of the New Mexico State Highway Commission, 191-194; restoration of Socorro sites, 198-201; funeral, 203-205

Bursum IV, Holm O. "Cuatro," 12, 93, 112,174-175, 200, 204
Bursum, Louise (later Wolfinger). 21, 22
Bursum, Lulu (Moore), 20, 25, 41-46, 51, 72, 75
Bursum, Maria (Hilton), 20-21
Bursum, Michael (brother of H. Bursum III), 73, 75
Bursum, Michael (son of H. Bursum III), 12, 45, 91, 93, 177, 204
Bush, George H. W., 118, 127
Bush, George W., 201

C

Caffey, David L., 26, 27
Camino Real (El Camino Real de Tierra Adentro), 23-24, 191, 195-198
Campbell, Jack M., 116, 119, 126, 129, 142, 159, 179
Campbell, J. Bart, 21, 22
Cargo, David F., 17, 77, 79-82, 90, 95-98, 115, 120, 128, 141-144, 154-155, 159, 165, 174, 176-180, 181, 186-188
Cargo vs. Campbell, 142-143
Carruthers, Garrey, 194
Carter, Anderson, 151-155, 165, 167-169, 186-188
Cather, Willa, 46, 96
Catron, Thomas B., 26-27, 29, 34-36
Celler, Emanuel, 178
Chacon, James, 58, 95
Chavez, David, 53, 66-67
Chavez, Dennis, 50-51 65-68, 81, 83, 120-121, 123-125, 178
Chavez, Jr., Dennis, 64-65
Chavez, Jr., Fabian, 47-49, 63, 67, 83, 124, 179, 180
Chavez, Tibo J., 52, 163
Cheney, Richard, 84, 127, 135
Christiansen, Asher, 100
Civil Rights, 37-38, 52, 146, 150-151

Cline, Dorothy, 37
Coca, Benjamin, 118
Coll, Max, 190
Collins, Seaborn, 83
Colts, 26, 46, 56
Conrad N. Hilton Foundation, 198-199
Conservative Coalition, 189
Constitutional Convention of 1910, 36-38
Coogler, Ovida "Cricket," 54-55, 68
Cordova, Dennis, 82
Corterier, Peter, 173-174
Cowart, George, 9
Cowart, Jane, 9
Curry, George, 30, 35
Cushing, Ned, 103
Cutting, Bronson, 15

D

Davidson, Bob, 9
Dead Senator Bill, 120, 123, 125
DeCola, A. C., 167
de Gaulle, Charles, 173
Delgado, Lorenzo, 107
Dewey, Thomas E., 58, 99-101, 136
DeYoung, Leonard, 97
Diaz, Porfirio, 35-36
Dillon, Maurine, 41
Dillon, Richard C., 58, 62
Dole, Bob, 118, 148
Domenici, Pete V., 9, 91, 181
Dorr, Robert, 97, 116
Draft Goldwater Movement, 131, 136, 139-140, 153
Duckworth, William H., 84-86, 120

E

Easley, Mack, 123, 164

Eastern New Mexico University, 115
Edwards, James, 142
Eisenhower, Dwight D. and administration, 78, 101-102, 106-108, 131, 139, 147, 151
Elle of Ganado, 32
ERD (now EBP), 193-194
Espinosa, Gilbert, 57
Espinosa, Reginaldo, 56, 58-59, 63, 95
Evans, M. Stanton, 128, 144

F

Falkner, Herbert, 63
Fall, Albert Bacon, 34-36, 59, 183
Farrell, John A., 85
Fernandez, Antonio, 122-123, 152, 178
Fernandez, Teresa Leger, 184
Fettinger, George, 189
First State Bank, 195, 198, 200, 204-205
Foreman, Ed, 153, 180-181
Foreman, Lillian, 153
Foster, Frank, 86, 115
Franklin, Martina, 19, 59-60
Friends of El Camino Real Historic Trail, 198

G

Gabor, Zsa Zsa, 169
Gallegos, J. O., 53, 61-63
Garcia, Francisca, 203
Garcia, Julio, 97, 107, 134
Garcia Opera House, 203-204
Garcia, Tom, 82, 155
Gardner, William A., 9, 107, 115, 141
Geronimo, 195
Gizzi, John, 144
Goldwater, Barry, 105, 135-140, 146-148, 155, 158-159, 160-161
Gomez, Art, 37

Gonzales, Emma, 97
Gonzales, Mrs. Bill, 82
Gottlieb, Sidney, 58
Greene, Rowena. 135
Grisham, Michelle Lujan, 183, 200
Gunderson, Carroll E., 62

H

Haaland, Deb, 183
Hamm, Ron, 12, 19, 39, 70-72, 113, 127, 129, 191-192
Hansen, LeRoy, 9
Harban, Ruth (Bursum), 31
Harden, Paul, 19, 23, 24, 195, 199-200
Harding, Warren G., 41
Harris, Charles, 35
Harrison, Will, 48, 51, 78, 81, 97, 123-124, 143, 152-153, 158-159, 174
Hartley, Earl, 158
Headen, Charles and Jessie, 195-196
Heflin, Reuben, 37
Hernandez, Benigno C., 40-41
Hernandez, M. P., 44
Herrell, Yvette, 183
Hillerman, Tony, 84
Hilton, Augustus "Gus," 21-22, 25
Hilton, Conrad, 22, 24-25, 38-39, 162, 169-171, 175
Hilton, Mary, 39
Hilton, Steven M., 199
Holloman Air Force Base, 193
Holtby, David, V., 27
Hoover, J. Edgar, 43, 59
Horn, Calvin, 65
Howe, Dennis, 168-169
Hubbell, Frank A., 40-41
Hughes, Robert, 104
Hughes, Thomas, 57, 95
Humphrey, Hubert, 172
Hunner, Jon, 71

Hutar, Patricia Miller, 16, 105-106, 110-111, 128, 131-132, 139, 144, 186-187, 201

I

Ingrahm, Anne, 76
Irion, Frederick C., 47, 68, 119, 142

J

Javits, Jacob, 105, 148
Johnson, Bob, 185
Johnson, Gary, 192, 195
Johnson, Lyndon B. 71-72, 124, 144, 146-147, 150, 158-159, 161
Jones, Lord Chalfont Alun Arthur Gwynne, 172
Jornada del Muerto, 197

K

Keith, Lany, 97
Keleher, Loretta, 45
Keleher, William A., 32, 34, 38, 45, 47, 49-50, 52, 54,
Kennedy, John F. 66, 78-79, 85-86, 94-95, 110, 113, 116, 118-119, 127, 133, 139, 143, 146, 150, 160
Kennedy, Robert F., 144
Khrushchev, Nikita, 109, 119
Kiker, Jr., Henry A., 155
King, Bruce, 48, 119, 179
King, Gigi, 160
Kitchel, Denison, 150
Kohler, Peter, 104
Korman, Seymour, 138
Kropp, Simon, 43

L

Lam, Cindy, 11, 12, 167, 204-205
Larson, Robert W., 31

Larrazolo, Octaviano, 58, 121, 124
Larrazolo, Paul, 124
Lee, Charlie T., 194
Lee, Floyd, 96
Lee, Frances (Marron), 9, 96-98, 107-108, 110-111, 165
Lee, Oliver M., 189, 194
Lee, Vincent M., 189
Leonard, Harold "Fats," 83, 152
Letoc, 23
Lindsay, Imogene, 156
Lodge, Henry Cabot, 131, 153
Loma Theater, 199-201
Lopez, Junio, 124
Lowden, Florence Pullman, 41
Lucero, Dave, 97, 107
Lujan, Ben Ray, 184
Lujan, Edward, 9
Lujan, Manuel, 45
Lujan, Jr., Manuel, 9, 45, 180, 181, 183
Lukens, Donald 'Buz,' 136-139
Luna, Solomon, 28, 30, 36, 38, 40, 46
Lusk, Georgia Lee, 52, 75

M

Mabry, Thomas, 47, 64, 122
Mahe, Eddie, 168
Mahias, Pierre, 173
Mapes, Paul, 160
Marron, Owen N., 34, 96
Martinez, Joe L., 65
Matlock, Albert, 115
McDevitt, Charles, 136-139
McKee, Jean, 105
McKeel, Benny, 97
McKim, Barbara, 134
McKim, George, 9
McManus, John B., 111-112

McMillan, Colin, 9, 134, 155
McMurray, Howard J., 65
Mechem, Dorothy, 8, 89
Mechem, Edwin L., 8-9, 165, 185, 188, 201-202; gubernatorial years 8, 19, 10, 16-17, 48, 59, 66-68, 73-74, 77, 79-80, 82-84, 86-87, 89, 108, 113-114, 116, 119-121, 123-127; senate years, 133, 151-152, 154, 159, 180
Mechem, Merritt C., 25, 41, 85
Melzer, Richard, 28
Menand, Louis, 151, 160-161
Mershon, John, 189
Meskwaki Nation, 20-21
Miles, John E., 43-44, 52-53, 61-62, 65-67, 89
Miller, Alberta, 156-158
Milton, Hugh, 43
Mitchell, Jr., John P., 9, 108, 114-115, 120, 134
Monette, Charlotte, 9
Monette, Chuck, 9
Montano, Hilario, 118
Montoya, Alfonso, 124
Montoya, Carlos, 137
Montoya, Della, 89
Montoya, Joseph A., 86, 111-112, 122
Montoya, Joseph M., 112, 120-126, 129, 152, 159, 165, 178-180, 187
Montoya, Tom, 54, 122-123
Moorman, Donald, 19
Moore, Paula, 54
Moreland, Cliff, 190
Morris, Tom, 178-180
Mossman, Fred, 97
Mulcock, James 'Bud,' 180
Murphy, Frank, 43
Murphy, Leo and Don, 9
Museum of New Mexico Board of Regents, 194-194
Myers, R. David, 65

N

Nadasdy, Leonard J., 12-13, 16, 95, 98-105, 114, 118, 131, 134, 137-139, 144, 172
NATO (North Atlantic Treaty Organization), 171, 173
Neal, Caswell, 90, 142-143, 159
Neuberger, Maurine, 111
Newell, J. Benson, 45
New Mexico College of Agriculture and Mechanical Arts (New Mexico A&M). See also New Mexico State University, 42-45, 67, 72-73, 75
New Mexico Highlands University, 115
New Mexico Institute of Mining and Technology (New Mexico Tech), 177, 198, 200
New Mexico Military Institute (NMMI), 60
New Mexico State Highway Commission, 83, 174, 191-194
New Mexico State University. See also New Mexico A&M. 45, 72, 115
Nixon, Richard M., 16, 78-79, 85-86, 94-95, 105, 125, 181, 186,188, 201
Nord, Tom, 114, 166
North Atlantic Conference of Young Political Leaders, 171-173
Norvell, David, 115, 120

O

O'Connor, Sandra Day, 46, 76
Oestreich, W. C., 64
Olsen, Harold, 63
Onate, Juan de, 23, 196
One-Person One-Vote Reforms, 141-143, 176-180, 185
Opgenorth, Henry, 44
Ortega, Victor, 82
Ortiz, Willie, 153
Otero County Commission, 194
Otero II, Miguel, 26
Owen, Gordon, 35

P

Palmer, Gabrielle, 197
Parker, Jim, 9
Pattison, Hoyt, 9, 12, 17, 67, 84-87, 107. 115, 120, 127, 138, 159, 184-185
Pattison, Joy, 12, 84, 188-190
Pattison, Luciester, 85
Pattison, Orville, 67
Pavlak, Andrew J., 199
Payne, Oliver, 157-158
Pearce, Steve, 182
Perlstein, Rick, 160-161
Pilabo, 23-24, 197, 204
Pino, Joe, 80, 97-98
Piro People, 23-24, 195-197
Po'pay, 24
Pousma, Richard, 80
Powell, Earl and Jane, 131
PreCheck, Inc., 194
Prentice, Lawrence, 120, 158
Pre-Primary Convention Law (and Primary Reform), 50-51, 63-65, 122, 126,128-129, 135, 155-158, 163-165, 180
Price, John, 114
Pruitt, Ralph, 185
Puckett, Earl, 76
Puckett, Hester, 70
Pueblo Revolt, 24

R

Rahn, Pete, 192-193
Rayburn, Sam, 94
Reader, Tom, 155-156, 158
Reagan, Ronald, 187-188
Redman, Jack, 120, 124, 151, 155, 159, 165
Reiche, Greg, 196
Remington, Barbara, 195-196

Rhodes, Eugene Manlove, 46
Richardson, Bill, 184
Richardson, Rich, 130
Riley, Carroll, 197
Robinson, Paul, 9
Rockefeller, Nelson, 135, 147, 151, 153
Roe, Jerry, 114, 117
Romero, Eugenio, 29
Romero, Trinidad, 25
Romney, George, 147
Roosevelt, Franklin Delano (FDR) and administration, 49-51, 58, 62, 78, 99
Roosevelt, Theodore, 29-31, 33
Roybal, David, 48, 180
Runnels, Dorothy, 182
Runnels, Harold "Mud," 181-182
Ryan, Jack, 9

S

Sadler, Louis R., 35
Salazar, Robert, 82
Salazar, Victor, 54
Sanborn, Burt, 134
Sanchez, Gregorio U., 60
Sanchez, James, 60
Sanchez, John, 204
Sanchez, Joseph, 37
Sanchez, Tony, 97
Sandoval, Henry, 57
San Miguel Catholic Church, 24, 195, 198-199
Schifani, Emanuel, 140-141
Schiff, Steve, 183
Schmitt, Harrison, 165
Scott, Hugh, 138
Scranton, William, 147
Sebastian, Caesar, 61
Seligman, Arthur, 47

Simms, Albert G., 178
Simms, Jr., John R., 74, 82-83, 122
Simms, Ruth (Hanna) McCormick, 178
Skeen, Joe, 9, 108, 114, 117-118, 182
Small, Xochitl Torres, 182-183
Smith, Esther, 84, 86, 107
Smith, Guthrie, 40
Smith, Margaret Chase, 111
Socorro City Council, 174
Socorro County Commission, 60-61, 174
Spencer, Elizabeth (Bursum), 12, 92-93, 112, 174-175
Spiess, Charles, 36
Springer, Charles, 36
Springer, Patricia, 97, 134
Spude, Robert L., 37
Stamatov, Suzanne, 51
Stapp, George, 97
Starr, Arthur, 43-44
Stockton, Alvin, 74
Syfert, Oscar, 156

T

Tabet, Ray, 82
Taft, Robert, 100-102
Taft, William Howard, 14-15, 30-36, 111, 176
Taxes for Public Schools, 49-50, 116, 119
Taylor, Elizabeth, 169
Teague, Harry, 182
Teipana, 23, 195-196
The Conscience of a Conservative, 148
Thompson, Aileen, 153
Tiano, Tony, 155
Tingley, Carrie Wooster, 49-50
Tingley, Clyde, 42-43, 49-53, 64, 73, 107, 116, 122
Trigg, Ralph S., 140-141
Trinity Site, 71
Tripp, Don, 9, 118

Tripp, Rosie, 9
Trujillo, Art, 153
Trujillo, Patricia, 134
Truman, Harry S., 54, 58, 99
Tucker, Merle, 9, 147
Twitchell, Ralph E., 26, 57

U

Ullrich, Richard, 134
University of New Mexico, 60-61, 76, 107, 115
U.S. Route 54, 192-194

V

Van Sickle, Scott, 166
Voting Rights, 37-40, 42, 57, 86-87, 111-112

W

Waddell, Marianne, 166
Waldhauser, Ted, 115, 120
Walker, Betty, 82
Walker, E. S. Johnny, 179-180
Warren, Adelina "Nina" Otero, 40, 75
Wells, Stephen G., 200
White, F. Clifton, 101-106, 131, 135-139, 148-153, 165, 187
White, Theodore, 79, 100-101, 106, 136, 139-140, 150
Wilson, Harold, 172
Wilson, Heather, 52, 183
Wilson, Mick, 109
Wilson, Woodrow, 39, 41
Witt, Boston, 90
Work and Sweat Drive, 61

Y

Young Republican Clubs, see Chapters 4, 6-11

Young Republican National Federation, see Chapters 7, 9, 11

Z

Zamora, Moise, 63
Zeikus, Brad, 9, 168-169

www.ingramcontent.com/pod-product-compliance
Lightning Source LLC
Chambersburg PA
CBHW011955150426
43199CB00020B/2868